The Dynamics of Shareholder Value

ROGER W. MILLS

The Dynamics of Shareholder Value

The Principles and Practice of Strategic Value Analysis

© Roger W. Mills and John Robertson, May 1998

All rights reserved. No part of this work covered by copyright hereon may be reproduced or used in any form or by any means - graphic, electronic or mechanised, including photocopying, recording, taping or information storage or retrieval systems - without written permission of the publishers.

Design and Typesetting: Mars Business Associates Ltd
Printed and bound in Great Britain by: Butler and Tanner Ltd

First published: May 1998

LIBRARY OF CONGRESS CATALOGING IN PUBLICATION DATA

Mills, Roger W.

The Dynamics of Shareholder Value,
The Principles and Practice of Strategic Value Analysis

Roger W. Mills

Included bibliographies and index

ISBN   1 873186 07 X

1. Finance, Valuation, Strategy

I. Title

A demonstration disk of a software package called Evaluator produced by ValuAd is available free of charge by contacting the publisher.

Publisher:

Mars Business Associates Ltd, 62 Kingsmead, Lechlade, Glos. GL7 3BW
Tel/Fax: 01367 252506   Email: johnr@cccp.net

Author:
Roger W. Mills.
Tel: 07771 888888   Email: DrRWMills@aol.com

Acknowledgements

Books are rarely the consequence of one person's effort and this book is no exception.

The trigger for this book occured shortly after I established a close working relationship with Price Waterhouse as their Consultant Professor on Shareholder Value. A practical "How to do it" book was seen as being an important addition to the shareholder value publications available in the market. I am very grateful to Mike Maskall and Philip Wright of Price Waterhouse who read my first book on Strategic Value Analysis and encouraged and supported the initiative to produce this book.

However, the greatest single acknowledgement must be given to Sean Rowbotham who played many roles; friend, critic and editor. His tireless effort, enthusiasm and support helped make this book happen in a very tight time frame. We had a rare opportunity to discuss a subject close to our hearts, on which Sean has sound theoretical and practical experience in the corporate world. A very productive and enjoyable partnership ensued that not only helped shape and structure the book but also produced invaluable dialogue about very contentious valuation issues. The result of this was joint development of frameworks/models to provide sound underpinnings for the illustrations and examples provided throughout the book. I look forward to a continuation of our partnership.

A special thank you also goes to Stephanie Gale-Burkitt, whose enthusiatic support throughout the writing of the book helped to ensure that it was completed within a very ambitious time frame.

Many thanks are due to a number of individuals who influenced the structure and content of the book; they are Mike Maskall, Jon Bentley and Fiona Carter of Price Waterhouse and Jenny Collett.

Extensive comments on chapters or parts of the book were received from the staff of Price Waterhouse; Hermann Aichele, Julian Alcantara, Christopher Baer, Lisa Dhanani, Elisabeth Edwards, Patrick Figgis, Axel Jagle, Loic Kubitza, Neil Lyons, Denise Maass, Andrew Wardle, and from James Rush of Preston Logan Associates.

Other people whose contribution should not go unnoticed include: from Henley Management College, James and Victoria DeBono, David Ewers, Kathy Hensman and Carole Print; from Price Waterhouse, Rebecca Carter, Jane Docherty; and finally, Greg Collett, Nigel Harris and Mike Melvill, of Valuad; Jim McNulty of SBC Warburg Dillon Read; and Ian Neill of ICL plc.

Preface

Valuation methods, often presented as being new approaches and associated with measuring shareholder value in the USA, have been attracting considerable interest in the UK, continental Europe and elsewhere in recent times. These new methods focus attention on the present value of estimated future short-term and long-term cash flows and, in fact, the principles on which they are based are not new. They are well established in project finance and investment appraisal for evaluating major projects and acquisitions. However, what is different is their application in valuing the business as a whole, and their use in managing the business. Often this involves developing a new, or at the very least a modified set of performance measures, to replace the previous dominance of accounting performance indicators for managing the business. More broadly, and what is often not well appreciated, is the usefulness and adaptablitiy of the approaches for evaluating difficult but important issues like joint ventures and intangible assets.

These new methods have all the appearance of being only financial tools, but they really are multidisciplinary. They draw not only on corporate finance, but also strategy, marketing and scenario analysis and come in different forms, although most share one common feature – an emphasis on discounted cash flow analysis. To the extent that they encourage thought about the return one is generating on investors' money, these new measures are welcomed by the financial community.

A multitude of global business issues which can lead a management team to implement a Shareholder Value creation strategy include; mergers and acquisitions, strategy development, resource allocation, market and product innovation, incentive compensation, investor communications, value reporting and performance measurement. This book focuses on Strategic Value Analysis in terms of the theory and how it is used in practice. It shows the linkage with Shareholder Value creation, competitive advantage, the cost of capital, risk and terminal value. It develops the use of free cash flow and alternative measures, and also addresses more complex areas such as mergers, acquisitions and joint ventures. Furthermore, it considers valuation issues relating to emerging markets, new issues, intangibles, cross border considerations and the use of alternative valuation tools such as real options.

Roger W. Mills,   May 1998.

Contents

PART 1: Valuation - The Dynamics of Shareholder Value — 1

Chapter 1: Introduction to Strategic Value Analysis — 3

Introduction; New measures of value; Problems with using profits or earnings for strategic analysis; The international dimension; Value reporting; Accounting measures and valuations; The empirical evidence; Overview of the book; Part I – Valuation in Context; Part II – Key Issues; Part III – Applications; Summary checklist; Concluding remarks.

Chapter 2: Calculating a free cash flow strategic value — 23

Introduction; Estimating free cash flow; Illustration – Estimating free cash flow; Relationship between the different drivers of free cash flow; Estimating free cash flow in practice; Estimating strategic value and free cash flow; Estimating terminal value; Business value, corporate value and strategic value; Summary checklist; Concluding remarks.

Chapter 3: The planning period and competitive advantage — 39

Introduction; The competitive advantage period and strategic theory; Introducing the dynamic of time through life cycles; Estimating CAP in practice; Options and CAP; Interrelationship between the planning period; the CAP and the termainal value; Summary checklist; Concluding remarks.

PART 2: Key issues — 61

Chapter 4: Alternative Measures of Strategic Value — 63

Introduction; Economic profit, Economic Value Added, (EVA®), and Strategic Value Added (SVA); Ten steps for calculating Strategic Value Added; Review of Strategic Value Added/Economic Profit approaches; A comparison of valuation results; Other valuation approaches; Technology and valuation; Summary checklist; Concluding remarks.

Chapter 5: Terminal Value — 83

Introduction; Discounted Cash Flow (DCF) methods; Important considerations in applying DCF approaches; Market relative valuation methods; Profit and Loss account relative valuation methods; Balance sheet market relative valuation; Asset value analysis; Options, CFROI and miscellaneous TV issues; Summary checklist; Concluding remarks.

Chapter 6: The Cost of Capital — 99

Introduction; Weighted Average Cost of Capital (WACC); Cost of equity; Cost of debt; Capital structure; Cost of capital - a divisional business unit perspective; The cost of capital in practice; New directions in estimating the cost of capital; Summary checklist; Concluding remarks.

PART 3: Applications — 125

Introduction

Chapter 7: Valuation in Emerging Markets and Cross Border Valuations — 129

Introduction; Differences in accounting practices; Data limitations; Treatment of risk and uncertainty; Estimating the cost of capital; Dealing with inflation pressures; Cross border valuations; Summary checklist; Concluding remarks.

Chapter 8: Mergers, Acquisitions and Joint Ventures — 153

Introduction; Returns to shareholders; Shareholder Value analysis (SV) in merger and acquisition analysis; The Evode Group; Evaluating joint ventures; Scenarios, options and strategic value; Summary checklist; Concluding remarks.

Chapter 9: Valuing New Issues and Intangible Assets — 173

Introduction; Orange – background; Valuing intangible assets; Summary checklist; Concluding remarks.

Chapter 10: Strategic Value Management — 189

Introduction; Value mapping and critical value analysis; Applying Strategic Value Management in practice; Key issues to consider in implementing Strategic Value Management; Summary checklist; Challenges for the future.

Bibliography — 209

Discount tables — 219

Appendix 1 — 223

Santos plc; Consolidated profit and loss accounts for the years ended 31st December; Consolidated balance sheets for the years ended 31st December; Notes to the accounts.

Appendix 2 — 226

Key concepts of modern financial theory

Glossary of terms — 235

Part 1: Valuation - The Dynamics of Shareholder Value

Chapter 1: Introduction to Strategic Value Analysis

'The three most important things you need to measure in a business are: Customer satisfaction, Employee satisfaction and Cash flow. If you are growing customer satisfaction, your market share is sure to grow too. Employee satisfaction gets you productivity, quality, pride and creativity. Cash flow is the pulse - the vital sign of a company.

Jack Welch, CEO General Electric [1].

Chapter preview

○ Strategic Value Analysis as a synthesis of the disciplines of marketing, finance and strategy.

○ The difficulties associated with using profits or earnings for measuring value from a strategic perspective, which relate to issues associated with creative accounting and differences in international accounting practices.

○ How the future value creating potential of a business can be measured by adopting a long-term Strategic Value perspective expressed in terms of discounted cash flow analysis.

○ The principles that underpin Strategic Value Analysis, i.e. how a limited number of key value drivers can be used to determine the value of a business and/or its strategies.

○ Strategic Value Analysis as a framework that can be related to number of 'new' metrics which have been developed for measuring value creation.

Introduction

There is nothing new about a concern with value in finance. Much has been written on the subject and many measures of value have been developed which focus on profitability, assets and cash flow. Most of those used for company valuation have drawn on information contained within the main financial statements, which is then related to market-based data. For example, the use of earnings and price to earnings multiples for comparable companies has long been popular practice.

While cash flow measures of value developed around the principles of discounted cash flow analysis have been popularised for appraising capital projects, their use in business valuation has only recently started to gain substantial acceptance in Europe, despite their well documented adoption in the USA since the early 1980s. The use of such measures in the USA has traditionally been associated with a drive towards shareholder value via the maximisation of returns to shareholders [2].

The move towards shareholder value has been driven by a number of significant trends [3]:

- Continued globalisation of capital markets;
- An increasing focus on corporate governance;
- Rising shareholder activism;
- Investors moving increasingly towards cash flow based evaluation.

This focus on only the shareholder has shown signs of shifting and it has been recognised by prominent businessmen that attention needs to be paid to more than one facet of the business [4]. Such views have also been evident in the popular literature on business strategy. For example, one well-respected view about the construction of any business strategy is that three main players need to be taken into consideration – the corporation, the customer and the competition [5].

The emphasis on customer and employee satisfaction has been recognised as being important, particularly in some European markets like Germany. Nevertheless, Europe is waking up to the needs of shareholders because of a number of influencing factors, which include:

- anaemic economic growth in Europe;
- low inflation;
- increasing privatisations and decreasing state subsidies;
- stiff competition from low labour cost countries;
- free(r) trade;
- deregulation of industry;
- increasing influence of shareholder interest groups;
- need for additional equity and debt capital.

All such factors have resulted in pressure being exerted on the return achieved on invested capital and a growing focus on shareholder value.

As many organisations recognise, in practice the customer oriented marketing view and the shareholder oriented financial view should form part of an interactive process that relates the product-market specifics to wider financial implications. In fact, as we will demonstrate in this book, Strategic Value Analysis can be seen as providing this interactive process that links customers to investors [6]. In Figure 1.1 we show that this linkage has three components; value creation, value preservation and value realisation [7].

Figure 1.1: Shareholder value links customers to investors

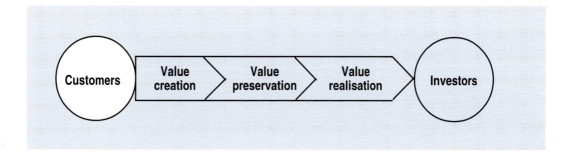

○ Value creation – The process whereby a company can maintain a return on capital greater than its cost of capital. This positive 'spread', which can be retained in the business or distributed to shareholders, represents the value shareholders are looking for when they make their decision to invest in a company. Value creation involves being able to offer something to your customers at a price that satisfies the condition of earning a positive spread.

○ Value preservation – The need to ensure that what is created is not simply wasted or lost through inefficiency or poor management.

○ Value realisation – The need to ensure that investors realise value through capital appreciation of their shares, share buy backs, and dividend pay-outs.

New measures of value

Valuation methods, often presented as being new approaches and associated with measuring shareholder value, have been attracting considerable interest in the UK, continental Europe and elsewhere in recent times [8, 9]. These have often been represented in the media by way of rating tables to show the best and worst performing countries and companies. An example of such a rating table is provided in Figure 1.2 where Market Value Added (MVA) is shown for the 'Top Ten Companies' in the UK.

Figure 1.2: Top Ten UK companies by MVA

Rank	Company	MVA(£m)
1	Shell	15,184
2	Glaxo Wellcome	13,479
3	Unilever	11,222
4	SmithKline Beecham	8,396
5	BAT	7,619
6	Marks and Spencer	7,268
7	BTR	6,623
8	Reuters	6,379
9	BT	6,179
10	Vodafone	5,530

Source: *The Sunday Times*, 10 December 1995, Analysis by Stern Stewart & Co.

MVA is the difference between the total market value (i.e. market value of debt plus equity) and the debt and equity capital that has been invested in the business (usually book values are a starting point to which a number of value based adjustments are made). According to this rating scale, Shell at the top of the league has produced nearly 2.75 times as much MVA as Vodafone at the bottom.

These new methods, like MVA, focus attention on the present value of estimated future short-term and long-term cash flows and, in fact, the principles on which they are based are not new. They are well established in project finance and investment appraisal for evaluating major projects, such as acquisitions [10]. However, their application in valuing the business as a whole, and their use in managing a business is different. Often this involves developing a new, or at the very least a modified, set of performance measures, to replace the previous dominance of accounting performance indicators for managing the business. More broadly, and what is often not well appreciated is the usefulness and adaptability of the approaches for evaluating difficult but important issues like joint ventures and intangible benefits [11].

These new methods have all of the appearance of being only financial tools, but they really are multidisciplinary. They draw not only on corporate finance, but also strategy, marketing and scenario analysis and come in different forms, although most share one common feature – an emphasis on discounted cash flow analysis. To the extent that they encourage thought about the return one is generating on investors' money, these new measures are welcomed by the financial community [12]. The following are examples of different forms of the new methods and all are reviewed in more detail in later chapters of this book:

○ Free cash flow analysis *.
○ Economic profit as popularised by Economic Value Added (EVA®) †.
○ 'Spread' methods.

---

* Often referred to under the heading of Shareholder Value Analysis.
† EVA is the registered trademark of the Stern Stewart company.

Free cash flow analysis is reliant on the net present value approach commonly used for purposes of investment appraisal [13]. Using it, projected cash flows for a planning period and beyond for each business unit in a corporation can be estimated by management, converted into a present value and aggregated. When divided by the number of common shares the result provides an estimate of the shareholder value per share. It focuses substantially on issues relating to the time period over which value may be created, the implications associated with the selection of an appropriate planning horizon, and the strategic implementation of the approach within business units [14]. It has a very strong link with scenario analysis and the analysis of business and market specific risks [15].

Economic profit measures focus on the economic value created over distinct time periods, such as a year. As illustrated in Figure 1.3, for any given time period economic profit is the difference between Net Operating Profit After Taxes (NOPAT) and the Capital Charge, i.e.

Economic profit * = NOPAT − Capital Charge

Figure 1.3: Economic profit

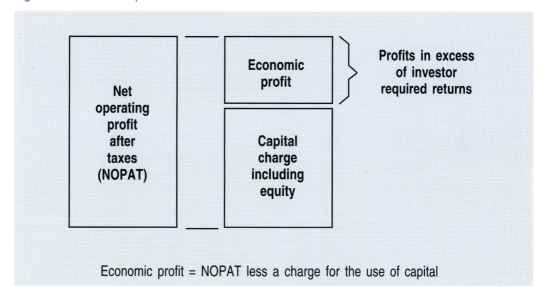

Economic profit = NOPAT less a charge for the use of capital

---

* Alternatively, it is expressed as:
   Economic profit = (NOPAT% − WACC%) x IC

Where,
   IC   = Invested Capital (IC); and
   WACC = Weighted Average Cost of Capital.
   With a NOPAT of 15%, a WACC of 10% and IC of 100, EVA is 5, i.e. 15 − 10, or (15% − 10%) x 100.

While economic profit focuses on a given time period, Market Value Added (MVA), which was introduced earlier, is used to show long-term total value creation or destruction. MVA represents invested capital plus the present value of projected economic profit figures. The one crucial difference between the two is that MVA embodies market expectations and it takes a forward looking perspective. In fact, the results of applying free cash flow analysis and economic profit measures can be shown to be the same in principle when using the same assumptions [16].

In addition to frameworks which draw on the net present value principle, there are those which view value creation or destruction by comparing the 'spread' between the return generated and some measure of the cost of capital. Approaches to calculating the return generated may differ and they can be measured using an internal rate of return calculation or by adjusting accounting returns into cash flow terms. One spread approach that has attracted much attention, known as Cash Flow Return On Investment (CFROI), is the subject of discussion in Chapter 4.

One important point to understand is that in reality all the methods that claim to be focused on shareholder value, including discounted cash flow, economic value added, cash flow return on investment and various accounting approaches, are not applied in the same way. In many cases, the fundamental assumptions are different, the calculations are different and the time horizon is different. Consequently, these various methods do not all produce the same answers or insights into a business' value and its prospects. As Black, Wright and Bachman say in *In Search of Shareholder Value*:

> *Look out for acronyms such as CAPM, CFROI, EVA™, and TSR, all of which manipulate the source data on cash flow, capital or its cost to show different aspects of value* [17].

Figure 1.4: Total Shareholder Return (TSR) generated by the top ten US companies

	TSR (%) * 1991-96 average
3Com	92
Tellabs	84
EMC	74
Cisco Systems	73
Oracle	67
Dell Computer	66
Intel	61
Andrew Corp.	60
Citicorp	60
Micron Technology	60

Source: Boston Consulting Group

---

* TSR (shareprice appreciation plus dividends) is the theoretical capital growth that would have been achieved by a share over the period under review, assuming all dividends were re-invested. TSR typically is represented as the change in capital value of a company over a one-year period, plus dividends, expressed as a plus or minus percentage of the opening value.

Of these measures, TSR is supposed to be the most difficult to manipulate and, like MVA, is often found illustrated in rating tables, as shown in Figure 1.4 for the 'Top Ten Companies' in the USA [18].

No one approach is necessarily right for all circumstances. As with much of good management, the trick is to know when it is most appropriate to use each measure. Best practice dictates the avoidance of single point measures, which can bias decision making and distort management effort. It is important to recognise that all such measures can be seen as addressing some of the shortcomings associated with conventional analysis. For example, a major criticism levelled against the UK and the USA has been short-termism. The poor relative competitive edge of these two countries is often viewed as being attributable to their failure to emphasise long-term investment, this in turn being the fault of their myopic financial markets. A noteworthy review of short-termism found little to support the view that financial markets play any significant part in promoting a short-termist perspective [19]. However, it did find managerial short-termism to represent a real problem. Many businesses in Britain do appear to adopt a very short-termist perspective, that is managing for today rather than tomorrow and beyond.

The new measures represent an important alternative to taking a short-termist perspective and draws on the principles of corporate finance and financial economics rather than accounting, for reasons we review in the next section*.

Problems with using profits or earnings for strategic analysis

Cash is fact, profit is opinion [20].

Creative accounting

One particular problem with using profits or earnings for strategic analysis concerns creative accounting. This represents a means by which companies are able to create a favourable picture of their performance while doing nothing necessarily illegal [21]. Creative accounting featured strongly in the UK press following the publication of a book by Terry Smith which was somewhat controversially entitled, *Accounting for Growth: How to Strip the Camouflage from Company Accounts* [22]. Smith demonstrated a number of approaches by which companies could use and had used considerable judgement to produce results which put them in the best possible light, while staying within the letter of the law.

There are a number of well-documented methods of creative accounting, but one potential creative accounting approach that can be used is to keep costs away from the profit and loss account by capitalising them. This is achieved by including them with fixed assets in the balance sheet. This is possible because accounting makes a distinction between costs that expire during an accounting period and are written-off through the profit and loss account, and assets, which do not expire during a single accounting period and are 'held over'. If a case can be made for such items to be treated as assets, that part which expires during an accounting period will be matched as a cost, the remainder being held in the balance sheet as an asset.

---

* A summary of these principles is shown in Appendix 2.

Items that may often be capitalised include:

○ interest;
○ research and development;
○ start-up costs.

To understand how the capitalisation of costs works, consider the extreme case of a company which, after charging interest payable of £10 million through the profit and loss account, makes a loss of £5 million. Ignoring depreciation and any taxation issues, if this company did not include this interest payable in its profit and loss account, the loss of £5 million would be £5 million profit. This is because the £10 million of interest payable would be included with the fixed assets in the balance sheet rather than with costs in the profit and loss account. The books would still balance irrespective of the treatment of the interest payable and, in the case of the capitalisation of the interest, both the assets and the shareholders' fund sides of the balance sheet would have increased by £10 million*.

When and why do companies capitalise interest costs? The practice may often be used, and not unreasonably, for a large project when the interest is considered to be an indistinguishable part of the cost of an asset. The effect of capitalisation is often very beneficial to the current year's profit but this may not be quite as much as just illustrated, because often the interest payable included within fixed assets will be depreciated together with the actual asset. For example, we will assume that our company with interest payable of £10 million incurs this in relation to a project with a planned time-scale of five years. Depreciating the project over five years means a reduction in profits for each year of £2 million, assuming a straight-line write-off.

The effect of capitalisation is therefore to defer the cost, unless the item never makes an appearance in the profit and loss account – a practice that has been associated with the treatment of investment properties by companies in the property sector.

In principle, a skilled reader of company accounts should be able to spot creative accounting practices. However, there is some evidence that casts doubt on the ability of analysts to detect them [23]. For example, one piece of research found that of 1,325 possible corrections that the 63 experienced investment analysts could have made in calculating financial ratios from a set of accounts full of 'window dressing', only 34 adjustments were made in total. What is more, 52 analysts made no corrections at all! [24]

The international dimension

In addition to the potential problems of creative accounting there are some other difficulties in working with accounting-based measures that need to be brought into the discussion. These difficulties can be seen if we take a more international perspective. By way of illustration, JBA Holdings, a business applications software vendor, reported interim pre-tax losses as a result of having adopted US accounting standards. In fact, the result of restating 1996 results was the conversion of pre-tax profits of £1.4 million to a loss of £2.42 million [25]. Such situations are by no means new, and were well illustrated in 1993 when Daimler-Benz became the first German company to list its shares in New York. Under German rules, it reported a $372 million profit; under tougher US ones, its loss was $1.1 billion! [26]

---

* The shareholders' fund side of the balance sheet is higher because the loss of £5 million is now a profit of £5 million – a change of £10 million.

Such differences have also been well illustrated in studies of the European Union (EU) where, unlike many other parts of the world, a 'harmonisation' of accounting and financial reporting practices has been under way. However, the harmonisation of accountancy practices in the EU has been shown to have had limited impact, as illustrated many years ago in a study of seven EU states [27]. The preparers of accounts were asked to draft accounts (in ECU) for the same hypothetical group of companies to provide statements, which should be directly comparable as between different jurisdictions. For the profit and loss account, participants were asked to use the maximum flexibility of local rules to provide three alternative figures:

1. that at which a real company would be most likely to arrive;

2. the highest profit possible; and

3. the lowest profit possible.

The results of the study are summarised in Figure 1.5.

Figure 1.5: Profit differences within the EU

(ECU millions)	Most Likely Net Profit	Maximum Net Profit	Minimum Net Profit
Belgium	135	193	90
Germany	133	**140**	27
Spain	131	192	121
France	149	160	121
Italy	174	193	167
The Netherlands	140	156	76
United Kingdom	192	194	**171**

The results of the study illustrated the potential for significant differences in reported net profits between EU member states. Also, that the range over which the profit may be measured could be different. To take extreme cases, the British profit could have been at worst 171 million ECU while the German profit could have been at best 140 million ECU. A major reason for the difference between the net profit figures concerned the treatment of goodwill. In an acquisition an acquiring company's financial reports include the target's assets and liabilities adjusted to a fair value to reflect the total consideration paid. In the typical acquisition situation, where the amounts paid exceed the fair value of net assets acquired, the difference is classified as goodwill. Combined net income includes the target company's operating results only from the purchase date forward. Goodwill amortisation, adopted as standard practice in EU countries other than the UK until recently, reduces such combined net income [*].

---

[*] New mandatory rules imposed by the UK Accounting Standards Board (ASB) now require goodwill to be shown alongside a company's assets. Instead of writing-off goodwill immediately against reserves, companies will now be required to show goodwill as an asset and amortise it against future years, profits. This will bring the UK in line with the practices adopted in most other countries.

This study is now some eight years old and it is not unreasonable to believe that there has been greater progress towards harmonisation in financial reporting practices. In fact, more recent research has investigated the effect of the initiatives that have been undertaken by the International Accounting Standards Committee (IASC) which has been striving to put in place a set of core standards for acceptance by the world's leading stock markets [28].

In terms of general comparisons between EU financial reporting practices and the rest of the world, few differences were evident, probably because the EU contains the UK, France and Spain, which are the ancestors for most of the accounting systems found internationally [29, 30]. As regards the situation within EU countries, the results suggested some important differences across the EU relating to specific issues (e.g. recognition of revenue on construction contracts, treatment of gains or losses on long-term monetary items, and the treatment of development costs).

The impression provided by the study is that the IASC has managed to reduce the number of options available to corporations, while at the same time permitting them to still employ the most commonly found practices. However, while the overall compliance rate with the IASC recommendations was found to be relatively high, considerable diversity still exists within the EU. What is more, harmonisation attempts by the EU appear to have had no influence on the extent to which EU practices are congruent with the IASC standards.

Until such time as standardisation is achieved it is appropriate to bear the following quote in mind:

> ...the sheer scale of international accounting differences including the effects of such complex figures as 'earnings' and 'net assets' means that income statement formats around the world are not only different, but also irreconcilable [31].

Value reporting

One plea often made is for the provision of more relevant information to those who use financial statements in making decisions about companies [32]. The view has been expressed that the financial reporting model is an anachronism that, despite increasingly tight regulation and extensive disclosure requirements, does not meet the needs of those who run businesses and invest in them [33]. To overcome this Price Waterhouse has proposed an approach called 'Value Reporting' which has seven core components [34]:

1. Perform a preliminary evaluation of the financial drivers of the company – the levers of shareholder value.
2. Determine how these drivers are embodied in the corporation's objectives and how the drivers are shaping business operations.
3. Understand how management has developed the strategies currently in place to achieve these objectives.
4. Determine whether the objectives and strategies are supported by performance measurements, and assess the quality of measurement data provided to management.
5. Assess whether management processes foster value creation.

6. Draw up the 'big picture' from all the foregoing activities and select the most relevant points to communicate with the investing public about value-creating strategies, processes, goals and results.

7. Review, on a rotating basis, how effectively the major processes of the company (such as capital planning, acquisitions, budgeting, strategic planning, product/service planning, management forums, and executive compensation) are functioning, and fix what needs to be fixed.

Value Reporting is characterised by a Statement of Shareholder Value Achieved, based on estimated future cash flows which analyses financial and non-financial 'value drivers'. These are the key variables that lead to the creation of shareholder value. Examples of the kind of financial variables represented by these value drivers include:

- sales growth rate;
- operating profit margin;
- cost of capital.

Non-financial drivers include:

- market share;
- customer satisfaction;
- product defects;
- 'intellect index', to gauge employees' skills;
- research and development;
- brands;
- indicators of administrative efficiency, such as process cost per sales transaction or office space utilisation.

This Statement of Shareholder Value Achieved expresses the underlying value of the business as a whole and per share. How such value is calculated is reviewed in the next chapter.

Accounting measures and valuation

We have identified many limitations associated with accounting measures, which limit their value in strategic financial analysis. By and large, these have been discussed within the context of external reporting, but they have some additional limitations, when considered as internal measures of performance, i.e.

1. Risk is excluded.
2. Investment requirements are excluded.
3. Time value of money is ignored.

1. Risk is excluded

Risk is of central importance in establishing the economic value of any asset. A firm's level of risk is determined both by the nature of its operations and by the relative proportions of debt and equity used to finance its investments. These two types of risk are respectively referred to as 'business risk' and 'financial risk': Earnings figures do not incorporate consideration of either type of risk.

2. Investment requirements are excluded

The relationship between changes in economic value and changes in earnings is further obscured by the fact that the investments in working capital and fixed capital needed to sustain the firm and to support future growth are excluded from the earnings calculation.

3. Time value of money is ignored

Earnings fail to measure changes in economic value because earnings calculations ignore the time value of money. Economic value calculations, by comparison, explicitly incorporate the idea that a sum of money received today is worth more than a sum of money received a year from now because it can be invested to earn a return over the next year. What is more, the discount rate used to estimate economic value can be adjusted to include not only compensation for risk-bearing, but also compensation for the expected levels of inflation.

The empirical evidence

Specific accounting based indicators of performance have been found in UK studies to fare poorly as measures of shareholder return, (what shareholders expect to receive by way of dividends and capital appreciation). For example, studies have found that there is little if any statistical relationship between shareholder return and earnings per share growth and virtually no relationship at all with return on equity [35]. However, by comparison cash flow measures fare much better than accounting measures of profitability as indicated by a considerable amount of empirical research, which has demonstrated that there is a significant relationship between cash flow and share prices [36]. Research undertaken in the UK supports previous work predominantly based on US data [37]. Using a sample of 98 firms listed on the London Stock Exchange over the period 1979 to 1992, strong evidence was found that cash flow variables have incremental information content beyond that contained in accrual earnings. However, both accrual earnings and cash flows were found to be important determinants of stock returns for UK companies.

As far as other markets are concerned, the evidence is far less comprehensive. In the Asia Pacific region, preliminary research has indicated that investors have not relied on earnings per share growth to value securities, but are concerned with their overall potential cash pay-out, adjusted for risk [38].

Overview of the book

In the remainder of this book the principles and practice of Strategic Value Analysis will be demonstrated. The structure of the book is as follows:

Part 1: Valuation – The Dynamics of Shareholder Value

Chapter 1: Introduction to Strategic Value Analysis
Chapter 2: Calculating a Free Cash Flow Strategic Value
Chapter 3: The Planning Period and Competitive Advantage

Part 2: Key Valuation Issues

Chapter 4: Alternative Measures of Strategic Value
Chapter 5: Terminal Value
Chapter 6: The Cost of Capital

Part 3: Applications

Chapter 7: Valuation in Emerging Markets and Cross Border Valuations
Chapter 8: Mergers, Acquisitions and Joint Ventures
Chapter 9: Valuing New Issues and Intangible Assets
Chapter 10: Strategic Value Management

Part 1: Valuation – The Dynamics of Shareholder Value

Within Part 1, the dynamics of shareholder value are considered. A key feature of Strategic Value Analysis is the strategic analysis of the business over an appropriate time horizon. This necessitates examining markets, customers, competences and capabilities. The result of such strategic analysis can then be expressed in financial terms using the principles of finance. Within Strategic Value Analysis, this involves using the principles of discounted cash flow analysis to calculate a value for the business based on managerial judgements determined from the strategic analysis. This value can be expressed using any of the different value metrics currently in vogue.

In simple terms, value resulting from such calculations can be used as the basis for comparison with the value as determined by the stock market if the business in question is a listed company. Recognition has to be given to the fact that any value will be dependent on the quality of the data used. Strategic Value Analysis can deal with this by providing and encouraging interrogation such that the value can and should be revised in the light of better quality data. One measure of strategic value, free cash flow analysis, relates data input with value output via a number of so-called 'value drivers'. Managerial judgement about the business strategy is captured in these value drivers, which are converted to period by period cash flows and ultimately a value. In generic terms these value drivers can be expressed as follows:

1. Sales growth rate.
2. Earnings Before Interest, Tax, Depreciation and Amortisation (EBITDA) margin.
3. Cash tax rate.
4. Fixed capital investment to support current levels of activity – known as replacement fixed capital investment – and to support future growth – known as incremental fixed capital investment.
5. Working capital investment.
6. Weighted Average Cost of Capital (WACC).
7. Planning period.

Cash flows are determined with reference to the first five value drivers. The resulting cash flows are known as 'free cash flows' and represent the cash freely available for distribution to the providers of debt and equity (and/or other long-term sources of funds). Funding requirements are not deducted in arriving at these free cash flows, but are taken into consideration via their inclusion in the calculation of the Weighted Average Cost of Capital (WACC) used as the discount rate. These free cash flows are typically estimated over a planning period and then, together with any terminal value, they are discounted to a present value using the WACC.

How such a valuation can be undertaken using these seven value drivers is reviewed in Chapter 2 where, based on a limited number of assumptions, a strategic value is estimated for Santos plc [*]. This is a fictional company originating as a group of retail bookstores which has recently started to diversify its base within the publishing sector. Its intended diversification is broad ranging such that it anticipates having a presence in the rapidly emerging Internet publishing market. In fact, Santos plc is used in much of this book to illustrate the principles of Strategic Value Analysis [†], (real-life illustrations are also provided in later chapters).

Within any valuation, the estimation of the cash flows is critical, as are assumptions about the Weighted Average Cost of Capital and the planning period. Both of these are the subject of individual chapters. Specifically, issues associated with the determination of planning period or Competitive Advantage Period are reviewed in Chapter 3. This chapter forges the crucial link between financial and strategic theory in valuation analysis.

By understanding what it is that drives performance in terms of shareholder value it is considered that management will be able to focus on what really matters. However, not all value drivers will be equally important and by building a value model it is generally possible to identify those which have the greatest impact on value. In fact, a good illustration of the use of these seven value drivers is provided in Evaluator, which evaluates current business strategies and draws extensively on the seven value drivers for purposes of initial analysis. It values and benchmarks a company's performance in terms of these seven value drivers against key competitors to indicate where strategies can be modified to enhance value and to formulate and implement appropriate courses of action.

---

[*] public limited company
[†] The financial statements for Santos plc are summarised in Appendix 1 page 223.

The approach outlined above and illustrated in the next few chapters focuses on the analysis of key value drivers within a fairly simple framework. It is important to recognise that in real life the modelling may well be much more complex. Spreadsheet modelling can be invaluable particularly when it is structured in the manner illustrated in Figure 1.6.

Figure 1.6: Modelling using Strategic Value Analysis

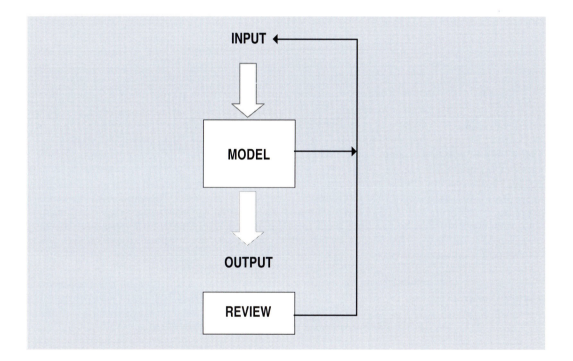

Imperfect input data is always the starting point. Very often what is required is not available, or what is required is not known at this stage. Such imperfect data can then be modelled using Strategic Value Analysis to give a 'first pass' picture of reality by way of output. There may often be some core assumptions adopted in developing the Strategic Value Analysis model which need to be challenged, as well as the data used as the input to the model. This challenging process represents the most valuable part of the process of building a more robust model of reality.

To achieve most benefit, such modelling needs to be carefully structured. At first this may focus on the seven value drivers, but often circumstances dictate a more detailed approach involving the analysis of:

1. operating effects;
2. financing effects;
3. tax effects.

The analysis of operating effects forces attention on the business case for the model to be built. For example, if looked at within the context of evaluating a proposed acquisition it seeks to ascertain what new management will be able to do with the operations that are not currently being practised. Consider the acquisition of Jaguar by Ford. In the hands of Ford such analysis probably corresponded with scope for research and development on existing and new models, access to new distribution channels, and so on.

As regards the financing effects, it is useful to look at the capital structure and the cost of capital afresh and separately. While financing effects can usefully be analysed separately, initially, the results must be fed back into the operating case because it would also be affected by any financial restructuring. Last, but by no means least, tax effects need to be looked at carefully and one approach is to make the best guess possible when analysing the operating and financing case, but then to examine them in more depth, with the outcomes being fed back into the overall model.

This three-step approach typically makes the overall process much more complex, but is often essential for major valuations. At this stage, the importance of specific valuation software for reducing potential spreadsheet error needs to be recognised.

Part 2: Key Valuation Issues

As indicated earlier, there are different measures of strategic value, each of which may have merit for different circumstances. How these can be calculated and how they potentially relate to one another we consider in Chapter 4. While they can be shown to be reconcilable with one another in principle, in practice they often produce different results. Why this may be so and the relative merits of each, are also discussed in the chapter.

One really important feature of the Strategic Value Analysis thinking is the emphasis it places on value creation beyond the planning period. As McKinsey and Company have shown, the contribution of such value, known as the terminal value, to the total may be very significant[39]. Issues associated with the determination of terminal values, as a basis for their calculation and when each may be appropriate, are covered in Chapter 5. This includes a review of some of the more important traditional methods in use for valuation generally. Of these terminal value approaches, one in popular usage involves the calculation of a perpetuity.

Key within the calculation of a perpetuity value are assumptions about the cost of capital (often the WACC), which is used as the discount rate to estimate present value. In fact, the cost of capital typically has a significant impact on value in strategic value calculations and there are many issues that need to be taken into account in its estimation. These issues and a review of the methods that can be used to estimate the cost of capital are covered in Chapter 6.

Part 3: Applications

The last four chapters of the book relate the principles of the earlier chapters to real-life situations. Many of the issues introduced in Chapters 1 to 6 are illustrated and extended.

In Chapter 7, some of the important issues associated with valuation in emerging markets and cross border valuations are considered. Much of the so-called conventional wisdom developed in the first six chapters is difficult to apply in an emerging market environment. A good example of such difficulties concerns the cost of capital. The techniques developed in Chapter 6 for estimating WACC need to be revisited when looked at from the perspective of determining a discount rate to be used in a new issue in Malaysia. These are illustrated using the data relating to Litrak, an infrastructure company listed at the end of December 1996.

Mergers, acquisitions and joint ventures represent an important application of valuation approaches. As regards mergers and acquisitions, all the evidence suggests in general terms that little financial benefit accrues to acquirers. However, mergers and acquisitions need not be financially unsuccessful. It is possible to use a framework built around Strategic Value Analysis for the evaluation of an acquisition opportunity. The nature of this framework and how it can be applied is reviewed in Chapter 8 with reference to the acquisition of a UK chemical company by Laporte plc. We illustrate how using the Strategic Value Analysis framework, the acquisition target can be evaluated on a stand-alone basis. This evaluation can then be reviewed against the potential value as seen through the acquirer's eyes. The important point is that the size of this value varies depending on the perspective of the acquiring company, such that the value derived by one potential acquirer may be very different from that seen by another.

In addition to reviewing valuation from an acquisition perspective, we also demonstrate how the same framework can be used in evaluating a joint venture opportunity. While the framework can be adapted for use, there are some challenging issues associated with joint venture analysis. As will be illustrated, one of these is that the main part of the value may arise from the terminal value and assumptions about the length of the planning period become critical.

In Chapter 9, the question of how to evaluate private companies and new issues is reviewed with reference to the flotation of Orange plc. In the case of Orange, the valuation was very dependent on information about peer group companies in order to estimate the WACC to use. This example provides an illustration of the application of techniques that frequently need to be used in practice to estimate the index of the market related risk, called the beta. Information about this is required to estimate the cost of equity using the Capital Asset Pricing Model (CAPM). The Orange illustration also serves to show a number of other important valuation 'complications'. First, the company was expected to be loss making for a number of years and second, estimates of its value were very heavily dependent on assumptions about the market for cellular telephones over a relatively long time horizon, i.e. beyond ten years.

The last chapter, Chapter 10, reviews the concept of Strategic Value Management. Many companies have embarked on applying the principles of valuation using discounted cash flow methods to manage their business on an ongoing basis. Essentially, such a programme involves driving the principles of valuation down throughout the organisation and can be undertaken using any of the valuation metrics which will be discussed in Chapter 4. Such a process, known as 'cascading' brings with it additional challenges in the form of needing to value the parts of the business which make up the overall company. This necessitates that attention is devoted to the cost of capital required by the individual businesses, which may be very different from that for the company as a whole. While a company might have an overall cost of capital of 10 per cent, this might represent a blend of the costs of capital of different business units. The challenge is how to measure these business unit costs of capital and also how to assess the relevant planning periods to use.

In addition to these technical issues associated with Strategic Value Management there are some others which are equally important which need to be taken into consideration. First, such an initiative is very often undertaken in conjunction with others like re-engineering, as part of an overall change programme. Second, and of particular importance, are the implementation issues. It is one thing to undertake a valuation, it is quite another to harness management into using the principles of valuation in managing a business.

Summary checklist

- Strategic Value Analysis represents a synthesis of the disciplines of marketing, finance and strategy.
- Despite recent moves to reduce creative accounting and the moves being made towards international harmonisation of accounting policies, scope still exist for manipulation of accounting measures. Profits are a matter of opinion while cash is a matter of fact.
- Profit and earnings as measures of strategic value suffer from the fact that they ignore risk and the time value of money and exclude investment requirements.
- The real value of the SVA framework is the questions it forces managers to ask about the dynamics of how their business creates value.
- Different measures can be used to assess value creation and these including free cash flow analysis, economic profit and 'spreads'.

Concluding remarks

In this chapter we have shown that profit measures, traditionally used for purposes of valuation, are a problem in estimating strategic value for a number of reasons:

1. Studies have shown that profit measures are not closely associated with shareholder returns.
2. Such measures are capable of manipulation and vary in definition across different national boundaries.
3. The long-term nature of strategic issues that relate to a world full of risk and uncertainty may often be overlooked in using such measures.
4. The application of profit measures tends to be highly user unfriendly and focused incorrectly in a business world in which managers have to satisfy multiple objectives.

However, despite these reservations financial statements typically represent the starting point for making strategic value estimates. With this in mind it will be shown in subsequent chapters how the information provided by such statements for the fictional company, Santos plc, can be used to estimate a number of strategic value measures. Such statements will be used to generate a cash flow 'picture' of the business.

By comparison with profit measures, free cash flow analysis assumes that in broad terms the value of a business can be determined by discounting its future cash flows using an appropriate cost of capital. These cash flows are captured within a number of value drivers and related to the dynamics of business.

Many organisations are embarking on the quest for value and using the new valuation metrics in the recognition that such approaches may help them face the challenge of managing in an increasingly turbulent and uncertain business environment. Often companies use more than one measure, and a good example of this has been provided by the large US chemical company, Monsanto. It is applying the CFROI* measure to link corporate actions with market expectations and, in addition, it has adopted the Economic Value Added metric for managing its business units [40].

What is the real benefit of adopting the new valuation metrics? All approaches can be seen as offering a means of asking the right questions about whether the business can satisfy the demands of its many stakeholders. As to which is best, the jury is still out. There is little doubt that there will be continued effort on the part of the proponents of all to demonstrate that their metric is best. All are preferable to the traditional alternatives, not least because they all force tough questions to be asked which might otherwise be neglected.

---

* See Chapter 4.

Chapter 2: Calculating a Free Cash Flow Strategic Value

Glaxo Wellcome is destroying shareholder value at the moment. But five years from now it could be creating more value than any other European drug stock...

Of course, investors must be prepared to look through two years of static earnings. But on anything but a short-term view, Glaxo is still an attractive investment.

Lex Column, Financial Times, 1 August 1997.

Chapter preview

- How to calculate the strategic value of a business using a free cash flow value driver framework.
- The principles that underpin the free cash flow estimation of strategic value, drawing particularly on information relating to an example company.
- Using publicly available data to estimate five cash flow value drivers.
- The relationship between the value drivers, life cycle effects and the type of business being valued.
- The relationship between the value of the planning period and the terminal value.

Introduction

This chapter is concerned with how future free cash flows and the value from a strategic investment opportunity (strategic value) can be estimated. This strategic value can be represented by two related parts, the period over which forecast plans are made, known as the planning period, and the period beyond, known as the continuing period. Associated with each of these will be a value, the size of which will depend on a number of factors, including the type of business to be analysed. For example, in the case of Santos plc referred to in Chapter 1. It will be shown how a value of £196.25 million can be calculated over a five-year timeframe and how the majority of this value (73 per cent) can be attributed to value created beyond the five-year timeframe.

Specifically, this chapter examines how strategic value comprising estimates for the planning and continuing period can be determined. The starting point for now is the estimation of the free cash flows using the first five of the seven value drivers discussed in Chapter 1, i.e.:

1. Sales growth rate.
2. EBITDA (Earnings Before Interest, Tax, Depreciation and Amortisation).
3. Cash tax rate.
4. Fixed capital investment.
5. Working capital investment.

For now, important issues relating to the remaining two value drivers will be ignored. This is because the determination of the cost of capital and the planning period are considered in separate chapters later on in the book. In this chapter, the emphasis is on providing an overview of the steps involved in undertaking a relatively simple strategic value calculation.

Estimating free cash flow

How can values for the free cash flow drivers be estimated? The answer is that they are typically estimates obtained by looking at a mix of past experience, management judgement about what is likely to happen in the future, and observations about the marketplace.

The importance of cash flow data should not be underestimated in measuring strategic value. The expression 'garbage in, garbage out' (GIGO) is very appropriate for issues relating to business valuation, where the quality of any business valuation can only be as good as the input data on which it is based. With this in mind let us review the issues associated with estimating the cash flow drivers.

1. Sales growth rate

Estimated future sales can be projected from market information to produce forecasts about the market for goods or services. Such market forecasts should be based on an analysis of market opportunities. A pricing policy will also have to be established in each sector in order to put a monetary value on the forecast sales quantities. Prices (in most markets) affect the quantity sold, so there will be an iterative process to estimate the sales volume at the most appropriate prices to provide what is thought to be the relevant sales receipts over the forecast period.

The current level of sales (for each product at current prices) is very much the starting point for sales growth analysis. Any expected growth in sales volume from, for example, prior investment in fixed and working capital must be added. There may also be some adverse influences on sales value, for example, as a result of a decrease in sales volume because of say divestment, or even a lowering of prices.

As a starting point it can be quite helpful to think of the first driver of business value as being sales growth. If the enterprise does not sell anything, then it cannot really be said to be in business! However, it is important to be realistic in assessing sales growth potential. Current and prospective competition, when combined with actual and potential barriers to entry typically influence sales growth potential.

2. EBITDA margin

EBITDA is used rather than other measures of earnings, such as operating profit to overcome many of the difficulties that may arise because of taxation and capital structure differences, particularly within a cross-border valuation context[*]. It can also be thought of as being closer to cash than other measures of profit because the depreciation of tangible assets and the amortisation of intangible assets are ignored in its calculation[†].

EBITDA reflects the earnings to be generated after the costs of doing business have been taken into consideration. Typically, once sales forecasts and more concrete sales plans are agreed, managers will need to consider the means of ensuring the supply of those sales to customers and the costs of doing so. Such costs will relate to:

1. the sourcing and costs of raw materials;
2. employing and training an adequate labour force;
3. establishing sufficient sales and distribution facilities;
4. marketing of the product/service;
5. ensuring adequate production facilities;
6. creating a management team able to manage the business.

In a not-for-profit organisation, activities will also generate costs that have to be charged against income receivable. However, in some not-for-profit concerns, the income may not be linked to the service in quite the same way that costs are linked to sales in a commercial enterprise. For example, a charity in which the income from donations and grants is

---

[*] In some circumstances, EBITDA information may not be available in which case the operating profit will typically need to be converted to cash flow by adding back depreciation and any other non-cash items. This is illustrated later in Figure 2.6 with reference to Santos plc.

[†] Depreciation can be thought of as being an apportionment of the sum paid for a fixed asset over its useful economic life. The simplest way to understand this is with reference to an illustration. Imagine a piece of machinery bought today for £100,000, which is expected to last for five years and to be worth nothing at the end of this time period. If paid for by cash then there would be a cash outflow of £100,000 at the time of purchase. However, for accounting purposes it would be written-off over the five-year period such that only a proportion, say one fifth or £20,000, would be charged against profit each year.

unrelated to the 'output' or activity of the charity. In this case, the not-for-profit undertaking has to ensure that the best use is made of its income by providing a cost-effective service. It is arguably more difficult to manage this – where one is measuring benefits against costs – than in the commercial world where the amount of profit is a measure of the degree of success.

This illustration also flags up that very different approaches may need to be adopted in generating forecast cash flows depending on circumstances. What drives cash flow is by no means common to all types of business operations; an issue that has to be considered in forecasting future cash flows. A sequence of events starting with sales growth may be difficult to apply in all circumstances.

It is important to realise that the EBITDA margin on sales also depends on the type of business. Generally, the principle is that the greater the need for investment in fixed assets and working capital, the higher the profit margin has to be on sales. For example, food retailers in the UK have relatively low amounts tied up in fixed assets and working capital. They may own some of their stores but rent others and have very little tied up in working capital by way of stocks and debtors. Such companies work on lower sales margins than heavy goods companies, like those supplying plant and equipment to industry, that have to plan for much higher margins on sales value. Such companies have large factories to pay for and the net profit on each sale has proportionately to be much higher than the retailer.

3. Cash tax rate

Once EBITDA has been estimated, a forecast amount of tax to be paid will have to be taken into account. Tax is often more difficult to consider from a general managerial perspective than the other cash flow drivers because it is very much a specialist area. For this reason general assumptions about the cash tax rate are often made when valuing a business. Nevertheless there are one or two issues that are important to understand.

First, tax payable on profits is an income tax paid by a venture on its income (or net profit) in just the same way that individuals have to pay income tax on their income. Companies in many countries must also pay capital gains tax on any gain made from liquidating an asset or investment held over time. For example, if an office building was sold for £10 million which had originally cost £4 million, there would be tax to pay on the capital appreciation of £6 million. However, in many countries the capital gains tax is not levied on the full capital gain because an allowance is made for the general rate of inflation. In this example, the allowance for inflation would mean that the £4 million original cost would be indexed to a higher figure and the resultant gain would be lower.

Second, a charge, for what has become known as deferred tax, is made in each year's accounts for a number of adjustments, including the amount of capital gains tax that would have to be paid if the asset were sold at the date the accounts were drawn up. The main point about deferred tax is that it is irrelevant as far as free cash flow is concerned. The concern is with the amount of tax actually paid in any year, that is the year during which any tax is payable.

Third, under taxation systems like that in the UK, interest payable is a tax-deductible expense whereas as a general rule, interest receivable and investment income are taxable income. In other words, for a company with a net interest expense the tax charge in the profit and loss account has been reduced by the tax shield effect of interest. To arrive at the true after-tax profits from operations, the tax charge must first be adjusted to reverse this effect. This can be estimated by multiplying the net interest payable figure in the profit and loss account by the marginal rate of corporation tax. The adjusted tax charge effectively represents the tax payable by the company if it had been entirely equity-financed and had no non-operating income. If this adjustment is not made, the way in which a company has been financed will distort the calculated return.

4 & 5   Fixed and working capital investment

Using information about sales growth potential, the EBITDA margin and likely cash tax payments, operating cash flows can be estimated. However, for valuation purposes free cash flow estimates are required in the form of deductions from operating cash flow for investment purposes. In other words, the distinction between operating cash flow and free cash flow is that the investment necessary to maintain existing cash flows and to support future cash flows. Such investment will be concerned with:

○ Replacement fixed capital investment, (RFCI) in the form of investment for the replacement of fixed assets to meet existing customer demands and investment in new assets to meet intended sales growth projections incremental fixed capital investment, (IFCI).

○ Working Capital Investment (WCI), i.e. investment in working capital such as stocks of materials.

Estimating these can be difficult in practice and many different approaches can be adopted. For RFCI the objective is to assess how much a company needs to reinvest in its existing core business at current prices, in order to maintain both the productive capacity and, where it is an issue, competitive position. In other words, how much should the company be charging against profits for the use of its fixed assets on a replacement cost basis? This number is often referred to as the 'maintenance capex' and its calculation forces an assessment of the real economic value of a company's assets. Companies tend to invest according to their free cash flow and so an analysis of free cash flow should give a reasonable guide to a company's future investment spending. This is because falling free cash flow is generally followed by falling capital investment and vice versa. Since companies are not obliged to disclose their RFCI, any assessment of its value is bound to be subjective. However, in some industries, maintenance capex can be estimated with some degree of confidence by referring to the replacement cost of capacity, e.g. airlines, car manufacturers and steel producers [82]. In other industries, however, the figure may bear little relationship to the eventual cost of replacing fixed assets. More generally, an estimate of maintenance capex must be put in the context of both actual capex and the historic cost accounting (HCA) depreciation figure. Actual capex over several years, relative to sales or fixed assets, gives a guide to how much a company has thought it necessary to invest in its assets – though this must be offset by an assessment of the proportion of that capex that was earmarked for expansion rather than maintenance. HCA depreciation in most cases provides a baseline figure for maintenance capex; a frequently used assumption is that depreciation is a good estimate for RFCI.

For the other two types of investment IFCI and WCI, there are many different forecasting approaches. One approach mentioned above, which will be illustrated in the next section, involves estimating the relationship between increased sales and increased fixed and working capital expenditure using historical data. It is important to note that this will very often need to be disaggregated substantially. For example, working capital investment will typically be analysed in terms of required expenditure on individual components, like stocks and debtors.

Perhaps the most difficult problem in this area arises when there are step changes in technology. If a competitor invents a new production process, which dramatically lowers cash operating costs, a company is obliged to decide whether to invest in the same technology or face steady loss of competitive position. Even if it judges that the return on that investment will be inadequate, once a rival's capacity is in existence it will tend to drive industry prices down to new, lower levels relative to input costs. In effect, this means that a decision not to invest is a decision to begin to leave the industry.

While reference has been made to fixed and working capital requirements to support future growth, they are not the only type of investment that may be necessary. Expenditure on research and development, product development as well as other less tangible items, may be required. The reality is that this is a cash flow approach which recognises that any cash outflow, however defined for accounting purposes, must be taken into consideration.

Illustration – estimating free cash flow

To see how the five cash flow value drivers can be used to provide a free cash flow estimate, let us consider a business with sales revenues today of £100 million and sales growth rate expectations of 5 per cent in the first year, 10 per cent in the second year, and 15 per cent in the remaining three years. With knowledge of this information the sales receipts would be as indicated by the 'End of Year' column in Figure 2.1.

Figure 2.1: Forecasting future sales receipts

Year	Start of Year £m	Growth Rate %	End of Year £m
1	100.00	5	105.00
2	105.00	10	115.50
3	115.50	15	132.83
4	132.83	15	152.75
5	152.75	15	175.66

Let us further assume that the values of the EBITDA margin and the cash tax rate for these years have been estimated as follows:

Year	1	2	3	4	5	Beyond
EBITDA margin	10%	10%	12%	12%	14%	10%
Cash tax rate	30%	30%	30%	30%	30%	30%

Applying these two value drivers to the projected sales revenues in Figure 2.1 gives the after tax operating cash flow shown in Figure 2.2:

Figure 2.2: From sales receipts to after tax operating profit

Year	Sales Receipts £m	EBITDA %	EBITDA £m	Cash Tax Rate %	Operating Cash Flow after Tax £m
1	105.00	10	10.50	30	7.35
2	115.50	10	11.55	30	8.08
3	132.83	12	15.94	30	11.16
4	152.75	12	18.33	30	12.83
5	175.66	14	24.59	30	17.21

As indicated in the preceding section, operating cash flow does not take account of important cash outflows that will need to be incurred to support the existing and the intended sales growth. In order to achieve the intended sales growth rates, fixed and working capital investment may need to be incurred. Replacement fixed capital investment (RFCI) is required to maintain the existing assets in a satisfactory form to meet existing customer demands, while incremental fixed capital investment (IFCI) needs to be incurred to meet the projected sales growth rates. For our example company, let us assume that the depreciation for each of the five years has been estimated as £5 million and that this depreciation figure is a good proxy for RFCI. As we have indicated, an estimate has to be made of the amount of incremental fixed capital that will be required to support incremental sales. One way to build this in is to assume that for every £1 of sales to be generated some fixed capital investment will need to be incurred. For example, this might well be expressed as a percentage of incremental sales, such as a rate of 10 per cent on every £1 of additional sales will mean that 10 pence of incremental fixed capital investment will be required. This has to be recognised as being a rather simplistic approach insofar as investment may not occur in even increments, but may be incurred in 'lumps', however, it does represent a starting point.

Typically, an investment in working capital will also be required as additional sales will be difficult to sustain without incurring incremental working capital. More stock may be needed and it may only be possible to achieve a growth in sales by extending credit and increasing debtors. In common with incremental fixed capital it can be assumed that for every additional £1 of sales to be generated, some working capital investment will be required. In other words, any increase in sales can only occur by taking on more stocks of raw materials and, possibly, by increasing accounts receivable (debtors). For purposes of the earlier example it will be assumed that incremental fixed capital investment (IFCI) and working capital investment (WCI) will be 10 per cent over the five-year assumed planning period.

All this can now be pulled together to estimate prospective free cash flows. These are illustrated in Figure 2.3.

Figure 2.3: From operating cash flow after tax to free cash flow

Year	1	2	3	4	5
	£m	£m	£m	£m	£m
Sales	105.00	115.50	132.83	152.75	175.66
EBITDA	10.50	11.55	15.94	18.33	24.59
– Cash Tax	3.15	3.47	4.78	5.50	7.38
Operating Cash Flow	7.35	8.08	11.16	12.83	17.21
– WCI *	0.50	1.05	1.73	1.99	2.29
– RFCI	5.00	5.00	5.00	5.00	5.00
– IFCI †	0.50	1.05	1.73	1.99	2.29
Free Cash Flow	1.35	0.98	2.70	3.85	7.63

Relationship between the different drivers of free cash flow

The relationship between the cash inflows and outflows is important to recognise. To achieve sales growth, expenditure will have to be incurred, the amount of which will depend on the magnitude of the sales growth and the capacity of the business to expand. The interrelationship between these cash flow drivers is vital to understand, particularly so in the case of the sales growth rate and incremental fixed and working capital investment. Without adequate fixed assets and working capital it may be impossible to achieve a target growth rate, let alone sustain it. However, one problem with fixed capital investment is that it may often be 'lumpy'. Beyond a certain level of production it may be impossible to produce more without investing in completely new plant and equipment. Thus, the assumption of a linear relationship between sales growth and investment is one that may not always be realistic.

The identification of key value drivers is vital and it is important to recognise that they may vary over the life cycle of a business and by type of business. In the case of the life cycle (illustrated in Figure 2.4), in the start-up phase sales growth will often play a dominant role. However, with the development of the market and the increased participation of competitors, attention to profit margins may well be more important. This is because there will often come a point beyond which increased sales will result in value destruction, i.e. additional sales revenue might well be outweighed by the costs associated with generating it.

---

* For year 1, incremental sales = £105m - £100m = £5m, and WCI = £5m x 10% = £0.5m

† For year 1, incremental sales = £105m - £100m = £5m, and IFCI = £5m x 10% = £0.5m

Figure 2.4: Value drivers over the life cycle

	Stage of life cycle			
Value Drivers	**Launch**	**Growth**	**Maturity**	**Decline**
Sales Growth	High	High	None	Negative
Operating Margin	Low/High	High	Medium	Low
Tax Rate	Low	Low	Normal	Depends
Working Capital Investment	High	High	Low	Reducing
Fixed Capital Investment	High >>> Depreciation	High > Depreciation	Low/Medium = or < Depreciation	Low/Reducing << Depreciation
Cost of Capital linked to level of business risk	Very High	High	Medium	Low
Planning Period	Short	Medium/Long	Long	Short/Medium
Continuing Value	Large	Large	Medium	Medium

As indicated above, not only will the stage of development have an impact on the value drivers, but also the type of business. An example of this is provided in Figure 2.5 for a systems solutions company. Work undertaken to identify the impact of the value drivers within four different businesses yielded very different results.

Figure 2.5: Impact of value drivers within ICL (the systems solutions company) *

Business	**1**	**2**	**3**	**4**
Value Drivers				
Sales Growth	Medium	High	High	Medium
Operating Margin	High	Medium	High	High
Tax Rate	Low	Low	Low	Medium
Working Capital	High	High	Medium	Medium
Fixed Capital	Medium	High	Low	Medium
Cost of Capital	High	High	High	High
Planning Period	Medium	Long	Long	Long

A business such as that characterised under Business 2 is dependent on substantial fixed and working capital investment to generate sales growth. In fact, this value driver profile can be likened to a start-up situation in which fixed and working capital expenditure will be essential for stimulating future growth. It is also worth noting that in some businesses such expenditure will be directed at intangible rather than tangible items. Future growth may be driven by research and development in industries such as pharmaceuticals, while in others expenditure on branding of products and product development may be the key.

---

* Courtesy of Mr I. Neill, Director of Strategic Planning, ICL plc.

Estimating free cash flow in practice

The usual starting point for estimating values for cash flow drivers, particularly when working with publicly quoted companies, is the information contained in the annual report and accounts. By way of illustration the information introduced in the last chapter relating to the fictional example company, Santos plc, will be drawn on. In this case we will show more fully how free cash flows can be derived from accounting data rather than by way of just the simple projection method used for purposes of exposition in the last section.

A free cash flow forecast for Santos plc for 1998 to 2002 and beyond is shown in Figure 2.6. Historical data for 1997 are also shown to the left of the black vertical line.

Figure 2.6: Free cash flow estimates

	1997 £m	1998 £m	1999 £m	2000 £m	2001 £m	2002 £m	Beyond £m
Sales	285.02	319.22	357.53	400.43	448.48	502.30	502.30
− Cost of sales	122.94	137.69	154.21	172.72	193.45	216.66	216.66
Gross profit	162.08	181.53	203.32	227.71	255.03	285.64	285.64
− Operating expenses	125.75	143.36	163.43	186.31	212.39	242.12	242.12
Operating profit *	36.33	38.17	39.89	41.40	42.64	43.52	43.52
+ Depreciation	13.03	13.38	13.89	14.47	15.11	15.83	16.64
Operating cash flow	49.36	51.55	53.78	55.87	57.75	59.35	60.16
− Cash tax †	9.39	10.90	11.45	11.96	12.42	12.79	13.05
Operating cash flow after tax	39.97	40.65	42.33	43.91	45.33	46.56	47.11
− Stock increase	9.29	6.84	7.66	8.58	9.61	10.76	0.0
− Debtor increase	6.19	5.70	6.38	7.15	8.01	8.97	0.0
+ Creditor increase	3.73	4.92	5.51	6.17	6.91	7.74	0.0
− RFCI	13.03	13.38	13.89	14.47	15.11	15.83	16.64
− IFCI	2.80	4.10	4.60	5.15	5.77	6.46	0.0
Free cash flow	12.39	15.55	15.31	14.73	13.74	12.28	30.47

The estimates beyond 1998 reflect an assessment of future prospects for each item, which has been influenced by past performance. Very often when undertaking such an exercise from an external perspective, guidelines for such assessment may be provided by the

---

* Excludes interest because it is concerned with the cash flow that is freely available to *all* the providers of capital to the business.
† Prior year tax charge plus tax effect of interest on additional debt taken on during the year.

analysis of information relating to peer group companies. It is important to note that when undertaking a thorough assessment of free cash flows the separate analysis of some important areas, like working capital investment (WCI) requirements, will be essential. This is because it can be very difficult to capture requirements meaningfully via one single WCI indicator, as illustrated in Figure 2.6 where WCI was broken down into its components.

It is also important to understand the difference between free cash flow analysis and the sort of cash flow statements often required to be produced to comply with accounting standards. As illustrated in Figure 2.7, such cash flow analysis does not reflect free cash flow. In the case of the statement shown for Santos plc, interest and dividends that relate to the financing of the business have been included. However, for the purpose of valuation, they must be omitted. This is because future free cash flows are discounted using discounted cash flow analysis with a cost of capital (WACC) figure, for the requirements of both shareholders and debt-holders. Inclusion of interest and dividends in the free cash flow estimates would represent double counting.

Figure 2.7: Cash flow statement

	1997 £m	1998 £m	1999 £m	2000 £m	2001 £m	2002 £m
Operating profit	36.33	38.17	39.89	41.40	42.64	43.52
+ Depreciation	13.03	13.38	13.89	14.47	15.11	15.83
Gross funds from trading	49.36	51.55	53.78	55.87	57.75	59.35
− Tax paid *	6.86	8.35	9.07	9.50	9.82	9.94
− Interest paid †	8.51	7.94	8.21	8.66	9.50	10.65
− Dividend paid ‡	5.85	5.30	11.64	12.20	13.75	13.92
Net funds from trading	28.14	29.96	24.86	25.51	24.68	24.84
− Stock increase	9.29	6.84	7.66	8.58	9.61	10.76
− Debtor increase	6.19	5.70	6.38	7.15	8.01	8.97
+ Creditor increase	3.73	4.92	5.51	6.17	6.91	7.74
− Fixed asset investment	15.83	17.48	18.49	19.62	20.88	22.29
Generated surplus / <deficit>	0.56	4.86	− 2.16	− 3.67	− 6.91	− 9.44
+/− Debt repaid / <raised>	− 0.64	4.76	− 2.26	− 3.77	− 7.01	− 9.54
+/− Share capital repurchased / <raised>	1.10	0.00	0.00	0.00	0.00	0.00
+ Cash increase	0.10	0.10	0.10	0.10	0.10	0.10
Finance repaid / <raised>	0.56	4.86	− 2.16	− 3.67	− 6.91	− 9.44

* Prior year profit and loss account charge.
† Current year profit and loss account charge.
‡ Prior year profit and loss account charge.

Although financing costs are omitted in determining free cash flows for purposes of valuation, they do need to be analysed for purposes of management information. This is because they are very important and may often limit managerial action simply because there has to be sufficient free cash available to meet the perceived requirements of the providers of funds. This need may well constrain an ambitious plan, such as that to achieve substantial future sales growth via the immediate purchase of plant and equipment and incremental working capital investment, particularly if it results in unsatisfactory cash flows in the short term. If there is a shortfall it will need to be met somehow. Alternatively, it may be that there are surplus cash flows, which raises a different issue - what to do with the excess cash generated. It could be invested in new growth opportunities, used to fund working capital requirements and/or to change long-term funding requirements. All these uses of a surplus will have the effect of generating a benefit, which must be factored into the valuation. In any event, both deficits and surpluses must be taken into consideration.

Estimating strategic value and free cash flow

How free cash flows can be estimated for Santos plc has been illustrated (summarised in Figure 2.6), but to estimate strategic value these cash flows must be discounted at the WACC. As indicated at the beginning of this chapter, such value is typically estimated by determining the value over the planning period and from the continuing period (the Terminal Value), which often represents the largest part of the total value.

Value of the planning period

Let us assume that the WACC of Santos plc after tax and when appropriately adjusted for inflation, is 12 per cent. This WACC will be examined in detail in Chapter 6 and represents the return required by the providers of both debt and equity finance. With knowledge of this WACC, the present value of the cash flows of Santos plc for the five-year planning period can be calculated as being £52.28 million, as shown in Figure 2.8.

Figure 2.8: Present value of free cash flows from the planning period

Year	1998 £m	1999 £m	2000 £m	2001 £m	2002 £m
Free cash flow	15.55	15.31	14.73	13.74	12.28
Discount factor	0.893	0.797	0.712	0.636	0.567
Present value	13.89	12.20	10.49	8.74	6.96
Cumulative present value	13.89	26.09	36.58	45.32	52.28

Estimating terminal value (TV)

A planning period of five years was used for the period 1998 to 2002 inclusive, but the issue now arises of how to estimate a Terminal Value (TV) for the continuing period beyond 2002. Santos plc has a share price of £1 and 106 million shares[*]. This implies a market

---

[*] See Appendix 1.

capitalisation of £106 million, while the value calculated for the five year time forecast period is £52.28 million, a substantial difference. In fact, the value calculated is only 27 per cent of the market implied value and therefore the question arises of how this difference can be accounted for. One commonly used way of estimating TV involves the calculation of a perpetuity value by dividing the assumed perpetuity free cash flow by the cost of capital *. For Santos plc, the free cash flow in the continuing period beyond 2002 is £30.47 million (see Figure 2.6), which when divided by the assumed cost of capital of 12 per cent produces a value of approximately £253.92 million. However, this is not the value required. In fact, what is needed is the present value of the perpetuity and not the value at the end of five years. This present value is substantially lower than £253.92 million and is in fact £143.97 million (£30.47 million ÷ 12 per cent x 0.567) see Figure 2.9. This is obtained by discounting the £253.92 million in five years to a present value.

Figure 2.9: Present value of the planning period and TV

	1998 £m	1999 £m	2000 £m	2001 £m	2002 £m	Beyond £m
Free cash flow	15.55	15.31	14.73	13.74	12.28	30.47
Discount factor	0.893	0.797	0.712	0.636	0.567	
Present value	13.89	12.20	10.49	8.74	6.96	
Cumulative present value	13.89	26.09	36.58	45.32	52.28	
Present value of terminal value					143.97	
Business value					196.25	

Business value, corporate value and strategic value

To calculate a business value, the present value of the planning period has to be combined with the present value to be derived from the business beyond it. In the case of Santos plc, assuming a five year planning period and a cost of capital of 12 per cent, the result is a total business value of £196.25 million (£52.28 million + £143.97 million). This value is now substantially higher than the market implied value of £106 million, but the difference can be explained.

The business value that has been calculated for Santos plc is not the same as strategic value. Business value represents the value generated by the free cash flows against which all providers of funds have a claim, but strategic value is concerned with that part of business value which is attributable to the shareholders. To understand how to arrive at this it is necessary to recall that business value was estimated by discounting the free cash flows at a cost of capital which took account of the benefit of both borrowed funds and funds provided by shareholders. To estimate strategic value the present value of

---

* The rationale for the approach and others that can be used for estimating a TV is provided in Chapter 5.

borrowed funds needs to be subtracted in order to find the claim on the value of the business attributable to just the shareholders. It may also be the case that investments are held in other businesses, the benefits of which are not captured in the business valuation process. Any such benefits have to be added to determine corporate rather than business value. In fact, two adjustments are required to calculate strategic value, which take the following form:

	Business value
+	Marketable securities or investments *
=	Corporate value
−	Market value of debt and obligations
=	Strategic value
÷	Number of ordinary shares
=	Strategic value per share

For Santos plc, the result of this calculation is shown in Figure 2.10.

Figure 2.10: Strategic value per share

	£m
Business value	196.25
Marketable securities	0.00
Corporate value	196.25
Market value of debt	70.92
Strategic value	125.33
Number of shares (millions)	106
Strategic value per share (£)	**1.18**

For Santos plc, the estimated business value is £196.25 million, there are no marketable securities (e.g. interest earning deposits) and the notes to the accounts for 1997 show creditors amounts falling due after one year of £70.92 million. If such creditors are taken as being a proxy for the market value of debt and obligations, they can be deducted from corporate value. The resulting £125.33 million is then divided by the number of shares for 1997 of 106 million, as shown in the notes to the accounts † and a strategic value per share of £1.18 is obtained.

---

* Surplus cash invested in marketable securities (non-operating assets) are assumed to create no additional value, i.e. their net present value is zero.

† Appendix 1, page 225.

How might the figure for strategic value be interpreted? Santos has a stock market listing and a current share price of £1.00. As implied earlier, this share price can be compared with the publicly quoted price determined by the forces of demand and supply to see if a value gap exists. This is the term applied to the difference between the publicly quoted share price and estimates of its value using specific company information. For Santos plc, there is a value gap of 18p at a 12 per cent cost of capital (£1.18 - £1.00).

What does this strategic value per share represent? It is the estimated value per share and it is very dependent on the assumptions made about the key value drivers. Change any of these and this value will also change. For example, an increase in the EBITDA margin, *ceteris paribus*, will result in a higher strategic value per share. By way of illustration, in one company that was analysed using this framework, an increase in the EBITDA margin to the levels currently being obtained by peer group companies had the effect of doubling the strategic value per share and formed part of the rationale for it becoming an acquisition target.

Let us pause at this point and reflect on the figure for strategic value estimated for Santos plc. It represents the value derived from a fairly simplistic view of the company. In reality, it would be reasonable to expect that estimates used in a full valuation would have to involve considerable detailed analysis. For example, many businesses provide multiple services and/or produce multiple products. For them, a more realistic process of valuation would be to calculate the cash flows relevant to, say, each business unit using planning periods that reflect the different distinctive capabilities of each, and then to discount them at a required rate of return relevant to each unit. All of these individual values could then be aggregated and the strategic value estimated. The ability to be able to go into such detail depends on information being available. Obtaining information can often be difficult, but a guide as to what may be available is provided in Figure 2.11.

Figure 2.11: Possible sources of available information

		Internal		External	
		Past	Future	Past	Future
Financial	Numeric	Management accounting	Budgets and forecasts	Competitors' results	Brokers' forecasts
	Text	Results narrative	Five-year plan	Brokers' view	Press opinion
Non-financial	Numeric	Operating performance	Capacity planning	Market share	Market research
	Text	Performance commentary	Strategic goals	Trade media	Technology forecasts
Source: Accountancy Age, 6 March 1997					

Two other issues that need to be flagged again with reference to the Santos plc example is the proportion of value accounted for by the TV and the significance of WACC. The size of the value from the continuing period, the TV, is the largest contributor to business value and such estimates of the TV are not unusual when a perpetuity calculation is undertaken over short time periods. For this reason it is preferable to forecast as far forwards as possible. Use of the perpetuity approach for calculating the TV does cause concern among practitioners who, because of the relative contribution it makes to total value, may also use a number of other approaches. A review of the alternatives is considered in Chapter 5 and important issues relating to the cost of capital are the subject of Chapter 6.

Summary checklist

- Five value drivers enable a free cash flow picture of a business to be generated.
- This free cash flow picture is generated over a planning period, the sixth value driver, beyond which a terminal value may be calculated for the continuing period.
- A seventh value driver, the WACC, is essential for converting cash flows into values. (This is covered in its own right in Chapter 6.)
- Robust and consistent valuations require that the nature of the interrelationship between all seven value drivers are examined.
- The Strategic Value Analysis framework is very effective in forcing clarity of thought about tough issues that drive the value of a business and to help to organise thought around the limitations imposed by having imperfect data.

Concluding remarks

The free cash flow strategic value approach is very powerful, but the outcome needs to be looked at carefully in terms of the assumptions used in arriving at any valuation. Garbage in can be all too easily reflected by garbage out. It is critical to ensure that data and assumptions used are as robust as possible. To this end, sensitivity analysis and scenario thinking can be used very effectively as will be illustrated in the next chapter. It is also important that such value is expressed in the most appropriate form, an issue considered in Chapter 4, once the all-important issue of how to determine the planning period has been considered.

Chapter 3: The Planning Period and Competitive Advantage

Although competitive advantage period (CAP) has unassailable importance in valuation, it is a subject that has not been explicitly addressed in finance textbooks in a way commensurate with its importance. Further, many analysts and strategic planners that adhere to a DCF framework reduce the model's validity by using explicit forecast periods that do not reflect CAP. We believe that CAP can play an important role in linking valuation theory and practice.

Michael Mauboussin and Paul Johnson, Credit Suisse First Boston, 1997 [41].

Chapter preview

○ The critical issues involved in estimating over what period of time (planning period) cash flows should be forecast.

○ The link between the value of a business captured during this planning period and beyond it (the continuing period).

○ The use of strategic frameworks as a starting point to ensure that the right questions are asked in relation to the length of the planning period used.

○ How the planning period may be estimated in practice by, first, looking at a Price Earnings interpretation, second, by using the concept of the market implied duration and, third, by applying scenario thinking.

○ How options thinking allows the planning period and terminal value issues to be viewed from a different perspective and, hence, generate additional insights into the valuation equation.

CHAPTER THREE

Introduction

How the value of a business can be estimated using the free cash flow approach focusing on a number of key value drivers was demonstrated with reference to Santos plc in Chapter 2. This value for Santos plc consisted of that from the planning period and an assumed period beyond, known as the continuing period. The value from the continuing period, the terminal value, for Santos plc represents 73 per cent of the total corporate value and, as such, the size of this proportion typically represents a major cause for concern. If the time horizon is extended this proportion falls, but this then raises the million dollar question – 'how far out to go?' The length of the planning period, together with the issue of competitive advantage and the Competitive Advantage Period (CAP), i.e. that period over which a firm enjoys a competitive advantage, are the subject of this chapter. As will be illustrated, there is often confusion between the planning period and the CAP, and the two are not necessarily the same. In reality, most valuation models use a planning period over which it is assumed that a return on capital is earned in excess of the cost of capital.

Figure 3.1: Relationship between planning period and terminal value

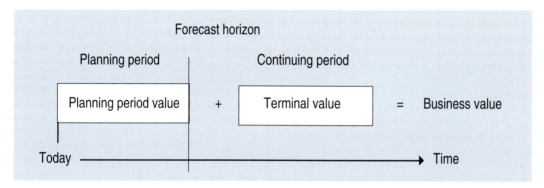

As illustrated in the example in the last chapter, a common approach is to forecast over a finite time period, such as five years, and then to capture any remaining value assumed to arise in a perpetuity calculation. The logic behind this is that once the market has been established, cash receipts can be viewed as being potentially indefinite, as long as necessary replacement investment in fixed assets or other areas, like marketing or research and development expenditure, is undertaken to maintain the existing position. The use of a perpetuity calculation is convenient because it means that cash flows do not have to be estimated forever. However, blind reliance on a standard period for assessing free cash flows and the adoption of a perpetuity calculation to capture value thereafter is inadequate. It is essential to look for ways of capturing future value as realistically as possible and to recognise that different business units may well have different time horizons over which they need to consider their long term strategic plans. The CAP is yet another variable in any valuation and can be considered to be a vital issue to assess. Unfortunately, while the principle underpinning its importance is understood, its estimation in practice is not. Quite simply, this is because its assessment is based on a good deal of qualitative judgement and it is difficult to be accurate in its determination. Often less energy is expended in its determination than with other issues, which fall more readily within the financial specialist's comfort zone and, unfortunately, there are no easy answers to this issue about what is an appropriate CAP. Certainly, this chapter does not suggest a simple solution, but it does offer some guidelines based on both theory and practice.

The Competitive Advantage Period (CAP) and strategic theory

The CAP is the time during which a company is expected to generate returns on incremental investment that exceeds its cost of capital. Economic theory suggests that competitive forces will eventually drive returns down to the cost of capital over time. In other words, if a company earns returns above the cost of capital, it will attract competitors into the industry, the consequence of which will be a reduction in industry returns.

The concept of CAP is not new and has existed in the finance literature for many years, although not necessarily under that name. It has carried various labels, examples of which are 'value growth duration' and 'T' [42, 43, 44]. For example, it was formalised by Miller and Modigliani throughout their seminal work on valuation [45].

A number of strategic approaches, which will be reviewed in the following sections, have been developed which can, in principle, be applied to determine the length of the competitive advantage period.

Understanding the external context

One approach commonly quoted within the context of business valuation and which will be reviewed shortly, is that associated with the 'five forces' framework developed by Michael Porter [46]. The competitive period can be explained using the five forces identified by Porter and illustrated in Figure 3.2.

Figure 3.2: Porter's five forces

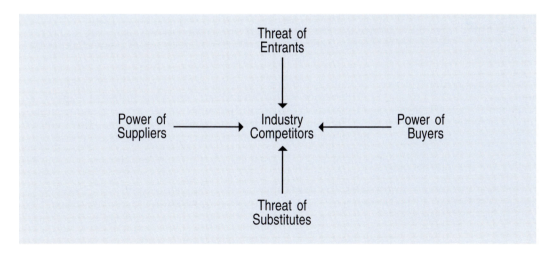

A company's competitive advantage may be threatened by potential entrants on the one hand and the possibility of substitute products on the other. It will also be affected by the relative power of suppliers and buyers and by the degree of competitive rivalry within the industry in which it exists.

In establishing the length of the competitive advantage period, a company's management needs to be aware of these forces. It may be aware of certain potential entrants to the market, but it may also know that the barriers to entry are such that it will take a new entrant to the industry four or five years before it becomes a serious threat. Similarly, it may be aware that in the market from which it buys its most important raw materials, mergers and take-overs are taking place, which will make the suppliers' market less competitive and raw materials more expensive. Again, it is a question of judging the length of time over which the suppliers' prices will rise.

Although the contribution by Porter has been invaluable, there has been considerable interest in terms of what makes firms that operate within the same industry different. There is evidence to suggest that the performance achieved by an organisation depends more on its relative performance within an industry rather than the industry sector in which it operates. For example, Rumelt analysed the returns of a large sample of American firms by reference to their profitability in different industries [47]. Rumelt's findings are summarised in Figure 3.3.

Figure 3.3: Contributions to variance of profits across business units

	%
Corporate ownership	0.8
Industry effects	8.3
Cyclical effects	7.8
Business unit specific effects	46.4
Unexplained factors *	36.7

By far the largest contributor to explaining differences in profits is business unit-specific effects, which account for 46.4 per cent of the contribution to variance of profits. In other words, there are no systematically successful firms or industries, but there are systematically successful business units. These are the businesses that enjoy competitive advantages and outperform their competitors year by year.

The Rumelt's evidence, therefore, suggests that the performance achieved by an organisation depends more on its relative performance within an industry than the industry itself [48]. In other words, good relative performance within an industry translates into the generation of superior returns. Further work in this area has stimulated the view that this relative performance relates to core (distinctive) capabilities that can give businesses an edge.

Analysis of the internal context

Porter also outlined a framework for value chains [49]. The underlying principle of this framework is that all tasks performed by a business organisation can be classified into nine broad categories:

○ Five primary activities: inbound logistics, operations, outbound logistics, marketing, sales and service; and

○ Four support activities: firm infrastructure, human resource management, technology development and procurement.

---

* sometimes referred to as the 'X' factor.

Many adaptations of the value chain framework have emerged over time. One potentially useful variant is illustrated in Figure 3.4.

Figure 3.4   Value Chain

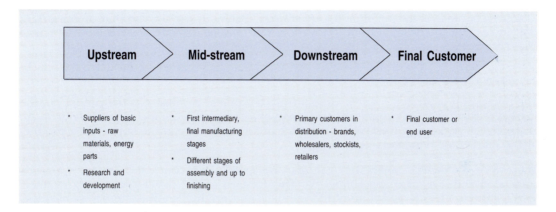

Since the value chain is composed of the set of activities performed by a business, it provides an effective way to diagnose the position of a business against its major competitors. Using this approach, it is possible to define the foundation for actions aimed at sustaining a competitive advantage, as opposed to the forces which determine industry attractiveness to the business. The latter are largely external and uncontrollable by the firm, whereas the activities within the value chain framework constitute the foundation of the internal controllable factors to achieve competitive superiority.

Research by Kay has identified four types of distinctive capability [50]:

1.   Reputation.
2.   Architecture.
3.   Innovation.
4.   Strategic assets.

1. Reputation

Enables a company to charge higher prices, or gain larger market share at a competitive price, for a functionally equivalent product. Examples of companies quoted by Kay for whom reputation is important are Lloyds Bank and Sainsbury's, the UK food retailing supermarket chain.

2. Architecture

Can be viewed in terms of a unique structure of relationships in or around the company that exists between the company and its suppliers. Via the development of a strategic architecture, an organisation should be able to commit the technical and production linkages across business units which will build on distinct skills and capabilities that cannot be matched or easily replicated by other organisations. Examples of companies held as having strategic architecture as a distinctive capability are Marks and Spencer and Benetton.

3. Innovation

Is seen as being a very strong source of competitive advantage, but one that is difficult to sustain because of the potential for replication. Patent protection can play an important part in reaping the benefits from innovation, but may be difficult to achieve in practice. One noteworthy exploiter of this approach has been the pharmaceuticals industry.

4. Distinctive capabilities

The ownership of strategic assets, differs from the others because it is the product of the market or regulatory environment rather than of a company's distinctive achievement. An example is a concession to exploit a resource or an exclusive right to supply as a product of the market, or regulatory environment *.

These four distinctive capabilities can also be seen in the core competences approach associated with Prahalad and Hamel [51]. This focused on the development of a strategic architecture to identify and commit the technical and production linkages across business units so as to build on distinct skills and capabilities that cannot be matched or easily replicated by other organisations. These competences can be thought of as being the collective learning of the organisation, particularly how to co-ordinate diverse production skills and integrate multiple streams of technology. Because of diversified information systems, patterns of communications, managerial rewards and so on, there will be an inevitable fragmentation of core competences and an impetus for learning will be required.

In principle, Kay's four distinctive capabilities should enable an organisation to achieve what are often regarded as being major sources of competitive advantage - size, market share, market selection, and market position. However, they will continue to add value only if their capability and distinctiveness are sustainable. In fact, one key issue Kay considered was the sustainability of these four distinctive capabilities.

On the basis of his research, Kay suggested reputation as generally being the easiest to sustain, strategic assets as being sustainable over long periods only if there are no changes in regulation or market conditions, and innovation as being the most difficult. In fact, some specific sources of sustainable competitive advantage were identified in research by Aaker (see Figure 3.5), who considered what the managers of 248 distinct businesses oriented towards service and hi-tech businesses thought were the sustainable competitive advantages of their businesses [52]. He found that sustainable sources of competitive advantage varied from business to business and arose from more than one source. This indicates that it is not sufficient for a business to base its strategy on a single source of competitive advantage and that the challenge for both management and investors is to be able to identify the sources for any given business. What is more, and is so often overlooked, is that identifiable sources of competitive advantage do not necessarily translate into a CAP for valuation purposes. For there to be a CAP for such purposes, there has to be sustainability. If a firm cannot sustain its competitive advantage, then by definition it will be unable to generate future returns in excess of the cost of capital, quite simply because others will be able to enter the market and erode excess returns.

---

* Associated with this grouping may be many distinctive capabilities often overlooked, like those associated with the skill of the workforce.

Figure 3.5: Sustainable competitive advantages in 248 businesses [53]

		High-tech	Service	Other	Total
1	Reputation for Quality	26	50	29	105
2	Customer Service/Product Support	23	40	15	78
3	Name Recognition/High Profile	8	42	21	71
4	Retain Good Management & Engineering Staff	17	43	5	65
5	Low-Cost Production	17	15	21	53
6	Financial Resources	11	26	14	51
7	Customer Orientation/Feedback Market Research	13	26	9	48
8	Product Line Breadth	11	23	13	47
9	Technical Superiority	30	7	9	46
10	Installed Base of Satisfied Customers	19	22	4	45
11	Segmentation/Focus	7	22	16	45
12	Product Characteristics/Differentiation	12	15	10	37
13	Continuing Production Innovation	12	17	6	35
14	Market Share	12	14	9	35
15	Size/Location of Distribution	10	11	13	34
16	Low-Price/High-Value Offering	6	20	6	32
17	Knowledge of Business	2	25	4	31
18	Pioneer/Early Entrant in Industry	11	11	6	28
19	Efficient, Flexible Production/Operations Adaptable to Customers	4	17	4	25
20	Effective Sales Force	10	9	4	23
21	Overall Marketing Skills	7	9	7	23
22	Shared Vision/Culture	5	13	4	22
23	Strategic Goals	6	7	9	22
24	Powerful Well-Known Parent	7	7	6	20
25	Location	0	10	10	20
26	Effective Advertising/ Image	5	6	6	17
27	Enterprising/Entrepreneurial	3	3	5	11
28	Good Co-ordination	3	2	5	10
29	Engineering Research Development	8	2	0	10
30	Short-term Planning	2	1	5	8
31	Good Distributor Relations	2	4	1	7
32	Other	6	20	5	31
	Total	315	539	281	1,135
	Number of Businesses	68	113	67	248
	Average Number of Sustainable Competitive Advantages	4.68	4.77	4.19	4.58

Introducing the dynamic of time through life cycles

Other sources of the potential underpinnings of CAP can also be found in other academic work. For example, Williams has extended the Porter framework by incorporating the time dimension into value chain analysis. He has classified industry environments into three types [54].

- Class I industries, characterised by competitively stable value chains, which over time are relatively unchanged.
- Class II industries, characterised by smoothly evolving value chains, which are reinforced through scale based learning.
- Class III industries, characterised by dynamic and unstable value chains, which accelerate rapidly to maturity.

In an alternative view of the product life cycle, Ansoff argued for an approach that considers the need provided by a product rather than the product itself [55]. This equates with looking at a demand life cycle, capturing ongoing, changing levels of need. Such needs are satisfied by technology and Ansoff used 'calculating power' as an example of a need that has existed for thousands of years. The changing level of need is represented by a demand life cycle, so in terms of calculating power, the need was initially met by using fingers (as reflected in the Arabic numeric system); then by abacuses; later by slide rules; then mechanical adding machines; electronic calculators; and currently by computers. Each technological development offered enhanced benefits such as speed, cost, capacity, or increased facilities. Ansoff suggested these to be demand technology cycles, with an 'S' shaped format suggesting emergence, rapid growth, slower growth, maturity and finally decline.

Within each demand technology cycle there will be a succession of product forms that satisfy the specific need at the time. Ansoff used the hand calculator as an example. Initially, it took the form of a large plastic box with a small screen and numerical operating keys. Its performance was limited to four tasks – addition, subtraction, multiplication and division. This was soon superseded by smaller hand held calculators performing many more mathematical and scientific functions. These in turn were succeeded by yet smaller versions and at much lower costs.

These cycles in the development of calculators suggest some interesting implications. If a company concentrates its product development, research and development and marketing efforts in a narrow aspect of the overall cycle, it may miss the opportunity to expand its market base. What is more, it may also overlook the fact that the demand technology cycle may be facing obsolescence. Companies need to decide in which demand technology to invest and when to move into a new technology. For some companies in some industries the choice is difficult as the demand technology cycles tend to have very short effective life spans, while others may become obsolescent very slowly and merge with the next generation. This means that in reality, CAP decisions may be very complex.

While it is widely acknowledged that products go through cycles, it is not well recognised that business designs also go through cycles and reach obsolescence. A business design refers to the totality of how a company selects its customers, defines and differentiates its offerings, defines the tasks it will perform itself and those it will outsource, configures its resources, goes to market, creates utility for customers, and captures profit. Slywotzky has adopted the term 'value migration' to illustrate that a business design can exist in only one of three states: value inflow, stability and value outflow [56]. These states emphasise the importance of relative value creation power, with a view to satisfying customer priorities better than competitors, thereby earning superior returns. More specifically, these three states (see Figure 3.6) are:

○ Value inflow. In the initial phase, a company starts to absorb value from other parts of its industry because its business design proves superior in satisfying customer priorities. Microsoft and EDS are among companies currently reckoned to be experiencing the value inflow phase.

○ Stability. This is characterised by business designs that are well matched to customer priorities and by overall competitive equilibrium. Companies such as Dupont are considered to be in this phase.

○ Value outflow. In the third phase, value starts to move away from an organisation's traditional activities towards business designs that meet evolving customer priorities more effectively.

Figure 3.6: Three stages of value migration

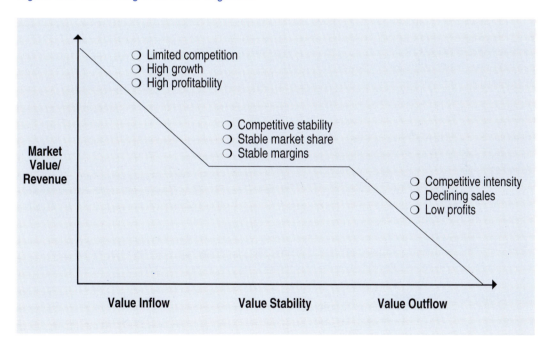

Value migration among business designs takes place at different levels:

○ Between industries, e.g. telecommunications, entertainment and computer;

○ Between companies in the same industry, e.g. BT, Energis, Vodaphone, Cellnet, etc;

○ Within a single company, e.g. fixed lines, mobile, multimedia.

Focusing on value migration at the industry level is a useful first step because it creates a context in which to evaluate individual business designs. It is not that value disappears, but that it moves – rapidly at times – towards new activities and skills and towards new business designs whose superiority in meeting customer priorities makes profit possible. To meet the challenge of value migration, managers must ask, 'Where in my industry can a profit be made? How is that changing? What is driving that change? What can my organisation do about it?' Beneath these questions lies a more fundamental inquiry – 'What is the changing pattern of what customers need, want and are willing to pay for, and what business designs respond most effectively to this changing pattern?' In every industry there is a limited set of key moves that allows advantage to be taken of the next cycle of value growth. Every business design has a limited value creation life cycle. Managers must act to create the next viable business design. The key questions are – 'Which move should I make? Which future business design element will be most important? Which future competitors do I have to worry about most?' This is where scenarios (for review later in this chapter) can be a very useful tool for helping to answer these questions.

Figure 3.7: Summary of strategic perspectives relevant to the CAP

Three broad areas of focus	Strategic tools
Understanding the external context within which a business operates, and performance relative to others within the industry.	Porter's five forces for industry analysis.
Analysis of the internal activities that comprise businesses and sources of sustainable competitive advantage.	Value chain of activities, distinctive capabilities and core competences.
Synthesis of the external and internal perspectives through the introduction of the dynamics of time and business as a game in a constantly evolving landscape and changing rules.	Life cycle analysis of products and technology. Three stages of value migration for industries and businesses.

Estimating CAP in practice

In determining CAP in practice, the assumption used about the time horizon will have a significant impact on the size of any Terminal Value (TV). TV, (the value arising from the period beyond the assumed CAP, known as the 'continuing period') is often a source of considerable concern in many valuations. This is important because it frequently accounts for a significant proportion of total value. For example, it represents 73 per cent of the market implied value in the case of Santos plc (see Chapter 2). In fact in some circumstances, such as a start up or a development in a new market, it may account for nearly all of the total value. A good real-life example of this was the valuation of the telecommunications company Orange plc (reviewed in Chapter 9), which was floated in 1996. Initial value estimates for the business in excess of £2.8 billion were produced by a number of analysts, of which £2.0 billion was the result of a terminal value estimate beyond a ten-year forecast period for free cash flows *.

Research has revealed that five years is popular as a planning period estimate for many UK companies [57]. When compared crudely alongside market PE multiples of between 17 and 19 years on current after tax earnings attributable to shareholders, there is the potential for a 'value gap'. One way of preventing a value gap is for a longer-term planning period to be applied, but this raises the immediate concern that planning for five years can often already be a complicated process. The fact that management looks typically only to a limited future period of say five years, is the real problem and there should be explicit recognition that the continuing period and the terminal value associated with it are directly within management's control. It is not a residual, but one of the most critical parts of the 'value future'. As such, it needs to be owned and actively managed, even though it may deal with a time horizon too distant to analyse prescriptively. If the valuation of this time period is seen to relate to the selected planning period, it is much more than a passive residual. In fact, it can be looked on as being the consequence of actions taken over the time period falling within the comfort zone of management action.

Two broad approaches for dealing with the CAP (and hence the terminal value) are:

1. Market Implied Duration.
2. Scenario Thinking.

1. Market implied duration

This approach can be thought of as involving the following steps [58]. First by a proxy for unbiased market expectations of six value drivers (other than CAP) is required, assuming use of a seven value driver model, i.e. sales growth rate, operating profit margin, cash tax rate, fixed capital needs, working capital needs, cost of capital and CAP. Second, a valuation model is built, including a terminal value calculation based on an assumed perpetuity. Finally, the time period over which the forecast is undertaken is 'stretched' over as many years as is necessary to achieve the company's current market price for its shares, i.e. the period over which the return on new investment stays above WACC is stretched to achieve market capitalisation. The resulting time period is the assumed CAP.

There is a belief that lengthening the CAP in this way can help to explain the 'X' factor [†], and a good illustration of this has been provided by Mauboussin and Johnson [59]. Based on a study of a selection of companies within the packaged food industry in the September 1982 to August 1989 period, using the approach described above they found that the CAP for this group roughly doubled in the seven-year period. In fact, this time period corresponded with most companies streamlining their business portfolios, cutting costs, increasing vital marketing expenditure, and increasing cash flows.

---

[*] A similar observation regarding the potential contribution from the terminal value was also confirmed by McKinsey and Company, which demonstrated that over an eight-year forecast period the terminal value in four industries accounted for anywhere between 56 per cent to 125 per cent of total value.

[†] Unexplained factors in Rumelt's research, see Figure 3.3.

While this approach is useful as a practical tool, particularly from the perspective of the external analyst, it does have some limitations that may be summarised as follows:

- It presupposes that the market price of the share is an appropriate reflection of future prospects, but there may be a radical shift in prospect that has not been detected by the market. Many acquisitions have been concerned with business transformations not reflected in the share price until the occurrence of a predatory move.

- What happens when there is no share price, e.g. for a private company or division/business unit? In this case there is no share price against which to 'stretch'. In our experience this can be dealt with effectively by undertaking market implied duration stretch on a carefully selected set of peer group companies, combined with scenario analysis (described in the next section).

From an external perspective, 'stretch' represents a useful starting point. However, whenever possible it should be combined with scenario analysis. Our experience has shown scenario analysis to be invaluable in understanding CAP from an internal operational perspective, as well as an external strategic perspective [60].

2. Scenario thinking

Scenarios start from the premise that there is more than one future and recognise the need to illuminate the major forces and trends driving a valuation, their interrelationships, and the critical uncertainties. Scenarios need not be heavily driven by mathematical or statistical analysis. Shell, for example, when applying this technique does not assign probabilities to its scenarios for several reasons. First, it intentionally looks at several scenarios that are more or less equally plausible, so that none is dismissed out of hand. Second, by definition, any given scenario has only an infinitesimal probability of being right because so many variations are possible. Third, the reason to be hesitant about all scenario quantification is that there is a very strong tendency for people to clutch at the numbers and ignore the more important conceptual or structural messages [61]. The value of performing this procedure is not so much the ultimate valuation number that it produces, but the insights discovered in the process of investigating the nature and existence of the opportunities available to management.

Specifically, the use of scenarios can help to avoid the shortcomings associated with traditional approaches to analysis, in which the assumptions used will often be extrapolated from the present situation with inadequate attention being paid to the impact of changes in the external environment of a particular business. With these traditional approaches, instead of a specific impact analysis there is an assumed vacuum, as if discontinuities and turbulence will not punctuate the external environment. Drawing on scenario analysis can make considerable improvements. When linked appropriately to free cash flow and strategic value calculations, it provides a distinctive way of grasping the key navigational questions about the future of a business. In terms of the CAP, the approach seeks to force questioning and thought about when the conditions signalling the end of the CAP might occur, i.e. a return greater than the cost of capital cannot be achieved. This involves asking key questions like – 'How can the free cash flow projections be validated for that period?' and 'Suppose the business under consideration is moving into a period of increasing turbulence?' To cope with that, it may become a significantly different business, or it may fail to cope and as a result under-perform relative to its original plan, which assumed little turbulence.

It is usually easy to imagine at least two different free cash flow projections, and the benefit of going through more than one projection and discovering the linkages typically enhances managers' learning, not least because many predictions are often mistaken. Scenarios help to avoid mistakes and can be seen in quite simple terms as being long term 'stories' about possible future external environments, framed as two or three credible pathways in which one's decisions might be played out.

Scenarios oblige the recognition of the dependencies that business performance has on external factors over which a firm has no control (like rain), but to which it might be able to respond in a timely manner (like an umbrella available before the next rainfall). They also encourage thinking through a welter of diverse speculations and the structuring of these into coherent pathways, which are relevant to a particular business. The pay-off is that in terms of the scenarios, the impact on the business of such external factors can be estimated. This enables an analysis of the potential value of the business to be undertaken, not with one straight-line calculation, but with different higher and lower values.

The risk of unwittingly making the analysis of strategic value abstract occurs when it is detached from the real business environment. This can occur when the assumptions underlying the numbers in a business plan, when put through the strategic value model, are not challenged but implicitly treated as a matter of faith. The risk is that of being mesmerised by numerical calculations while overlooking the possibility that the plan itself assumes a single-track extension of the current business into the future CAP.

By contrast, the link between strategy and scenarios forces attention on a wide-ranging search for developments in the external environment, favourable or not, which can help managers to anticipate and adjust for the potential impact on the value drivers of changes ocurring in the environment. It means surfacing and challenging the assumptions behind the numbers given for the value drivers. Developing scenarios does not mean mechanically changing business variables by a fixed percentage. Instead it means developing a comprehensive set of assumptions about how possible futures may evolve and how they are likely to affect industry profitability and the company's performance.

Scenarios start from 'What if ...?' questions. By depicting future pathways which are different from the pathway assumed in a particular plan (adopted or proposed), the uncertainties can be highlighted. As scenarios express, in a patterned way, uncertainties about what external factors could impact on the value drivers, there should be at least two scenarios, preferably equally credible, to be posed against each other. Comparison of their respective impact on one or more value drivers would clarify the issues or challenges distinctive to each scenario which managers could confront in the future. Those issues would surface by grasping the impacts of each scenario on value drivers such as sales growth rate, operating profit margin, fixed and working capital requirements, and the cost of capital. Thus the working out of different potential values for a business based on scenarios, gives more flexibility, realistic relevance and 'navigational' value to the analysis of strategic value.

By means of scenarios the variables which could impact on a business's long term value may be identified. For example, for a manufacturing business which has outperformed rivals in the past, credible ideas as to what trends would constitute one scenario including increasing customer power, loss of differentiation, more intense cost/price competition, and falling margins, can be identified. All of these arise from a mix of factors which range from the growth of international competition to the growing added-value ability of distributors.

Focusing on say the first five years of the example at hand, the impact on the five cash flow drivers of external conditions beyond the immediate control of the company may be illustrated by means of different credible scenarios. Armed with scenario outcomes the firm can mentally and practically prepare to see the earliest signs of change in its external environment. In effect it can, on a hypothetical basis, perceive in advance that if its key strategic challenges were to unfold – very differently from the alternative – what responses would be required. In other words, management can anticipate – initially on a 'What if?' basis – that to achieve, say, the sales receipts in the original plan, product and process technology changes would be required through a steep escalation in fixed and working capital investment needs.

Scenarios express and structure uncertainties about the future: of themselves they cannot resolve this uncertainty. But sharp and sensitive mental preparation by advance calculation of the value impact of alternative scenarios enables faster responses to be made. In this case, improved thinking about the substantive issues – the business challenges – raised by each scenario could lead to a planning process that enables an anticipated challenge, indeed a threat, to be converted by virtue of well-timed and scaled company response, into an opportunity.

The materials chosen for scenarios may be brief and prosaic, formulated without recourse to larger-scale constructions about economic, political and other macro changes. But they are sufficient to illustrate the point that current assumptions used for estimating the future value of a business must be specified in credible speculations about the future and structured in such a way as to show how different future conditions can impact on the key value drivers.

The process of calculating the present value and CAP implications of different scenarios enables managers to make two important gains in their strategic thinking:

○ They can see how the strategic value outputs derived from the inputs of their preferred or current plans, depend on assumptions which could be clarified and critically evaluated by comparisons made with the assumptions of credible alternative scenarios. Managers would therefore focus on the quality of their assumptions about changes in the external environment, as a precondition of any confidence in the numbers subsequently generated through the Strategic Value Analysis model.

○ Wrestling with each scenario's present value and CAP implications should sharpen managers' sense of the range of options they could have in driving forward their business in one direction or another. It gives a mental grip on how to weigh up in advance the risk/gain possibilities under each scenario.

There is however a third benefit. Each scenario helps to clarify the dominant strategic challenges associated with it – and how different (or similar) would the responses to each challenge have to be. Here is where the real and rapid advance in strategic thinking can occur. Consequences revealed through free cash flow analysis and strategic valuation help to clarify the first candidates for an effective strategic response. For example, this could be how an initial reactive response towards a threat might be converted into an opportunity, or how an attempt to respond to two different scenarios, instead of wagering on one against another, might yield a strategy aimed at resiliency against more than one possible future.

In our experience it is rare for the outcome of the application of scenario analysis to produce a CAP corresponding with the stretched market implied duration CAP. The consequence of this is that the terminal value issue, so neatly dealt with by virtue of the definition of market implied duration, raises its head again. Typically, the CAP resulting from scenario analysis is considerably shorter than that for the stretched version. This means that the all-important question of terminal value arises. In very simple terms, the terminal value implied is the difference between the market implied price and the value of the scenario. Analysis of the terminal value arising from this difference can be undertaken to see the assumptions implied. For example, a significant difference between the perpetuity value of the terminal value determined from scenario based calculations and the market implied terminal value can be examined in terms of the implications by way of prospective growth assumptions. This examination can be by way of an extension of the scenario activity, in which external financial observations are challenged in terms of their managerial implications for the value drivers within the strategic value model. In other words, 'What rate of growth is implied by the difference and what would be needed to make it happen?' *

Options and CAP

While the approaches described in the previous section may be appropriate for many businesses, there are some for which it is helpful to review and approach from a slightly different perspective. These are those businesses for which the bulk of their value can be seen to lie beyond the planning period and within the terminal value. They may be businesses currently generating little profit or cash, or even generating negative free cash flows, but to which the market place ascribes a high value. This value is seen to be a speculative estimate of the future value they may be able to deliver. For such businesses, there is no CAP readily observable, all is speculative and may, or may not happen.

As indicated in earlier chapters, the theoretical underpinnings for the use of the strategic value approach is drawn from the economic theory of the firm which contends that corporate investment decisions should be guided by the rule of net present value maximisation. However, it can be argued that when conventionally used it fails to recognise the strategic reasons for an investment, such as investing in a not-so-profitable project in order to acquire future growth opportunities [62]. This is important because with technology growing rapidly there will be more investments made for competitive reasons alone and such investments typically will fail the DCF test [63, 64, 65, 66]. The second important criticism of conventional analysis is that it fails to take account of the value of active management. Such management might correspond with waiting for major uncertainties, say over future market conditions, to unfold in order to avoid losses, or by undertaking specific research and development expenditure intended to lead to new patents. Active management aims to produce valuable information, thereby reducing uncertainty over the future. Furthermore, subsequent to making an investment, management can revise operating plans that underlay an original cash flow forecast, like altering input and output mixes or temporarily shutting down plant, in order to maximise operating cash flows. Quite simply, active management can affect value but it is not accounted for in conventional net present value analysis.

In fact, it has been argued that conventional net present value analysis is not only incomplete, but it may also lead to costly errors [67]. These errors arise from two sources.

---

* For an illustration of scenario thinking see page 50.

54 CHAPTER THREE

First, investments guided by the positive net present value criteria may be made too hastily. This is a problem because most capital investments are irreversible and thus justifiable only if the expected profit margin is sufficiently large. Second, and conversely, worthwhile investments may be rejected inadvertently based on the same criteria. In reality, any theory of investment needs to address the question: how should a corporate manager facing uncertainty over future market conditions decide whether to invest in a new project? One way around this is to regard any capital investment decision as being more than a 'black box' in which the decision is made without managerial intervention. Management has to decide when to invest, how operating plans should be modified during the life of the project, and whether to abandon a project in midstream. By guiding a project/investment from beginning to end, management may be able to squeeze its cash flow distribution towards a higher rate of return. This has led to the development of the idea that because management control can impact on a project's payoff in terms of potential profits and losses, control opportunities can be seen as being analogous to 'call' and 'put' options and therefore, may be analysed using options pricing theory. This theory has its origins in the valuation of stocks and shares, where a stock option is an explicit contract conferring certain rights to the holder, who exercises the option only when it is profitable to do so. In fact, an option is a contract which makes an agreement, but not an obligation to buy (a 'call' option) or sell (a 'put' option) at an agreed price at a future date.

The options approach can be extended in principle to capital projects, so that the opportunities inherent in a capital project can be viewed as implied contracts that allow management to choose only those actions that have positive cash flow effects. However, a difference arises in that the underlying assets of the options in a capital investment decision are real assets like the development of a new plant, rather than financial assets, like stocks and shares. As a consequence, the options imbedded in the investment decisions are referred to as 'real' options as opposed to financial options.

As illustrated in Figure 3.8, the value of a real options business can be seen in terms of the value generated from existing assets plus the value from growth opportunities.

Figure 3.8: Value components of a real options business

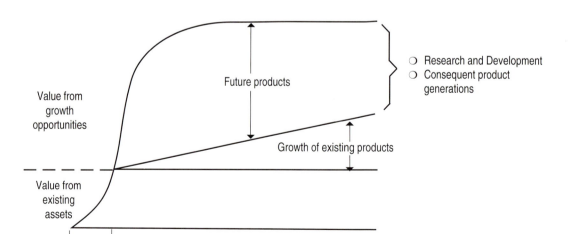

Source: *In Search of Shareholder Value*, Price Waterhouse, 1998 [68].

If Santos plc is viewed as a real options business, its business value may be expressed as follows:

Business value = Present value of existing assets + Present value of growth opportunities

The present value of the existing assets of Santos plc may be estimated by capitalising its 1997 free cash flow. The assumption underlying this approach is that, at this point in time, the business has reached a steady state with sufficient investment to produce a constant free cash flow of £12.39 million in perpetuity, the value of which is £103.25 million, i.e. £12.39 million ÷ 0.12.

In Chapter 2 we calculated a business value for Santos plc of £196.25m, hence the present value of growth opportunities is £93 million, i.e. £196.25 million – £103.25 million. The key issue is to understand the source of these growth options and the ability of the business to sustain their generation.

To date, options literature has had relatively little influence on management practices. Attention to real options has been scant, partly because modelling investments as options is a highly complex subject that is generally presented in a technical fashion. However, options have great potential relevance to managers, given that the manager's role is to use his/her skill to maximise shareholder wealth [69]. Ownership and control of an investment project can often generate follow-on opportunities, which are additional to the project's cash flows. For example, the purchase of a computer software company entitles the owner to the company's free cash flow, but the assets in place are not the only opportunity purchased. Along with the assets is likely to come the chance to learn about other software companies that might be for sale. The company may include highly skilled individuals who could be used to produce extra at little cost but with high value. Because such follow-on investment opportunities are relatively intangible and speculative, their expected cash flows are rarely examined directly. Nevertheless, these opportunities may have important value.

Illustrations of options pricing theory has emerged with reference to a number of examples, including investments in oil reserves, scale versus flexibility in utility planning and price volatility in commodities. Other examples of its use have also been emerging in recent times, for example, the pursuit of research and development projects [70]. A specific illustration of the options approach as applied to research and development has been provided by Merck [71]. The company wanted to enter a new line of business that required the acquisition of a number of appropriate technologies from a small company. Under the terms of the proposed agreement, Merck would pay $2 million over a period of three years. In addition, Merck would pay royalties to the company should the product ever come to the market. Merck had the option to terminate the agreement at any time if dissatisfied with the progress of the research.

In terms of analysing the strategic value of the project, Merck was unable to rely on traditional techniques. Project returns were difficult to model both because of the high degree of uncertainty regarding the size and profitability of the future market segments and because sales were not expected to commence until the latter part of the decade. The project had clear option characteristics: an overwhelming potential upside with little current downside exposure.

In keeping with the earlier discussion, two factors would determine this project's option value – the length of time the project could be deferred and project volatility. As regards the first of these, the longer Merck had to examine future developments, the more valuable the project would be. With more time, Merck would be able to collect more information and therefore make a better decision. In terms of project volatility, the high degree of uncertainty of project returns influences a project's value as an option because of the asymmetry between potential upside gains and downside losses. In the case of this project, Merck's downside loss potential was limited to the amount of the initial investment.

Merck used the Black-Scholes option-pricing model containing the following five factors to determine the project's option value [72]:

1. Exercise price.
2. Stock price.
3. Time to expiration.
4. Project volatility.
5. Risk-free rate.

These five factors were defined by the analysts at Merck as follows:

1. Exercise price. This represented the capital investment to be made approximately two years hence.
2. Stock price. This represented the value of the underlying asset, i.e. the present value of the cash flows from the project (excluding the capital investment to be made and the present value of the up-front fees and development costs over the next two years).
3. Time to expiration. This varied over two, three and four years with the option being exercisable in two years at the earliest. The option was structured to expire in four years because Merck thought that competing products, making market entry unfeasible, would exist by then.
4. Project volatility. This was represented by a sample of the annual standard deviation of returns for typical biotechnology stocks obtained from an investment bank.
5. Risk-free rate. A US Treasury rate of 4.5 per cent was used over the two to four-year period referred to in the time to expiration of the model.

The resulting option value from these five factors revealed that the option had significantly more value than the up-front payment that needed to be invested.

Options approaches may not be used in isolation [73]. In Merck it costs on average $359 million and takes ten years to bring a drug to market, and seven out of ten products fail to return the cost of the company's capital. Companies like Merck, therefore, have to face an enormous annual research and development expenditure. For example, it spends well over $2 billion annually on research and development and capital expenditures combined, and much of this is on risky, long-term projects that are notoriously difficult to evaluate.

To evaluate such expenditures the company uses a technique known as Monte Carlo simulation to produce a frequency distribution showing the probability that a project's net present value will exceed a certain level.

Options pricing theory is regarded as being useful in valuing financial instruments associated with shares or a commodity because they can be readily valued in the capital markets. Options pricing theory is, however, less likely to provide such readily quantifiable insights when considering an investment, the value of which is not driven exclusively by some traded asset. The valuation of a textile plant in an emerging market, for example, is unlikely to be accomplished more efficiently by using sophisticated options pricing techniques. In these instances, use of scenario-based cash flows combined with strategic value analysis as discussed earlier may be more beneficial [74]. As indicated, scenarios are a powerful tool for consolidating/clarifying one's perceptions about alternative future environments in which today's decisions might be played out.

History shows that investment opportunities with the greatest value creation potential often arise at points of discontinuity caused by technological innovation, deregulation, or shifts in consumer behaviour. Yet investing in these opportunities is risky since potential losses could be substantial. Companies have two obvious choices in such uncertain growth situations. Either they can commit themselves to full investment and hope it pays off (high risk approach), or they can wait and re-evaluate once market trends become clearer (low risk approach) – by which time bolder competitors may have taken the lead.

However, in many markets there is a third possibility – that of acquiring a growth option which buys a company the ability to participate in future growth without substantial risk. Growth options have three distinct features. They carry no obligation to make a full investment; they are considerably cheaper than full investment; and they give the buyer a preferential position from which to make a full investment over competitors without an option. A good example of this, which will be discussed later in Chapter 8, covers the use of joint ventures and strategic alliances.

Today's business environment is volatile and unpredictable because of growing market globalisation together with exchange rate fluctuations and more rapid technology induced changes in the market place. Irrespective of the causes of volatility, uncertainty requires managers to become more sophisticated in the way they look at, assess and account for risk. With this in mind, thinking in terms of options provides the means by which managers develop a better understanding of available choices or possibilities they can create. Ultimately, options approaches create flexibility which, in an uncertain world, mean that greater realism can be introduced into valuations undertaken. The bottom line is that managers will increasingly have to manage in such a way as to keep their options open.

Interrelationship between the planning period, the CAP and the terminal value

As mentioned in the introduction to this chapter there are no easy answers to what is an appropriate CAP, in fact any decisions concerning the CAP cannot be taken in isolation. As Figure 3.9 shows, the planning period adopted is related to the CAP which, in turn, is related to the terminal value calculation. Similarly, the terminal value calculation used makes certain assumptions regarding the CAP which, in turn, influences the planning period chosen.

Figure 3.9: Dynamic interrelationship between planning period, CAP and terminal value

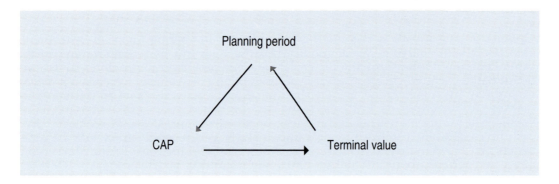

Two practical possibilities exist for the relationship between the planning period and the CAP:

○ First, the planning period is equal to the CAP, which implies that there is no new value created beyond it because the returns on new capital have fallen to the cost of capital. As will be illustrated in Chapter 5, the most appropriate terminal value calculation is the simple perpetuity.

○ Second, the planning period is less than the CAP and hence there is new value being created beyond it that needs to be captured by the valuation. As will be illustrated in Chapter 4, this is the situation for Santos plc and in such circumstances, there are alternative possible approaches that can be used to take account of this additional value. One such approach is that of the real options approach reviewed in this chapter. However, there are other possible solutions, which are reviewed in Chapter 5.

Summary checklist

○ A critical determinant of any valuation is what period of time should be used for the planning period.

○ Literature from strategic theory provides the starting point for understanding what could be the underlying determinants of the CAP.

○ A market-based perspective of the CAP can be derived using the seven value driver framework to derive a market implied duration.

○ From an internal as well as an external perspective, scenario thinking is invaluable in understanding what may underpin the CAP.

○ It is important to make explicit assumptions about whether the planning period used in any valuation is the CAP and, if the two are not the same, what will be the implications for the valuation.

○ It is important not to overlook the unique view provided by adopting an options thinking approach to valuation and the CAP for those types of business where all potential value seems to lie within the terminal value

○ Pragmatism dictates that cross-checking results using a number of different approaches may assist in gaining a deeper understanding of the CAP.

Concluding remarks

The determination of an appropriate planning period to use in any valuation is always a problem. As we have indicated, there are some approaches that can be used in its estimation, but the exercise is far from being a science. With this in mind, we should not be surprised to find rules of thumb to be common practice. A five-year planning period, combined with a perpetuity assumption seem to be popular for mature businesses, while high-growth businesses tend to favour longer planning periods and more aggressive terminal value assumptions.

The potential of options thinking and options approaches for evaluating certain types of business is an important emerging development. Where there are major concerns about the proportion of value accounted for by the terminal value, the options approach can be invaluable for facilitating thinking. This will be illustrated in Chapter 8 with reference to the evaluation of a joint venture opportunity in the Peoples' Republic of China.

Scenarios provide an invaluable means of trying to unravel and understand CAP. However, there are occasions where even they have limitations and another perspective is required. In such circumstances, options theory has much to offer but its application to the real world, as distinct from financial applications, is in a state of relative infancy. Doubtless there will be substantial developments in this area.

Part 2: Key valuation issues

Chapter 4: Alternative Measures of Strategic Value

> *... the reality is that all of the methodologies that claim to be for Shareholder Value Analysis, (including discounted cash flow, economic value added, cash flow return on investment and various accounting approaches) are not the same. In many cases, the fundamental assumptions are different, the calculations are different and the time horizon is different. Consequently, these various methods do not all produce the same answers or insights into a business' value and its prospects.*
>
> Richard Bassett, Managing Director CPS Alcar, 1997 [75].

Chapter preview

- The different methods that can be used for measuring strategic value, each of which relies on discounted cash flow analysis principles.

- The basic principles that underpin alternative valuation methods.

- How the economic profit approach, as popularised by Economic Value Added (EVA ®), * can be shown to produce the same result as the free cash flow approach outlined in Chapter 2, under certain conditions.

- How not all approaches for calculating strategic value lead to the same result, typically because of fundamental differences in assumptions, calculation bases and time horizons.

- The importance of technology in valuation modelling.

---

* EVA® is a registered Trade Mark of Stern Stewart & Co.

Introduction

In previous chapters Strategic Value Analysis has been discussed primarily in terms of using value drivers to produce a free cash flow forecast and the measurement of the total value generated from such free cash flow estimates for the planning period and beyond. However, this is by no means the only way in which strategic value can be expressed or calculated. A number of alternative measures of value are currently attracting much attention and these are the subject of this chapter.

As indicated in the opening quote to this Chapter, while these measures can be shown to produce the same result in principle, whether this is the case in practice will be dependent on the assumptions made. Often differences do arise for many reasons (we will explore this later), not least of which is the purpose for which the measure is used.

Economic profit, Economic Value Added (EVA®), and Strategic Value Added (SVA)

As indicated in Chapter 1, a valuation method called EVA® has been attracting much attention. It is one of a number that seek to analyse a business in terms of the economic profit earned in a given time period after deducting all expenses including the opportunity cost of capital employed. In other words, a business is only 'truly' profitable in an economic sense if it generates a return in excess of that required by its providers of funds, i.e. shareholders and investors. As illustrated in Figure 4.1, this type of approach can encourage three courses of action for improvement. These correspond with improving the return on capital, decreasing the cost of capital and decreasing the capital employed within the business. Action taken on any of these should improve performance in terms of the economic profit created.

Figure 4.1: Three courses of action for EP (economic profit) improvement

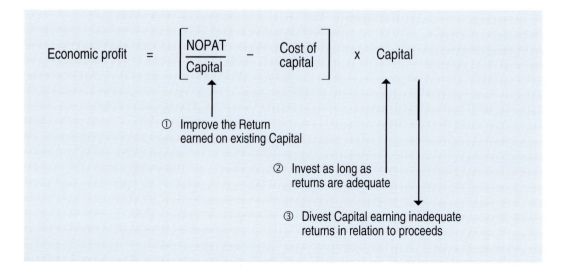

Economic profit is not a new idea. Alfred Sloan, the patriarch of the General Motors Corporation is reckoned to have adopted the principles of economic profit in the 1920s, and the General Electric Co. coined the term 'residual income' in the 1950s, which it used to assess the performance of its decentralised divisions [76].

In this section an economic profit measure known as Strategic Value Added will be reviewed. It will be demonstrated that Strategic Value Added can be calculated in principle using the same information that we used in Chapter 2 to calculate a free cash flow strategic value for the example company Santos plc. As a starting point, the free cash flow strategic value calculation from Chapter 2 is summarised in Figure 4.2.

Figure 4.2: Strategic value calculation for Santo

Free cash flow statement	1997 £m	1998 £m	1999 £m	2000 £m	2001 £m	2002 £m	Beyond £m
Sales	285.02	319.22	357.53	400.43	448.48	502.30	502.30
− Cost of sales	122.94	137.69	154.21	172.72	193.45	216.66	216.66
Gross profit	162.08	181.53	203.32	227.71	255.03	285.64	285.64
− Operating expenses	125.75	143.36	163.43	186.31	212.39	242.12	242.12
Operating profit	36.33	38.17	39.89	41.40	42.64	43.52	43.52
+ Depreciation	13.03	13.38	13.89	14.47	15.11	15.83	16.64
	49.36	51.55	53.78	55.87	57.75	59.35	60.16
− Cash Tax	9.39	10.90	11.45	11.96	12.42	12.79	13.05
Operating cash flow after tax	39.97	40.65	42.33	43.91	45.33	46.56	47.11
− Stock increase	9.29	6.84	7.66	8.58	9.61	10.76	0.0
− Debtor increase	6.19	5.70	6.38	7.15	8.01	8.97	0.0
+ Creditor increase	3.73	4.92	5.51	6.17	6.91	7.74	0.0
− RFCI	13.03	13.38	13.89	14.47	15.11	15.83	16.64
− IFCI	2.80	4.10	4.60	5.15	5.77	6.46	0.0
Free cash flow	12.39	15.55	15.31	14.73	13.74	12.28	30.47
Discount factor (12%)		0.893	0.797	0.712	0.636	0.567	
Present value		13.89	12.20	10.49	8.74	6.96	
Cumulative present value		13.89	26.09	36.58	45.32	52.28	
Value from planning period	52.28						
+ Terminal value	143.97						
Business value	196.25						
+ Marketable securities	0.00						
Corporate value	196.25						
− Market value of debt	70.92						
Strategic value (£m)	125.33						
Number of shares (m)	106						
Strategic value per share (£)	**1.18**						

66 CHAPTER FOUR

The value generated over the five-year planning period can also be looked at in terms of the additional value generated, such that the business value generated of £196.25 million could be compared with the business value at the outset. This can be estimated from the balance sheet, or as a result of using a perpetuity value based on the free cash flow for 1997. Taking the first perspective, a corporate value equivalent can be estimated from the 1997 balance sheet, i.e. a long-term debt plus equity figure. From Santos's balance sheet, summarised in Figure 4.3, this is £169.12 million (£70.92 million + £98.2 million).

Figure 4.3: 1997 Balance Sheet for Santos plc

	1997 £m	1997 £m
Fixed assets		104.20
Current assets:		
Stock	71.25	
Debtors	47.50	
Cash	0.80	
	119.55	
Creditors falling due within 1 year		
Creditors	40.98	
Taxation	8.35	
Proposed dividend	5.30	
	54.63	
Net current assets		64.92
Total assets – current liabilities		169.12
Creditors falling due after 1 year		70.92
		98.20
Capital and reserves		
Share capital		10.60
Share premium		38.70
Revaluation reserve		2.10
Profit and loss account		46.80
		98.20

By comparing the £196.25 million and this £169.12 million, £27.13 million is expected to be generated by way of additional value over the five-year planning period *. However, this £27.13 million could also be expressed in terms of the value added each year and this is exactly what economic profit approaches like Strategic Value Added seek to do. To illustrate this, the calculation of Strategic Value Added for Santos plc is summarised in Figure 4.4, from which it can be seen that £27.13 million is the cumulative value of annual Strategic Value Added.

While the resulting strategic value in aggregate and per share is the same in this case using both the free cash flow and Strategic Value Added approaches, the method of calculation is different. Under the free cash flow approach incremental fixed and working capital

---

* Reviewed later in this chapter under the heading of Market Value Added (MVA).

requirements are incorporated within the cash flow statement, whereas with economic profit approaches like Strategic Value Added, they are built into the capital base that is multiplied by the performance spread for each time period. For example the opening capital * in 1999 in Figure 4.4 reflects the incremental fixed and working capital requirement estimates for 1998. This opening capital of £180.84 million is used to generate a NOPAT of £28.44 million. As a percentage return on opening capital, this £28.44 million represents approximately 15.73 per cent. Given a cost of capital of 12 per cent, the 'performance spread' is 3.73% which, when multiplied by the opening capital, produces a Strategic Value Added of £6.74 million.

Figure 4.4: Strategic Value Added analysis of Santos plc

	1998 £m	1999 £m	2000 £m	2001 £m	2002 £m	Beyond £m
Opening capital	169.12	180.84	193.97	208.68	225.16	243.61
+ Stock	6.84	7.66	8.58	9.61	10.76	0.0
+ Debtors	5.70	6.38	7.15	8.01	8.97	0.0
− Creditors	4.92	5.51	6.17	6.91	7.74	0.0
+ IFCI	4.10	4.60	5.15	5.77	6.46	0.0
+ RFCI	0.00	0.00	0.00	0.00	0.00	0.0
Closing capital	180.84	193.97	208.68	225.16	243.61	243.61
NOPAT †	27.27	28.44	29.44	30.22	30.73	30.47
Return on capital (%)	16.12	15.73	15.18	14.48	13.65	12.51
Cost of capital (%)	12.00	12.00	12.00	12.00	12.00	12.00
Performance spread (%)	4.12	3.73	3.18	2.48	1.65	0.51
Strategic Value Added (£m)	**6.98**	**6.74**	**6.16**	**5.18**	**3.71**	**1.24**
Perpetuity value						10.33
Discount factor	0.893	0.797	0.712	0.636	0.567	
Present value(£m)	6.23	5.37	4.39	3.29	2.10	5.86
Cumulative present value	27.24					
+ Opening capital	169.12					
Business value	196.36					
+ Marketable securities	0.00					
Corporate value	196.36					
− Market value of debt	70.92					
Strategic Value (£m)	**125.44**					
Number of shares (m)	106					
Strategic value/share (£)	**1.18**					

---

* Sometimes referred to as the initial capital.
† Net operating profit less tax, e.g. for 1998, £38.17 million − £10.90 million (see Figure 4.2).

68   CHAPTER FOUR

Assuming depreciation is a good proxy for RFCI, NOPAT may be calculated via two routes; first, operating profit less cash tax, e.g. for 1998 (£38.17 million -- £10.9 million) = £27.27 million (see Figure 4.2), or second, operating cash flow after tax less depreciation, e.g. for 1998 £40.65 million – £13.38 million = £27.27 million (see Figure 4.2).

The difference with the Strategic Value Added approach is that value is calculated year-on-year. Performance spreads for each of the five years of 4.12 per cent, 3.73 per cent, 3.18 per cent, 2.48 per cent, 1.65 per cent and 0.51 per cent are multiplied by the opening capital to produce estimates of Strategic Value Added for each year of £6.98m, £6.74 million, £6.16 million, £5.18 million, £3.71 million and £1.24 million respectively. These are then discounted to a present value together with the estimated Strategic Value Added for the continuing period (beyond 2002). The result is a cumulative present value of the Strategic Value Added estimates of £27.24 million. However, from the foregone discussion and the courses of action identified in Figure 4.1, it can be seen that the calculation of Strategic Value Added is dependent on the definition used for the opening capital, NOPAT and the cost of capital.

In addition to measures of annual Strategic Value Added a related performance measure that was introduced in Chapter 1 and referred to earlier in this chapter called Market Value Added (MVA) would typically also be calculated. In Figure 4.4, the MVA for Santos plc is £27.24 million. In fact, there is more than one way of calculating MVA but, in simple terms, it is the market's assessment of the net present value of all past and projected capital investment projects of a company. If the market anticipates that a company will continue to earn profits above its cost of capital, it will have a positive MVA. If the market anticipates that profits will not exceed the cost of capital, the company's MVA is negative.

Figure 4.5:   Strategic Value Added and value

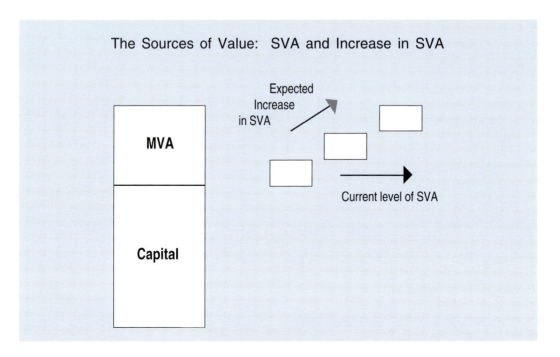

The Dynamics of Shareholder Value

MVA and Strategic Value Added are both closely related insofar as Strategic Value Added is an internal measure which may encourage the market to build a premium or discount to the market value of a company. It is possible for Strategic Value Added and MVA to move in opposite directions. For example, organisations implementing aggressive expansion strategies or making costly acquisitions may simultaneously have a negative Strategic Value Added and a positive MVA if the market anticipates that the earnings will soon exceed the capital costs.

Ten steps for calculating Strategic Value Added

The steps used to calculate the year-on-year Strategic Value Added values in Figure 4.4 were:

1. Calculate net operating profit after tax (NOPAT). Referring to Figure 4.2, if it is assumed that depreciation and capital expenditure for purposes of replacement are identical, then NOPAT must be equal to the operating cash flow after tax, less depreciation. For 1998, NOPAT is calculated as £40.65 million less £13.38 million, which equals £27.27 million.

2. Calculate NOPAT as a percentage of capital employed. For this, 'net opening capital employed' is required for each time period, which also requires making estimates of additional (incremental) fixed and working capital needs.

3. Calculate the Weighted Average Cost of Capital (WACC). For this, exactly the same issues need to be addressed for both the Strategic Value Added and free cash flow calculations and these will be reviewed in Chapter 6.

4. Calculate the 'performance spread', i.e. the difference between the NOPAT as a percentage of capital employed and the WACC.

5. Multiply the performance spread by the opening capital of the planning period to find the Strategic Value Added for each year.

6. Discount the Strategic Value Added for each year at the cost of capital and sum them to find the present value of the total Strategic Value Added for the planning period.

7. Determine the terminal value using the perpetuity approach and discount it to a present value, i.e. = £10.33 million (£1.24 million ÷ 0.12) in the case of Santos plc which, when discounted into present value terms equals £5.86 million (£10.33 million × 0.567).

8. Sum the cumulative present value of the Strategic Value Added for the planning period, the present value of the terminal value and the opening capital.

9. Adjust the corporate value by deducting the market value of any debt and adding the value of any marketable securities.

10. Divide the result by the number of shares, if a limited liability company, to give a value per share.

Review of Strategic Value Added/Economic Profit approaches

There is currently great enthusiasm for Strategic Value Added type measures. They do indeed have much to offer and the intention in this section is to illustrate that their use, as with any of the other measures, needs to be reviewed in line with their limitations.

1. Link with accounting practices

One of the supposed advantages of Strategic Value Added is the use of numbers derived from a conventional accounting system. Essentially the calculation of Strategic Value Added seems at first sight to require only one significant adjustment to a conventional profit and loss account - that is, the deduction of an appropriate capital charge. Managers familiar with the notion of 'bottom-line' profit are likely to be able to adjust relatively quickly to this revised approach. In addition, it may appear that the costs and time involved in adapting the system to incorporate this adjustment are unlikely to be significant. However, life is not as simple as this. For example, there are some significant drawbacks with this approach because accounting rules are not intended to ensure that the profit and loss account and balance sheet are reliable guides to the economic worth of a business. In fact, there are two key reasons why the accounting value of a business should not be regarded as necessarily a useful guide to its 'true' economic value:

1. Financial statements are prepared under the historic cost convention; assets are recorded at their original cost, therefore economic profit may be distorted in times of inflation. Cash revenues and cash costs are measured at current prices, but fixed assets and depreciation are measured at potentially out-of-date historical cost. The result is an understatement of capital employed and an overstatement of operating profits, the combined effect of which causes a potential overstatement of Strategic Value Added. This problem could be addressed by valuing capital employed either on a replacement cost or market value basis, though the information required to make the necessary adjustments may not be readily available. However, adjusting asset values to replacement cost implicitly assumes that all assets will be replaced and yet this may not necessarily be the case in reality.

2. Many important and valuable assets are usually excluded from the balance sheet altogether. Such assets include intangibles such as brands, customer loyalty, the reputation of the business and so on.

Furthermore, accounting numbers are open to manipulation, as illustrated in Chapter 1. As a brief reminder you may recall that there are two specific problems. First, there are a number of items included in a set of accounts, which are extremely subjective, and therefore open to manipulation. (For example bad debt provisions, asset lives for depreciation, etc.). Second, a number of choices exist in the way in which some items may be accounted for like research and development expenditure, depreciation, stock, etc.). At best, this subjectivity and choice of treatment could potentially reduce the comparability of Strategic Value Added of different companies, or different business units within a company. At worst, it could be exploited to deliberately manipulate the implied economic profit achieved.

It is important to recognise that accounting depreciation, which effectively reduces the measure of capital invested, potentially distorts the true profitability of a business. Over the life of an asset, the capital charge will reduce year-on-year and Strategic Value Added will apparently increase. It is argued that this could encourage managers to continue to employ older assets with low net book values and to defer investment in new assets since, in the short-term at least, this will reduce Strategic Value Added. Positive net present value investments may, therefore, be foregone as a result. The theoretically correct solution to this problem is to value assets at their economic value (the present value of future net cash inflows) and to charge 'economic depreciation' as opposed to accounting depreciation. Economic depreciation represents the change in the present value of an asset during the year. The effect of this is that the asset is revalued upwards to incorporate the net present value of the investment and the economic profit over the life of the asset is then expected to be zero.

Last, but by no means least, there are also a number of practical accounting difficulties involved in this approach within a business. Strategic Value Added can potentially be used to measure the value of business units, product markets and even at the level of individual products and customers. To perform such analysis it must be possible to measure the relevant profit and capital invested separately. While profits may already be measured, the ability to measure separate revenues and costs accurately is affected by the presence of shared costs and transfer price arrangements for the transfer of products and services within the business. The separate balance sheet requirement is potentially even more onerous, since such information may not be currently produced by the accounting system. Constructing balance sheets for business units for the first time may prove a time-consuming and costly exercise.

2. The impact of the capital base

The value of the starting capital base used in a Strategic Value Added calculation is an important issue. Strategic Value Added calculations based on a relatively low capital base such as book value make it easy to generate a stream of large positive numbers for Strategic Value Added. Quite simply, other things being equal, a lower capital base will result in higher returns on opening capital, higher performance spreads, and hence higher Strategic Value Added. Likewise, the use of market values will have a significant impact on the Strategic Value Added. If we had used market value in calculating return on capital for 1998, the result would have been 15.41 per cent.

	£m	
Market capitalisation (106 million shares @ £1)	106.00	
Value of debt (assumed to be equivalent to market value)	70.92	
Opening capital	176.92	(A)
NOPAT (from Figure 4.4)	27.27	(B)
Return on opening capital (B ÷ A x 100)	15.41	%

Deducting a 12 per cent cost of capital from this 15.41 per cent results in a performance spread of 3.41 per cent and a Strategic Value Added of £6.03 million (£176.92 million x 3.41), rather than £6.98 million. Applying this approach to the whole time period will result in a different Strategic Value Added and a different strategic value.

3. The effect of Strategic Value Added measurement on decision-making

We have seen illustrated that Strategic Value Added can be used as a valuation tool, giving the same results as conventional free cash flow calculation. The use of economic profit measures like Strategic Value Added does not, however, guarantee decisions will be taken which are consistent with the net present value rule. Firstly, at a technical level, the equivalence between cash flow and economic profit based valuations only applies if 'flow through' accounting is used. Under 'flow through' accounting, also referred to as the 'comprehensive income' approach, all transactions flow through both the profit and loss account and the balance sheet so that:

> Closing book value of equity   (including share repurchases, less new issues of equity)
>
> = Opening book value of equity + Accounting profit − Dividends

Under this approach all asset write-downs or upward revaluations should 'flow through', but accounting in many countries like the UK does not correspond with such practices. For example, any surplus on fixed asset revaluations may be taken to reserves and not credited to the profit and loss account.

As well as the above technical issues, there are some very important behavioural issues, which might affect the likelihood that economic profit encourages correct decision-making by managers. First, consider the effect of an economic profit system for measuring and rewarding managerial or strategic and investment decision-making. A manager may be inclined to accept an investment which generates superior economic profit in the early years of its life, even though its overall net present value may be inferior to alternative opportunities. At best, this may mean that value-maximising opportunities are spurned. At worst, negative net present value projects may be accepted on the basis of short-term economic profit improvement and shareholder value is destroyed. On the other hand, positive net present value investments may not be undertaken if they involve short-term reductions in economic profit. Second, consider shorter-term operational decisions. Towards the year-end a manager, who otherwise would not achieve the annual economic profit target, might take short-termist actions which, although ensure that the target is met, harm the long-term value of the business. Such actions might include reducing training, marketing, research and development and maintenance expenditures in order to boost short-run economic profit.

Many proponents of economic profit approaches recognise that this is a potential problem and offer possible solutions. First, they argue that a long-term bonus scheme based on Strategic Value Added economic profits should be used, in which economic profit bonuses earned are only paid out some three years or more later so that the longer-term implications of decisions can be identified. Second, they propose a number of adjustments to the basic economic profit approach, some of which are intended to encourage managers to take the proper long-term view when making decisions. These adjustments include capitalising and amortising what they describe as 'strategic investments', such as research and development, training, restructuring costs and so on, so that the effect of these expenditures is spread over the period in which the business is expected to benefit from expenditures.

4. The conceptual basis for assigning a capital charge to measure business

One claimed benefit of the Strategic Value Added approach is that it encourages managers to be more aware of the costs relating to capital employed in the business. It is worth noting, however, that there are some potential problems with this, which stem from concerns regarding the appropriateness of charging business unit managers with a cost for the capital employed in the business. Some argue that if capital investment decisions are not under the influence of business unit management, then in principle it is not appropriate to charge management with the cost of capital employed. Second, even if investment decisions are made at the business unit level, then basing the capital charge on the book value of capital may be misleading. The book value of capital employed arguably is largely a result of decisions made in the past by managers. Potentially, this gives an unfair advantage to some managers, while penalising others. The market value of capital is the more relevant measure on which to base the capital charge since it reflects more accurately the investors' view of the capital invested on which adequate returns are required. The seriousness of this problem therefore depends on the extent to which the book value of capital employed differs from market value. This will vary from business to business and industry to industry. Some proponents of Strategic Value Added type approaches argue that this problem may be overcome by focusing not on the absolute level of economic profit but instead on the change in economic profit year-on-year. In this way, even if the capital base from which the capital charge is calculated is distorted, the trend in economic profit can still be assessed. They also recommend a number of adjustments to book capital, which are intended to ensure that measured capital is a closer approximation to the market value of capital invested in the business.

Figure 4.6: Different perspectives of the value of Santos

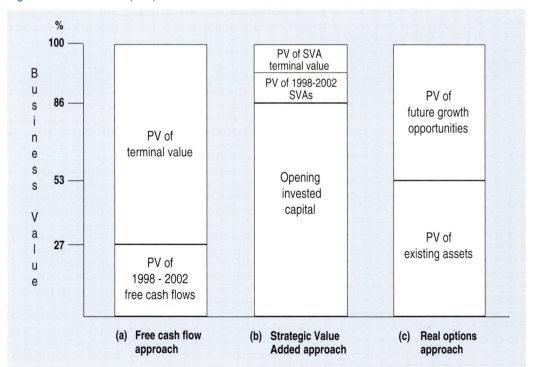

74 CHAPTER FOUR

A comparison of valuation results

Using Santos plc, the different approaches to valuation discussed so far can be summarised. In effect, as shown in Figure 4.6, these approaches represent different lenses through which to view the value of Santos.

(a) Free cash flow approach

As shown in Figure 4.6 (a), the free cash flow approach splits the value of Santos plc into two parts:

Value	=	PV of 1998-2002 free cash flows	+	PV of terminal value
	=	27%	+	73%

Figure 4.7: Analysis of free cash flow for Santos plc

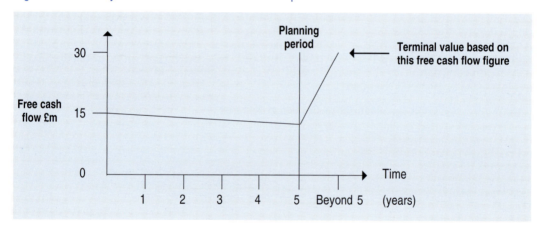

Figure 4.8: Analysis of capital base and associated returns (relative to cost of capital)

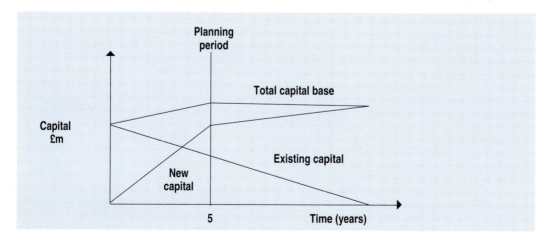

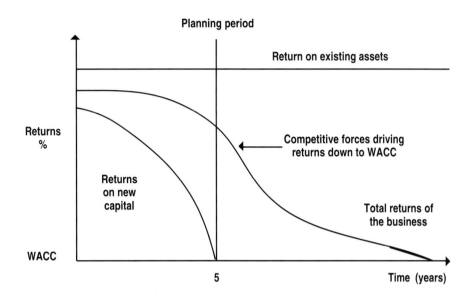

The capital of the business is split into the capital that exists today and that which will come into existence in the future through new investments that are made over time. If existing capital is assumed to continue to make its historic returns in perpetuity and new capital makes the returns as outlined in Figure 4.4., then as illustrated in Figure 4.8, it is possible to represent pictorially how the value created is being captured.

Figure 4.8 shows the total returns of the business decline during the five-year planning period in response to the decreasing returns on new capital. At the end of the planning period the returns on new capital have fallen to the cost of capital and no new value is being created. However, the value that is being created in the continuing period comes from the existing capital base of the business and is the result of past investment decisions. In essence, this is the value that is being picked up by the terminal value. Eventually the total returns of the business fall to the cost of capital as the new capital makes up an increasing proportion of the capital base of the business.

(b) Strategic Value Added approach

This splits the value into the three parts as illustrated in 4.6 (b), i.e.:

Value	=	Opening invested capital	+	PV of Strategic Value Added stream, 1998-2002	+	PV of Strategic Value Added TV
	=	86%	+	11%	+	3%

The underlying premise with this approach is that a business starts off with opening invested capital to which is added the new value created from additional investments over the planning period of £21.38 million, plus that created beyond of £5.86 million. If the planning period equates to the CAP this means that returns on new capital investments fall to the cost of capital at the end of the CAP and hence there should be no new value created beyond the CAP, thus there would be no terminal value. It can be seen in the case of Santos plc from Figure 4.9 that the CAP extends beyond the five-year planning period and hence there is a small terminal value capturing this extra value created. Extrapolating the curve in Figure 4.9, the CAP can be seen to lie between five and six years.

Figure 4.9: Analysis of Strategic Value Added for Santos plc

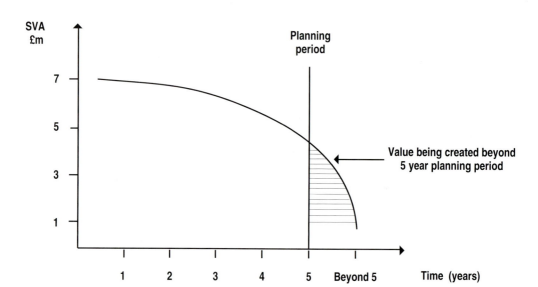

(c) Real options approach

As illustrated in Figure 4.6 (c), the real options approach can be used to shed further light on how value is being created by Santos plc. Using simplified assumptions *, as outlined in Chapter 3, existing investments generated free cash flows in perpetuity, which when valued represent 53 per cent of the total value, while future growth investments make up the balance of 47 per cent. This perspective on the value of Santos plc does force consideration of several questions such as:

○ How sustainable are the returns that generate the free cash flows from the existing investments?

○ What is the specific nature of the growth options that will generate the future value?

○ How likely is the business to continue generating and realising the benefits of these future growth options?

---

* For a more sophisticated modelling approach see CFROI.

Other valuation approaches

Equity cash flow approach

This approach involves discounting equity cash flows by the cost of equity (as opposed to WACC). In very simple terms, adjustments are made to free cash flows for interest after tax and debt repaid or issued. The resulting equity cash flows are then discounted at the cost of equity. The equity cash flows are not just the expected dividend stream of the firm, they represent all the cash available for equity holders.

In order to use this approach, the forecasted future performance of a firm needs to include projections of the outcome of its specific financial policy, so that the schedule of debt repaid or issued, plus associated interest implications are known. In principle, firms may adopt one of two broad financing policies, (while in real life they tend adopt a mixture of the two):

○ Equity is neither issued nor bought back, so that any incremental financing is undertaken using debt, with any excess cash being used to reduce debt. Dividend pay-out remains constant.

○ The amount of debt, and hence gearing, is kept at a constant level so that any incremental financing comes as a result of issuing equity with any excess cash being paid out as dividends.

If the second of these financing policies is adopted, the calculation of equity cash flows for Santos plc and the subsequent valuation of its equity is as illustrated in Figure 4.10.

Figure 4.10 : Equity cash flow calculation for Santos plc

	1997 £m	1998 £m	1999 £m	2000 £m	2001 £m	2002 £m	Beyond £m
Free cash flow	12.39	15.55	15.31	14.73	13.74	12.28	30.47
− Interest after tax	5.96	5.56	5.75	6.06	6.65	7.46	6.92
+/− Debt repaid / <issued>	− 0.64	4.76	− 2.26	− 3.77	− 7.00	− 9.55	0.00
Equity cash flow (£m)	7.07	5.23	11.82	12.44	14.09	14.37	23.55
Discount factor (14.03%)		0.877	0.769	0.674	0.591	0.519	
Present value		4.59	9.09	8.38	8.33	7.46	87.12
Cumulative present value		4.59	13.68	22.06	30.39	37.85	
Value from planning period	37.85						
+ Terminal value	87.12						
Business value	124.97						
+ Marketable securities	0.00						
Corporate value	124.97						
− Market value of debt	0.00						
Strategic value (£m)	124.97						
Number of shares (m)	106						
Strategic value per share (£)	**1.18**						

In calculating the terminal value using this approach, the assumption made is that the level of debt will remain constant in perpetuity. This means that no debt is issued or repaid and the interest after tax also remains constant. Thus, as shown in Figure 4.10, the equity cash flow for the period beyond 2002 is £23.55 million which, assuming a simple perpetuity calculation and a cost of equity of 14.03 per cent *, translates into a terminal value of £87.12 million (£23.55 million ÷ 0.1403 × 0.519).

An equity cash flow valuation may not reconcile exactly with the measures discussed earlier. One source of difference relates to the modelling of the debt/equity ratio as between the WACC used in calculating strategic value and Strategic Value Added, and the cost of equity used in the equity cash flow approach. In practice, the more the debt/equity ratio varies over the planning period, the greater is the difference each approach produces.

The key argument for using the equity cash flow approach is that it is often very difficult to estimate the market value of debt accurately, which potentially distorts the Weighted Average Cost of Capital and second, the deduction for the value of debt from the total market value of a company to arrive at the value of equity. In practice, this approach is favoured in valuing banks and financial institutions for a number of reasons including regulatory considerations. It is also favoured in emerging markets characterised by high levels of inflation, where the notion of a long-term stable target debt to equity ratio is often unrealistic.

Equity economic profit approach

There is also a variant of the Strategic Value Added approach, which involves comparing the return on equity (as opposed to total capital) with the cost of equity (as opposed to WACC). For each year an equity economic profit is calculated using the following formula:

$$\text{Equity economic profit} = (\text{Return on equity \%} - \text{Cost of equity \%}) \times \text{Equity invested}$$

For the same reasons as were discussed with reference to Strategic Value Added, the annual return on equity in this calculation is typically adjusted to convert it from accounting terms into cash flow terms. When expressed in present value terms, the sum of the equity economic profits (including the terminal value), should result in the same value as using any of the other measures reviewed so far. However, for reasons identified in the introductory quote to this chapter, this is often not so in practice.

Cash Flow Return On Investment (CFROI)

Cash Flow Return On Investment (CFROI) compares the cash flow to the total assets employed to generate those cash flows [77]. It is a reporting tool too all of the firm's stakeholders and is an inflation-adjusted measure of corporate performance, calculated in the same manner as an internal rate of return. It entails comparing real returns to the real cost of capital, in contrast to the other approaches which are expressed in nominal terms.

---

* The calculation of this will be illustrated in Chapter 6.

The essence of CFROI is to look at cash-in versus cash-out, much as in a capital project appraisal. CFROI is intended to measure the performance of a business from the investor's point of view because it looks at the cash investors have put in versus the amount they are getting out. It can be used to give a cross-sectional measure of returns and as a valuation method.

Three adjustments are made in order to calculate a CFROI:

1. Depreciation, amortisation and other non-cash charges are added back to the income stream and accumulated depreciation is added back to net assets to estimate 'gross assets'.
2. All numbers are adjusted for the effects of inflation to ensure that apples are compared with apples. The view is taken that just as one would never add US dollars to Deutsche marks without making a currency translation, the currency from one period should not be added to currency from another period without an inflation adjustment. For North American and Western European economies and average classifications of assets, this adjustment yields about a 20 to 40 per cent increase to the asset base.
3. Asset life is included explicitly in the calculation.

The proponents of this approach argue that it is preferable to approaches like Strategic Value Added because it does not focus on the measurement of the difference between a calculated return on capital (which is reliant on accounting principles and practice), and an estimated cost of capital. The suggestion by its supporters is that even when measures like Strategic Value Added have been adjusted to convert them from accounting to cash flow numbers they are still not comparable. This is because by being based on historical cost accounting, such measures suffer from the effect of non-zero past inflation rates on accounting statements and these effects vary widely across companies and countries.

As well as making a case for calculating the return differently, proponents of the approach look at the issues of estimating terminal value and the cost of capital very differently. Issues associated with the estimation of terminal value are reviewed in the next chapter and those relating to the cost of capital are covered in Chapter 6.

Technology and valuation

The demands of complex valuation circumstances and approaches like CFROI, typically necessitate the use of specific valuation software. In selecting software there are some important considerations, which include:

- ease of use;
- ability to rank areas of the business on which to focus;
- ability to tell what needs to be done to achieve a particular goal;
- ability to communicate complex financial concepts in a straightforward way;
- provision of a pre-formatted and consistent framework;
- robustness;
- connectivity to existing IS systems;
- use of diagrams and flow-charts;
- compatibility with training/implementation programmes.

Summary checklist

○ The various approaches that can be used to calculate strategic value can be grouped as follows:
1. Free Cash Flow (FCF).
2. Strategic Value Added (SVA).
3. Equity Cash Flow.
4. Equity Economic Profit.
5. Cash Flow Return On Investment (CFROI).

○ These approaches can also be summarised by their distinguishing features as illustrated in Figure 4.11.

○ Mathematical equivalence can be demonstrated between the measures under certain circumstances.

○ All the methods are reliant on the principles that underpin discounted cash flow analysis.

○ The choice of method will very often depend on the circumstances in which it will be used.

Figure 4.11: Resumé of valuation approaches

Approach	Free Cash Flow	Residual Income/ Economic Profit and Performance spreads	Cash Flow Return on Investment (CFROI)
Proponent	L.E.K. Partnership	Stern Stewarts' EVA ®	Braxton Associates
	Price Waterhouse	Marakon Associates	Boston Consulting Group
	McKinsey & Co		Holt Associates
Post tax cost of capital	Nominal as per CAPM	Nominal as per CAPM	Real market derived rate
Cash flows	Nominal	Nominal	Real

Concluding remarks

The main methods that can be used for estimating strategic value have been reviewed in this chapter. It has been illustrated that, with reference to Santos plc in principle the same result can arise from using different methods. However, this may not be so in practice because the fundamental assumptions used, hence the resulting calculations, may be different. If this is the case, the various methods reviewed in this chapter will not produce the same answers or insights into the value of a business and its prospects.

Differences in assumptions used can often be traced to the purpose for which a method is required. In that regard, some valuation methods are more suitable for one application than another. For example, in pricing a new issue or analysing a prospective merger and acquisition opportunity, free cash flow calculations are probably most appropriate, but in designing an executive compensation scheme based on meeting time constrained performance targets, Strategic Value Added may have more to offer. Valuation is not an objective science. There is no single true value, rather there are values which will be driven by the demands of the purpose for which they are undertaken. As illustrated in the boxed insert below, companies like Monsanto in the US recognise the need to use more than one measure.

Monsanto - An illustration of the use of valuation metrics in practice

Our objective was to put in place a system of economic based metrics that correctly measures shareowner value and that drives decisions so that shareowner wealth is continually enhanced over time. We selected Economic Value Added (EVA) as Monsanto's overall metric. The EVA financial management system will be supported by Total Business Return/Cash Flow Return on Investment (TBR/CFROI) at the planning level.

EVA is based on cash flow. It's derived by taking net income, making adjustments to eliminate accounting distortions, and subtracting a charge for capital used to generate that income. The appealing features of EVA are that it's easy to understand, it can be used by all employees, and it can be tied to incentive compensation plans. As a result, EVA can truly drive the type of behaviour needed to create greater shareowner value.

TBR/CFROI is an investor oriented tool that measures a company's return to its shareowners over a period of time. TBR/CFROI can be used effectively to better determine the performance expectations in our stock price. These expectations can then be translated into EVA targets for the company and its business units.

The power of combining these 2 metrics is that management now has at its disposal the most sophisticated techniques available to understand investor expectations. We can set business targets for achieving or exceeding these expectations, and then translate these goals into actions.

Source: Monsanto - 1995 Annual Report

Chapter 5: Terminal Value

Zeneca's cauldron is bubbling over with new potions. In the short term, marketing costs will restrain margin growth and cash flow. But Zeneca should have little trouble meeting & beating its target of 15% annual earnings growth to the turn of the century. The real strategic issue lies beyond that horizon.

Lex Column, *Financial Times*, 12 March 1997 [78].

Chapter preview

○ The principles and potential application of three different approaches that can be used to calculate Terminal Value (TV):

1. DCF.
2. Market relative valuation.
3. Asset valuation.

○ The contribution that the perpetuity approach can make in challenging valuation assumptions.

○ The important interrelationship between the TV and the planning period chosen.

○ The potential application of CFROI and real options approaches for considering TV issues.

84 CHAPTER FIVE

Introduction

Terminal Value (TV) and some of the approaches like the perpetuity method, that can be used in its estimation were introduced in Chapter 2. As illustrated with reference to Santos plc, this value which arises from the continuing period is often a source of considerable concern because it accounts for a significant proportion of total value. Of even more concern, in some circumstances such as a start-up or the development of a new market, the TV may account for a very large proportion of total value (see Figure 5.1).

Figure 5.1: Terminal value multiples applied in UK telecom issues [79]

Issuer	Broker's research	Date	Discount rate	Terminal value (multiple of normalised earnings) *
Ionica	SBC Warburg	June 1997	16-17%	6-8x
General Cable	BZW	April 1995	13%	7x
Orange	ABN Amro Hoare Govett	May 1997	13%	7x
Atlantic Telecom	ABN Amro Hoare Govett	May 1997	16%	9x
Colt Telecom	Kleinwort Benson	October 1996	15%	9x
BskyB	BZW	September 1994	11%	10.5x
TeleWest	Kleinwort Benson	October 1994	15-17%	12x

In estimating TV the following sequence of steps has been identified as being important [80]:

1. Select an appropriate technique.
2. Decide on the planning period.
3. Estimate the valuation parameters and calculate the TV.
4. Convert the TV into present value terms.

The second of these steps, the selection of an appropriate planning period was covered in Chapter 3. As regards the selection of a method, there are many potential alternatives that have not yet been reviewed which are the subject of this chapter. A case can be made for using each of them, but some stand up to better scrutiny than others. Nevertheless, the plain fact of the matter is that the selection of a TV method is rather like any area of consumer choice – it is dictated by preference, prejudice and gut-reaction, as much as logic. Many of those used are often referred to as traditional approaches and typically they are dependent on information about profitability or assets and, perhaps, a peer group set of companies. Some of these approaches are relevant in particular circumstances. For example, where exit from the market is under serious consideration

---

* Multiple = 1 ÷ (WACC − anticipated growth). For example, where cost of capital = 12 per cent and anticipated growth = 2 per cent, multiple = 1 / (0.12 − 0.02) = 10

because of an anticipated major deterioration in the market, liquidation value may well form the basis of a sound TV estimate. In contrast, for situations where the focus of attention is on building market share, a going concern measure rather than liquidation value would likely be more relevant for estimating TV.

In view of the potential significance of the TV in any decision, the structure illustrated in Figure 5.2 can be used to guide the assessment and selection of an appropriate method and its estimation.

Figure 5.2: Selecting an appropriate TV method

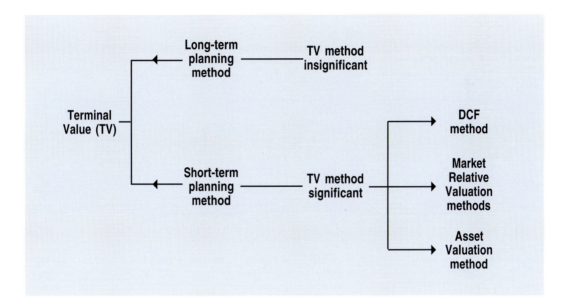

The starting point illustrated in Figure 5.2 is consideration of the time period. If the time period under consideration is very long, say in excess of 20 years, as may be the case of valuing a concession, then the TV estimation is relatively insignificant. For example, the value of £1 in year 20, is 0.149, assuming a discount rate of 10 per cent. This means that the relative importance of the TV to the total value becomes insignificant over such periods by comparison with frequently used short-term time periods, like five years. In year five at 10 per cent the discount rate is 0.621, meaning that every TV pound counts substantially towards the total value.

In the case of a short-term time horizon being used TV and the choice of a method for its calculation become important. Methods that can be used for estimating TV when a short-term view is taken are shown in Figure 5.2 as:

○ Discounted Cash Flow (DCF);
○ Market Relative Valuation methods;
○ Asset Valuation method.

Discounted Cash Flow (DCF) Methods

As illustrated in Figure 5.3, a number of issues have to be taken into consideration in estimating a TV using DCF analysis.

Figure 5.3: Issues in estimating TV using Discounted Cash Flow methods

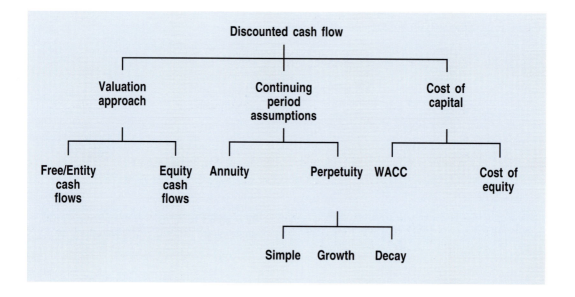

The way in which a DCF TV is estimated will be influenced by the:

○ valuation approach(es) adopted;
○ continuing period assumptions;
○ cost of capital.

Many of these issues are interrelated. For example, as illustrated with reference to Santos plc in Chapter 4, DCF TVs can be calculated from a free cash flow figure, a Strategic Value Added (economic profit), number, or the cash flow attributable to just the shareholders, known as an equity cash flow, but they differ because of the discount rate used. For calculating an equity cash flow TV the relevant cost of capital will be the cost of equity, while for the others it will be one that captures the cost of debt and an assumed long-term debt to equity relationship. The end result of using these two alternative valuation approaches can be shown to be the same in the world of *ceteris paribus* (other things equal) assumptions, although in our experience in practice this is rarely so. What is more, irrespective of whether an equity cash flow valuation or a free cash flow valuation method is adopted, there will still be choices to be made about the assumptions for the planning period and the continuing period beyond.

Annuity TV valuation

Where future cash inflows are constant over a finite time period, a TV can be calculated using the annuity approach. An annuity is a series of payments of an equal, or constant, amount of money at fixed intervals for a specified number of periods. Circumstances in which it might be appropriate to use for purposes of a TV calculation can be seen with reference to the following example. The computer repairs division of a major computer company is limited by developments in the market place believed to make such an operation redundant in say ten years time. If this is the case, an annuity approach is arguably appropriate, although in all probability it would also be compared with a liquidation value.

The formula for calculating the present value of an annuity is:

$$\text{Annuity TV} = \text{FCF}_{T+1} [1 \div (1 + \text{WACC})^1 + 1 \div (1 + \text{WACC})^2 + \ldots 1 \div (1 + \text{WACC})^n]$$

Where,
FCF_{T+1} = Normalised free cash flow for the continuing period *;
WACC = Weighted Average Cost of Capital (in the case of Santos plc 12%).

In the case of Santos plc, if it is believed that £30.47 million of free cash flow would be received for years 2002 to 2003 inclusive, the annuity value of this constant inflow at 12 per cent at the end of 1997 would be:

$$\text{Annuity TV} = £30.47\text{m} \times 3.605$$
$$= £109.84\text{m} \dagger$$

The figure of 3.605 used in the calculation is the sum total of the individual discount factors for 12 per cent over a five year time period and can be found readily in annuity tables ‡.

Perpetuity TV valuations

As illustrated in Chapter 2, many proponents of DCF valuation methods use perpetuity TV calculations. There are different perpetuity methods that can be used which, in simple terms, assume that:

---

* Normalised cash flows reflect the impact of events like the business cycle. In a cyclical business the size of the TV will depend on whether it is measured during upturn, downturn or a period of relative stability. It is important to recognise this influence rather than just simply taking the last year of the planning period as forming the basis of the perpetuity cash flow calculation.

† In common with all TV estimates this value must be discounted to convert it into present value terms.

‡ See page 221.

88 CHAPTER FIVE

○   only the cost of capital can be earned in the continuing period; or
○   more can be earned than the cost of capital; or
○   less can be earned than the cost of capital.

To correspond with these choices, the following TV calculations can be used:

○   simple perpetuity;
○   perpetuity with growth;
○   perpetuity with decay.

Simple perpetuity

The simple perpetuity approach is often represented as assuming constant cash flows beyond the planning period. It can be thought of as being reliant on the same principles as those associated with calculating an annuity, but instead we consider a special case in which constant free cash flows are assumed to be received for an infinite rather than a finite period *.

The simple perpetuity TV is typically calculated as follows:

$$\text{Terminal Value} = \frac{FCF_{T+1}}{WACC}$$

Where,

FCF_{T+1} = Normalised free cash flow for the continuing period;

WACC = Weighted Average Cost of Capital.

For Santos plc, the free cash flow in the continuing period beyond 2002 is £30.47 million (see Figure 2.6). Assuming this to be the normalised free cash flow, when divided by the assumed cost of capital of 12 per cent, the result is a value of approximately £253.92 million. However, this is not the value required for purposes of undertaking most valuations. Typically what is needed is the present value of the perpetuity and not the value at the end of five years. This present value is substantially lower than £253.92 million and is in fact £143.97 million (£30.47m ÷ 0.12 x 0.567), i.e. £253.92 million received in five years discounted to a present value.

---

* The simple perpetuity can be derived from the growing free cash flow perpetuity formula (discussed in the next section). For now, it is important to stress that the simple perpetuity does not mean that growth will necessarily be zero, rather it indicates that any growth will add nothing to value, because the return associated with growth will equal only the cost of capital. In other words, it reflects the fact that the cash flows resulting from future investments will not affect the value of the firm, because the overall rate of return earned on them will only equal the cost of capital – hence the method is often referred to as the 'convergence formula'.

Perpetuity with growth

There may be circumstances like the valuation of a telecommunications business (see Figure 5.1) in which it is believed that it will be possible to earn a return above the cost of capital in the continuing period. In such circumstances the perpetuity with growth approach is often argued as being more appropriate. It can be calculated as follows:

$$\text{Terminal Value} = \frac{FCF_{T+1}}{WACC - g}$$

Where,

FCF_{T+1} = Normalised free cash flow for the continuing period;

WACC = Weighted Average Cost of Capital;

g = Expected growth rate in free cash flow into perpetuity.

An assumed a growth rate in free cash flow into perpetuity of 2%, then this results in the following TV estimate:

$$= £30.47m \div (0.12 - 0.02)$$

$$= £304.7m$$

Assuming a perpetuity growth rate of 2 per cent, the resulting TV is £304.7 million, 20 per cent higher than using the simple perpetuity method. Clearly, the growth rate used has a significant impact on the TV and overall value and it is important to be able to justify the rate selected. An example of the use of perpetuity with growth assumptions and its justification can be seen with reference to the UK telecommunications company Orange plc. The rationale for the use of the approach was that within the UK market growth forecasts for the mobile industry had been substantially underestimated. In the advertising campaign, which preceded the award of the two mobile licences for the UK market in 1983, Cellnet's market forecast was for 100,000 subscribers while Vodafone's estimate was 250,000 for the total market! Today, the UK cellular base consists of about six million subscribers and forecasts for the market out to the year 2001 range from 10 million to 18 million. In fact, some manufacturers estimated the eventual penetration of mobile phones at 1.2 per person. The rationale behind such forecasts was that buying the service and the handset need not be linked and handsets may well be as cheap as digital watches in due course.

This approach has to be used cautiously because of the impact of growth assumptions on total value. In the case of a belief in real growth opportunities existing in the market, a reality check is essential. This reality check could be as simple as calculating what volumes would be say 10 to 20 years ahead, based on such a growth rate and making comparisons with the total potential market, competitive forces, and the like. It is also worth noting that perpetuity with growth calculations are sometimes used to take account of inflation. The assumption is that the cash flows in the continuing period should grow at a rate in perpetuity that reflects the inflation rate. Essentially, the logic of this is that if the free cash flow used in the continuing period calculation is not assumed to grow at the rate of inflation, it represents a real number that should be discounted at a real number. Given that WACC in the formula is expressed in nominal terms, conversion to a real rate is achieved by deducting expected inflation as g from the denominator. Opinion is divided about such practice. Those who favour it do so because it is consistent with general principles, i.e. real cash flows should be discounted at a real rate. Those who dislike it argue (among other points) that it is more realistic to assume that any growth will probably require at least additional working capital expenditure, and that replacement (maintenance) fixed capital investment is likely to exceed depreciation.

Perpetuity with decay

This is a very conservative approach which can be thought of as a special case of the perpetuity with growth method, i.e. growth is negative in perpetuity. It assumes that after the planning period the company will be unable to earn even its cost of capital and in terms of the perpetuity with growth formula discussed earlier, it is calculated as follows:

$$\text{Terminal Value} = \frac{FCF_{T+1}}{WACC - (-g)}$$

Assuming a negative growth in free cash flow into perpetuity of 3 per cent results in the following TV estimate for Santos plc:

$$= £30.47m \div (0.12 - (-0.03))$$

$$= £203.13m$$

Assuming a decay rate of 3 per cent the result is a substantial reduction in the TV from the simple perpetuity. However, by implication the circumstances under which such conditions would prevail would suggest an exit strategy as being appropriate, in which case an asset-based valuation would often be argued as being more appropriate.

Key issues in estimating terminal value using the perpetuity approach

TV is often the largest contributor to total value when using a perpetuity calculation and a relatively short planning period. The further into the future that the planning period extends, the lower is the relative contribution made by the continuing period. For example, over a five-year planning period results similar to Santos plc are not uncommon, on average, where TV represents 60-70 per cent of total value. Over a ten-year period this will often switch, with 30-40 per cent of total value coming from the TV. The underlying message is that it is desirable to project as far forward as possible with the planning period, but this is often counter to the planning period culture within many companies [81]. This tends to mean the adoption of relatively short planning periods and perpetuity TV calculations are not uncommon. However, there can be good justification for using the perpetuity approach even under such circumstances. The reason is best understood with reference to the following questions that can be used with executives involved in reviewing the strategic value of their business for the first time:

1. 'Do you believe your business has a life in excess of the planning period you adopt?' The response to this is typically yes.

2. Would it not be a good idea to use a period longer than your current planning period?' The answer is typically yes, but it would not be worth the effort because of the highly speculative nature of forecasting over long time periods.

3. 'Do you have faith in your planning period assumptions and numbers?' The result is typically a reserved yes, with greatest confidence being felt with earlier rather than later numbers.

Given such 'yes' responses there is a good case for using the perpetuity approach as a starting point, based on their numbers from the planning period. The advantage of this approach is that it relates long-term value to assumptions about business potential based on managerial judgement and insight. In fact, reflection on this approach by managers usually prompts the observation that the TV according to this approach is dependent on their assumptions about the time period in which they have greatest comfort and the other value drivers, not least of which is the cost of capital.

Important considerations in applying DCF approaches

1. All DCF methods are heavily dependent on expected future cash flow estimates and estimates for the cost of capital. Given this, the approach is easiest to accept for companies where cash flows are currently positive and can be estimated with some reliability for future periods and for which a proxy for risk, that can be used to obtain discount rates, is available. The problem is that they often represent the only practical alternative for companies with quite the opposite characteristics.

2. DCF TV calculations should really reflect a company's business cycle. With this in mind it is important to forecast far enough out to capture a complete business cycle and to use normalised figures as the input into the TV formula. Industry dependence on macroeconomic conditions typically differs in different stages of the business cycle and it is important to recognise that TV estimates are particularly sensitive to the phase of the cycle on which the estimates are based.

3. In considering use of the perpetuity with growth method, it needs to be recognised that few companies can expect to exceed the cost of capital for long periods of time. As a guideline, caution needs to be exercised in adopting a high growth rate and for purposes of realism, assessment of the feasibility of key assumptions (like the sales growth rate against the market potential), should be undertaken over a limited time horizon. One alternative to the perpetuity with growth that we have found used in practice involves estimating a growth rate corresponding with expected economic growth (e.g. GNP) plus inflation in a second time period of say five years beyond the assumed planning period, followed by a third time period using a simple perpetuity assumption.

As illustrated, in many cases the largest proportion of total value is generated from the continuing period. For this reason, many practitioners also look to other methods, but DCF methods have much to offer, because they can be interpreted and applied to support user judgement. In fact, they can be invaluable in terms of trying to understand the underlying issues involved in a valuation, although their acceptance in the market place for the specific case under consideration may be limited. For example, this is particularly the case for new issues where the use of Price Earnings (PE) multiples and the like have long been accepted practice.

Market Relative Valuation methods

Market relative valuation methods can be used in valuing the whole business and not just the TV. They are often used in Initial Public Offering (IPO) valuations, with the most popular method being the Price Earnings (PE) ratio. However, as illustrated in Figure 5.4, other methods like Price:EBITDA, Price:Sales, and Market:Book are used, and will be reviewed in this section. Such methods are reckoned to give the most consistent results for steady, organically growing companies. For companies in periods of change and restructuring, these techniques have several shortcomings.

Figure 5.4: Market Relative Valuation Methods

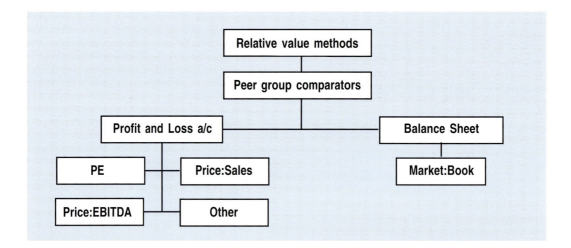

All these methods seek to determine the value of a business by making a comparison between the financial characteristics of similar peer group companies, for which there is also a stock market valuation, and the company to be valued. The basic premise is that the relationship between the market value and some measure of financial performance for a number of peer group companies represents an appropriate basis for inferring the market value of the company to be valued.

Peer group comparators

A poorly selected peer group will make any relative valuation tenuous and great care needs to be exercised to ensure that companies for inclusion are realistic from an investor's perspective. Even if a satisfactory peer group has been selected, care should be taken not to exaggerate the effects of supply and demand on the underlying share price of some of the peer groups constituents, particularly the less liquid ones. Further, one has to ask how to use the peer group data that are collected. For example, in terms of a PE relative valuation should the highest or the lowest average ratio, be used? For example, at the time of writing the UK food sector had around 22 companies with published PEs [*]. The

---

[*] *Financial Times*, 31 October 1997, p.47.

historic sector PE was 17.43, the highest PE was 64.6 and the lowest PE was 7.3. This may be yet further complicated by the need to take account of the level of premium generally expected for acquiring control of a company.

As regards TV estimates using relative valuation methods, there is one further major problem. The multiple(s) required are those for five years, ten years or even longer and not today. Predicting such multiples is a minefield! Reflection on the Asian crisis in 1998 paints a simple but vivid picture of this. Plunging share prices have been reflected in substantially deflated PE ratios. Predicting what these will look like in five years time is anyone's guess!

Profit and loss account relative valuation methods

As indicated in Figure 5.4, a number of profit and loss account relative valuation methods can be found in practice. A common feature of all of them is that information from the profit and loss account of the business to be valued is compared with a market determined multiple for a peer group set of companies. Before considering the individual methods, it is important to recognise that significant problems may arise in the interpretation of profit and loss accounts. There will always be legitimate exceptional or extraordinary costs, which should, as much as possible, be reversed out. However, other problems arise from so-called 'creative' accounting (the legitimate use of accounting practices to create the best possible picture of a company) and genuine differences in accounting conventions and practices *.

The most common earnings relative valuation method is the Price Earnings ratio, which is the subject of the next section. This method draws on 'bottom-line' information, (i.e. after the deduction of costs, charges and the like) and therefore may be more subject to the aforesaid influences than the two others methods discussed subsequently; Price: EBITDA and Price: Sales.

Price Earnings ratio (PE)

The Price Earnings ratio (PE) is calculated by dividing the market price of a share by the earnings per share (or the total market value by total earnings attributable to shareholders), i.e.

$$\text{PE ratio} = \frac{\text{Market price of share}}{\text{Earnings per share (EPS)}}$$

EPS in this ratio is calculated by dividing profit attributable to ordinary shareholders by the weighted average number of shares in issue. While it is considered to be an important indicator of corporate performance, it is influenced by both the principles applied in deriving profit and by the capital structure, i.e. the decision to fund a business using share capital or borrowed funds.

---

* These issues were reviewed in Chapter 1.

The latest published EPS figure is typically used to calculate the historic PE and the estimated current year's EPS is used to calculate a prospective PE. For example, consider a company with reported EPS of 10p last year, which is estimated to earn 12p per share this year. If the company's shares stand at £1.20, the historic PE is 12 (£1.20 ÷ 10p) and the prospective PE is 10 (£1.20 ÷ 12p).

As a method of valuation, the PE can be thought of as representing the number of years to recoup the sum invested, assuming the same EPS each year. Another way of looking at it is that it indicates how much investors are willing to pay for a company's current earnings. Potential high growth companies tend to have high PEs, while those with little or no growth have low ratios. In general, a high historic PE compared with the industry group average suggests either that the company is a leader in its sector or that the share is overvalued, while a low PE suggests a poor company or an undervalued share. It is worthwhile being cautious of companies with very high PE ratios. The company may be a 'glamour stock' due for a tumble or, if it is the PE of a very sound high quality company, the market itself may be in for a fall.

The way the PE ratio is applied for valuation purposes is by using the financial data of the company to be valued, in conjunction with that for a selected peer group consisting of listed companies ideally in the same business and same country, i.e.

$$\frac{\text{Price}_{\text{Peer Group}}}{\text{Earnings}} = \frac{\text{Price}_{\text{Target}}}{\text{Earnings}}$$

For example, if an analysis of the PEs of peer group companies revealed a ratio of 10 to 1, and the earnings of the target were £1 million, this would imply a value of £10 million. However, this typically ignores the fact that the prices used in estimating the PE ratios for the peer group relate to a relatively small proportion of the shares trading, not the price for gaining control. For this reason assumptions about control premiums are often built in, as are discounts on the price due to the reduced liquidity associated with private companies.

As indicated earlier with reference to the Asian currency crisis, the PE ratio of a company depends not only on its attraction to investors and the industry in which it operates, but also on the level of the stock market. For example, the crash of 1987 saw sector PE ratios collapse between 15 October and 2 November as follows:

Sector	15 Oct.1987	2 Nov.1987	Decrease
Building materials	16.6x	12.5x	24.7%
Food producers	18.0x	14.0x	22.2%
Textiles	16.4x	11.1x	32.3%
Retail banks	8.5x	6.3x	25.8%
Chemists	18.8x	12.4x	34.0%
Property	35.0x	24.6x	29.7%

This illustration has raised the question of whether it is right that a sharp fall over the whole market, which has not been attributed to changes in the underlying profitability or cash flows of constituent companies, should result in a sharp fall in the value of those companies.

A PE ratio may also be estimated using comparable transactions. The assumption in this case is that the marketplace provides an appropriate reference point for transactions that have occurred within the same industry as the potential company to be valued. Although numerous transactions are never recorded in the press, a variety of published sources are now available to give the buyer an indication of how the world may value companies that are similar to the potential acquisition. However, the challenge is to find reliable sources of comparable transaction details from press articles or on-line databases.

This technique should also come with a health warning. It is desirable, but not always possible, to select similarly structured transactions to that being valued, e.g. a hostile take-over bid, the acquisition of minority stakes etc. The limitations of such comparable transaction analysis relates to the possible lack of suitable comparisons. It is necessary to consider prevailing market conditions at the time of each transaction such as market premiums, sector earnings ratios relative to market and/or other recent comparable ratios.

Price: EBITDA (earnings before interest, tax, depreciation and amortisation)

As illustrated, earnings may be subject to a number of influences, such as creative accounting. One response is to move further up the profit and loss account in search of a 'purer' measure of profit. One such purer measure is reckoned to be Earnings Before Interest, Tax, Depreciation and Amortisation (EBITDA), which represents a proxy for gross operating cash flow before investment and financing requirements [82]. This measure of profit seeks to overcome the limitation of earnings as used in the PE ratio calculation because of historical cost depreciation calculations. In many countries, depreciation is calculated by rules of thumb which respond slowly, if at all, to changing circumstances.

By stripping out depreciation, EBITDA avoids many problems that stem from different accounting and depreciation practices. In addition, it strips out interest payments and hence is blind to the impact that a company's capital structure can have. So, using EBITDA is a double-edged sword, since by removing much that is misleading (depreciation practices), it also removes valuable information relating to capital structure and taxation [83].

In determining the multiple from peer group companies, enterprise (corporate) value is typically used in preference to equity value. This is because EBITDA represents the profit before interest and is, therefore, potentially available to both providers of debt and equity. As such, frequent practice is to relate EBITDA to enterprise value, this being a measure of the value of the business and comprises equity plus debt less marketable securities. In estimating the enterprise value to EBITDA ratios of peer group companies, the value (preferably market value) of debt, net of marketable securities, will typically be added to the market capitalisation and then divided by the EBITDA. For example, with a market value of debt of £320 million, a market capitalisation of equity of £680 million and an EBITDA of £100 million, the resulting enterprise value to EBITDA ratio would be:

$$\frac{(£320m + £680m)}{£100m} = 10:1$$

The way the enterprise value to EBITDA ratio is applied for valuation purposes is, in principle, the same as the PE. Financial data of the company to be valued are used in conjunction with that for a selected peer group consisting of listed companies which are ideally in the same business and same country, i.e.

$$\frac{\text{Enterprise Value}_{\text{Peer Group}}}{\text{EBITDA}} = \frac{\text{Enterprise Value}_{\text{Target}}}{\text{EBITDA}}$$

Price: Sales

This 'back of the envelope' type approach is sometimes used when no profit information is available, as is sometimes the case in countries where financial reporting requirements are minimal, or financial reporting standards are relatively poorly developed. It is also sometimes used when valuing loss-making companies, or those operating where accounting regimes differ widely. The link between sales revenue and share price is tenuous to say the least and, as such, this approach is best not used unless there is little other choice.

Balance sheet market relative valuation

Market :Book (MB)

The MB method relates market capitalisation to the book value of equity and it draws on information from the balance sheet rather than the profit and loss account. One approach for calculating an MB TV is to estimate the book value of assets that the business is expected to have at the future date in question and then to use a representative MB ratio to calculate an estimated market value of the company in so many years time. As with profit and loss account based market relative valuation methods, great care must be exercised with this approach because of the potential for creative accounting in finance statements and the need for consistency in definitions used. Debate often arises with this method in the treatment of intangible assets, like goodwill and brands.

The way the Market : Book ratio is applied for valuation purposes is also the same in principle as the PE. Financial data of the company to be valued are used in conjunction with those for a selected peer group consisting of listed companies, ideally in the same business and same country, i.e.

$$\frac{\text{Market}_{\text{Peer Group}}}{\text{Book}} = \frac{\text{Market}_{\text{Target}}}{\text{Book}}$$

Asset value analysis (AVA)

In addition to DCF and Market Relative Valuation Methods, analysts commonly look at the realisable value of the underlying assets as well. Asset valuation analysis (AVA) methods measure the economic value of assets as if they were sold. Such methods are a reasonable approach for companies that deal predominantly in assets that are relatively easily valued, like property companies. However, they represent a real problem for companies dealing with intangible assets, such as drugs companies involved with patents, trademarks and brands.

If the collective use of assets within the business conveys a benefit greater than the sum of the individual assets, then realisable values will be irrelevant because they will always be lower than the economic value. However, calculating realisable values is useful for many reasons. It is useful at least to check that any realisable value is not greater than the economic value. A second reason is the inherent uncertainty of economic values. The advantage of considering realisable values is that it gives some indication of the extent of the loss if expectations about the earnings of the firm are disappointed. However, the relative importance of realisable values depends on the control the shareholder has over the firm. Shareholders will only be in a position to enforce the sale of the firm's assets or their redeployment if they are planning to own a controlling interest in the firm.

Realisable values are not easy to calculate in practice because the information typically available in the published financial statements is expressed in terms of historic cost and sometimes adjusted upwards following a revaluation. Furthermore, such a valuation only reveals the values of individual assets and not what value might result from them being grouped together.

Asset value analysis is often considered to be most suitable for:

- Asset-rich companies, especially after prolonged asset appreciation;
- Situations where cash flows are unpredictable or negative;
- Situations where asset revaluation has not been conducted for many years;
- Turnaround situations;
- Break-up situations (unbundling).

Options, CFROI and miscellaneous TV issues

It is important to note that there are circumstances in which a completely different TV perspective may be adopted. Firstly, in some businesses, like bio-technology or high technology, nearly all value arising using strategic value approaches may arise from the terminal value. As a consequence, there is an increasing tendency to look at such businesses from the real options perspective reviewed in Chapter 3. Second, as illustrated in the last chapter, with the CFROI approach residual value is calculated differently from any of the preceding methods that have been reviewed. It separates the future cash flow stream of a business into a portion generated from existing assets and a portion generated from future investments. The CFROI approach to the latter portion uses the idea of competitive life cycles to forecast future CFROIs. Assumptions about sustainable growth rates in new investments and what is known as the 'hold' and fade' assumption enable an estimate of the future cash flow from new investments to be generated and avoids the need to estimate terminal values using perpetuity assumptions. Hold and fade assumes that current returns and growth cannot be sustained in perpetuity and any unusually high growth rates or performance will be challenged by competition. Any unusually low growth rates or performance will force a revitalisation of the assets and the replacement of management.

The 'hold' assumption within hold and fade is concerned with the number of years that a company can maintain a rate of return in excess of the WACC. This has been developed as a consequence of observations of the US equity market and the view that on average companies are not able to 'beat' the market for more than seven or eight years at the most [106]. After this seven or eight-year period, performance will gradually decay until eventually the return on investment will equal the WACC. This decay rate is known as the 'fade' period, and can be quite long – over 20 years in many cases.

Summary checklist

❍ The DCF approach forces explicit consideration of the factors driving the value of a business beyond the planning period.

❍ In choosing which particular DCF formula to use it is important to consider what is driving value creation or destruction and for how long this situation is expected to last.

❍ Any DCF TV is highly dependent on the year selected to represent the cash flow to be valued. Often this is the last year of the planning period, but this may not be the most appropriate figure to use. For example, in cyclical businesses care would need to be exercised in understanding where the company is in the business cycle and the trend in the cycle.

❍ The cost of capital used can have a very significant impact on a DCF TV. (This is such an important topic that issues associated with its determination form the substance of the next chapter.)

❍ The DCF approach can usefully be supplemented by using a number of others to cross-check results.

❍ There are many market relative valuation approaches that can be used to estimate TV, all of which are reliant on being able to identify comparable peer group companies.

❍ It is wise to use as many 'reality' checks as possible to ensure that the characteristics of the situation being valued are consistent with the underlying basis of the TV calculation.

Concluding remarks

The main methods adopted for calculating terminal values have been reviewed and a preference for the DCF-based approaches has been identified. They have one real benefit over market relative valuation approaches because if used properly they force the exercise of managerial judgement and do not place reliance on an externally driven multiple. Nevertheless, it needs to be recognised that relative valuation methods are widely used. In fact it is rare for one single TV method to be adopted and the use of multiple methods is common practice.

Chapter 6: The Cost of Capital

What is British industry's cost of capital? Many academics say around 12 per cent. Most stockbrokers think it is in single digits

Lex Column, *Financial Times*, 23 June 1998 [84].

'This is not a precise science. If academics are honest, the best they can claim is that they are 3 percentage points either way

Financial Times, 7 October 1996 [85].

Chapter preview

- The importance of the Weighted Average Cost of Capital (WACC) as the benchmark that is used to assess whether value is created or not for the providers of capital to a business.
- How to calculate the WACC using a three-step process which involves calculating both the cost of equity and the cost of debt, and estimating the target capital structure.
- How to calculate the cost of equity using the Capital Asset Pricing Model (CAPM), or Arbitrage Pricing Theory (APT), or the Dividend Valuation Model (DVM).
- How to calculate the cost of debt including situations where there are multiple sources of debt.
- How capital structure affects the cost of capital and the question of whether there is an optimal capital structure.
- Issues involved in estimating the cost of capital from a business unit perspective.
- Market related methods for estimating the cost of capital.

Introduction

How can a business evaluate whether a potential investment is really worthwhile? In every day life it is common practice to answer this question with reference to the rate of return that will be earned on funds invested. If money needs to be borrowed to undertake such a potential investment then there will be a cost associated with it, typically expressed as the percentage return required by the lender. Common sense would dictate that the return required from an investment should at the very least cover the cost of funds needing to be raised to finance it. What applies in everyday life also applies in corporate life. Organisations have to ensure that the opportunities in which it invests are those that will at minimum satisfy the returns required by the providers of funds. In other words, the cost of capital should equate with the opportunity cost of the funds tied up; i.e. the return which would be achieved from their next best use.

The cost of capital is important to understand for many reasons. As indicated previously only if a return is generated in excess of the cost of capital will shareholder value be created. It is also important to view it in terms of its impact on business value. This can readily be understood by recalling the valuation approaches reviewed in Chapter 4 and the perpetuity terminal value calculation reviewed in the last chapter. In terms of the strategic value model developed for Santos plc, a 1 per cent increase in the cost of capital reduces the strategic value per share from £1.18 to £1.01.

The importance of understanding the role of the cost of capital in value creation may be simple, but in practice its estimation is far more problematic, as will be seen in this chapter. One source of complication is that the providers of funds to a company are not typically a homogeneous group with identical requirements and expectations from their investment. At one extreme they may comprise long-term debt-holders seeking a secure and fixed rate of interest, while at the other they may be ordinary shareholders who accept that the return received is most likely to be contingent on the company's performance. Somehow the requirements of all providers have to be captured and there are different ways of achieving this that have been encountered in earlier chapters. One commonly accepted way is via the Weighted Average Cost of Capital (WACC) in which the requirements of all providers of funds are expressed in one percentage rate of return. Alternatively, costs associated with borrowed funds may be taken out of the cash flows resulting in equity cash flows, which are then discounted at the return required by the providers of equity (see Santos plc example in Chapter 4). Whichever method is used, determining the cost of capital is a real challenge. This is for many reasons, not least because there are different views about the methods to be adopted for calculating the cost of equity.

Apart from the issues associated with estimating the cost of capital for the company as a whole, there is one other important consideration. This relates to the need by many businesses to have capital allocation procedures delegated to parts of the overall business. In large organisations it is unsatisfactory and undesirable for all capital allocation decisions to be made at the centre. It often makes sense to delegate the authority for making such decisions. However, such procedures may also need to recognise that different parts of the overall business will need to generate different returns, dependent on the degree of risk involved.

Understanding the cost of capital is one of the major challenges for management. Those who understand it should be able to ensure that their organisations benefit. However, as will be seen from what follows, its estimation requires a good deal of tough analysis and the exercise of sound judgement. It is also important to recognise that it is all too easy to become side-tracked by some of the issues relating to the determination of the cost of individual components that make up a corporation's capital structure. Nowhere is this more the case than for the cost of equity for which a number of approaches have been developed to try and capture the rate of return required by shareholders. These approaches in themselves are challenging, but there is one important issue to acknowledge, any approach is only as good as the data on which it is based.

Weighted Average Cost of Capital (WACC)

As indicated in the introductory quote to the chapter, opinions differ about the size of the cost of capital. To understand the source of such differences we will review the cost of capital, which is often referred to as the weighted average cost of capital, or WACC for short, with reference to three steps involving estimation of the:

1. Cost of equity.
2. Cost of debt.
3. Capital structure.

These three steps and the building blocks associated with them are illustrated in Figure 6.1.

Figure 6.1: Three steps for estimating WACC

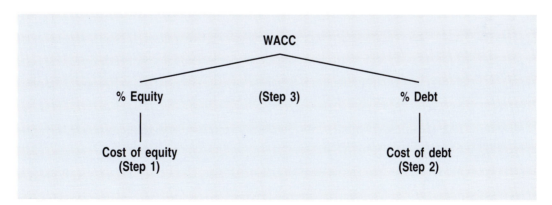

Of the three steps, the most difficult and controversial issue concerns the estimation of the cost of equity.

1. Cost of equity

Among the approaches available for calculating the cost of equity are the Capital Asset Pricing Model, Arbitrage Pricing Theory and the Dividend Valuation Model.

1.1 Capital Asset Pricing Model (CAPM)

Modern financial theory suggests that the cost of equity can be estimated from analysing what return investors require when buying a share. Their requirement can be estimated using the Capital Asset Pricing Model, known as CAPM. The underlying premise of the approach is the more risk an investor is required to take on, the higher the rate of return that will be expected. It is in a class of market models called risk-premium models which rely on the assumption that every individual holding a risky security will demand a return in excess of the return they would receive from a risk-free security. This excess return is the premium to compensate the investor for risk that cannot be diversified away.

The CAPM cost of equity can be estimated using the following formula:

$$\text{Cost of equity} = \text{Risk-free rate} + (\text{Beta} \times \text{Equity risk premium})$$

For example, Santos plc was shown in Chapter 2 as having a WACC of 12 per cent. As will be demonstrated, this was calculated using the CAPM to determine a cost of equity of 14.03 per cent, assuming a risk-free rate of 6.94 per cent, a beta of 1.222, and an equity risk premium of 5.8 per cent. In terms of the CAPM cost of equity formula, this can be shown as:

$$\text{Cost of equity} = 6.94\% + (1.222 \times 5.8\%)$$
$$= 14.03\%$$

Within the CAPM the variable specific to the type of business is the beta. Both the risk-free rate and the equity risk premium are assumed to apply to all companies within the market. Each of these three will now be examined in turn.

Beta

Beta is a relative measure of volatility that is determined by comparing the return on a share (stock) to the return on the stock market. In simple terms, the greater the volatility, the more risky the share, which will be reflected in a higher beta.

The type of risk that beta in the CAPM measures is called systematic, market, or non-diversifiable risk. This risk is caused by macroeconomic factors like inflation, or political events, which affect the returns of all companies. If a company is affected by these macroeconomic factors in the same way as the market is, then the company will have a beta of 1, and will be expected to have returns equal to the market. Similarly, if a company's systematic risk is greater than the market, then the company will be priced such that it is expected to have returns greater than the market. For example, if a share has a beta of 2.0, then on average for every 10 per cent that the market index has returned above the risk-free rate, historically the share will have returned 20 per cent[*]. Conversely, for every 10 per cent the market index has returned below the risk-free rate, historically the share will have returned 20 per cent below.

---

[*] Beta is often measured by using standard regression techniques to analyse monthly returns historically over a five year time horizon.

Care needs to be exercised in interpreting betas. Other statistics, like the standard deviation associated with the beta, may be all too readily overlooked. For example, a standard deviation of 0.33 on a beta of 1.0 indicates that with 99 per cent confidence (assuming a normal distribution), the beta lies somewhere between 0.01 and 1.99. For this reason, reference may often be made in practice to the betas of comparable peer group companies.

Care also needs to be taken in interpreting betas for companies with unusual capital structures. For example, two companies identical except for their capital structure may be perceived very differently by the market. If one is all debt financed and the other is all equity financed, it is reasonable to expect greater volatility in the returns and the share price of the all debt financed company. This is because in prosperous times the debt will be an advantage, but the converse will apply in periods of economic downturn. In other words, there is a financial risk that will be captured in historical measurement of the beta that will be reflected in a higher number, despite the fact that the companies are identical in all other respects. In effect, the historical measurement is picking up noise relating to the capital structure which needs to be removed. This is achieved by a process known as ungearing and regearing the beta (or unleveraging/releveraging the beta in US terms) [86]. The calculation necessary to ungear the beta is:

$$\text{Ungeared Beta}^* = \text{Published Beta} \div (1 + (1 - T_c)(D/E))$$

Where,

T_c = corporate tax rate;
D/E = debt/equity ratio.

This ungeared beta then needs to be regeared at the target debt/equity ratio using the following formula:

$$\text{Regeared Beta}^\dagger = \text{Ungeared Beta} \times (1 + (1 - T_c)(D/E_{Target}))$$

Where,

T_c = corporate tax rate;
D/E_{Target} = target debt/equity ratio.

The basis of the first part of this calculation, i.e. ungearing the beta, can be seen with reference to Santos plc in Figure 6.2.

---

* Sometimes called the asset beta.
† Sometimes called the equity beta.

Figure 6.2: Ungearing the beta of Santos plc

Beta	1.222
Marginal corporate tax rate	30%
Equity value	£98.20
Debt value	£70.92

The published beta of Santos plc is 1.222. To ungear this we use the formula:

$$\text{Ungeared Beta} = \text{Published Beta} \div (1 + (1 - T_c)(D/E))$$

$$= 1.222 \div (1 + (1 - 0.3)(70.92 \div 98.2))$$

$$= 0.81$$

This calculation has been undertaken using 1997 book values, but it should be recognised that market values for both debt and equity could be used *. From Appendix 1, Santos plc can be seen to have a current share price of £1 and note 4 indicates there to be 106 million shares. If we assume that the book and market values of debt are equal, the ungeared beta for Santos using market value is:

$$\text{Ungeared Beta} = 1.222 \div (1 + (1 - 0.3)(70.92 \div 106))$$

$$= 0.83$$

The result is not very different from that obtained using book values because both are fairly close to one another. It is also important to note that those who use this type of calculation may define debt as being net debt (after the deduction of cash and bank balances).

Once ungeared, the beta needs to be regeared at a 'target' debt equity ratio. So, for example, if we were to assume that Santos plc would prefer a target debt to equity ratio of 50:50 the implied beta would be:

$$\text{Regeared Beta} = 0.83 \times (1 + (1 - 0.3)(50 \div 50))$$

$$= 1.41$$

---

* Opinion is divided about the use of book or market values.

With a target debt to equity ratio higher than the current one, the calculations indicate a higher beta to reflect the increase in financial risk. Caution needs to be exercised in using and interpreting this approach. Definitions used in calculations may vary and it is a good idea to check that the calculation is really warranted, i.e. that the beta calculation has really been influenced by the capital structure.

How this type of calculation might be used in practice is illustrated in Chapter 9 with reference to the flotation of Orange plc , where published betas from 'comparable' companies were used to estimate the cost of equity for the company. Each of the comparable companies had different debt/equity ratios than that targeted for Orange plc, hence the need for the adjustment.

An alternative to using a published beta the is use of a predictive, or fundamental beta. This type of beta uses company-specific data (profit and loss account and balance sheet) to arrive at a multiple-factor beta, which is based on risk indices like company success, size and growth. The company specific data are regressed against systematic portfolios of risk indices, which results in a single factor weighted beta*.

Risk-free rate

The risk-free rate represents the most secure return that can be achieved. From a UK perspective, anyone wishing to sleep soundly at night might invest all available funds in government bonds which are largely insensitive to what happens in the share market and, therefore, have a beta of nearly zero. The risk-free rate within CAPM is hypothetically the return on a security or portfolio of securities that has no default risk whatsoever, and is completely uncorrelated with returns on anything else in the economy. Theoretically the best estimate of the risk-free rate would be the return on a zero beta portfolio. This means a perfect proxy for the risk-free rate would be a security with a beta equal to zero and no volatility. To find a perfect security is empirically impossible so a proxy is used that meets these requirements as closely as possible.

One of the issues that must be dealt with alongside the search for possible proxies is the maturity of the proxy. In developed economies, government securities tend to be the best candidates for the risk-free rate, since the government in many countries guarantees payment. However, government securities may have different maturity dates and different yields. For example, in the USA very long-term bonds with 30 year maturity dates exist, as well as short-term and medium-term bonds of ten years. Preference for a medium-term rate is not uncommon because it often comes close to matching the duration of the cash flow of a company being valued. A current Treasury-bill rate, because of its short-term nature, does not match duration sufficiently well. In order to use such a rate it would be necessary to apply rates expected to relate to each future period, not just today. In effect, the ten-year rate is a geometric weighted average estimate of the expected short-term Treasury-bill rates over the time period to be evaluated.

---

* It is important to note two types of risk are accounted for within CAPM thinking. In addition to the market-related risk captured in the beta, there is the risk which can be identified with a specific business. This is known as unsystematic, specific, or diversifiable risk and can be eliminated through individual investor action to carry diversified portfolios. Investors who choose not to be fully diversified will not be compensated for the total risk of their holdings, because the only risk which is priced and compensated for in the market is the systematic part. This distinction between types of risk is important and is considered more fully in the next chapter.

Equity risk premium

The equity risk premium * is the excess return above a risk-free rate that investors demand for holding risky securities. The risk premium in the CAPM is the premium above the risk-free rate on a portfolio assumed to have a beta equal to 1.0. If an individual security is more or less risky, then it will have a higher or lower risk premium. The risk premium can be estimated in a variety of ways, which will be discussed under the headings of *ex post* (historical) analysis and *ex ante* (forward-looking) analysis.

(a) Ex post analysis

Ex post, or historical analysis is a popular way to estimate the risk premium, the rationale being that history is a good predictor of the future. When history is used the first question to be answered is, 'How should the return be calculated?' Returns over time can be calculated by a simple arithmetic or compound (geometric) average, each of which can be interpreted differently. A geometric average implies that investors use a buy and hold strategy with dividends reinvested. This is an appropriate performance measure if investors hold for more than one period. The arithmetic average measures the average one-period performance and is appropriate if investors buy and sell every period. The choice depends on the perceived holding period of the investor. For example, if the holding period is assumed to be ten years, then the appropriate measure would be the average of a series of ten-year geometric returns.

Until recently it seemed to be accepted practice in the UK to use an estimate of 8-9 per cent for the equity risk premium. However in recent regulatory rulings in the UK much lower figures have been used for a number of reasons. First, the historical average of 8-9 per cent applies to a period that was by all accounts, on average, different to the current situation. While required rates of return on bonds – real interest rates – have gone up since the early 1980s, required rates of return on shares seem to have gone down slightly [87]. The basis for the contention that the expected real return on equities has fallen is that the dividend yield on equities has fallen. This, combined with a roughly constant long-run expected growth rate of dividends, implies that the required return on equities has fallen roughly in line with the fall in dividend yield. A fall in the expected real return on equities combined with a rise in the real interest rate arguably results in a significant fall in the risk premium.

A slightly more sophisticated version of this argument argues that the level of the risk premium is a function of other variables such as dividend yields, inflation and interest [88]. Estimates of a relationship between equity premiums and dividend yields, long-term bond rates and inflation have been used to estimate a current level of the risk premium for the USA, which is reported as being currently around 2 to 3 per cent. For the UK the application of a similar procedure gave a current estimate of between 4 and 5 per cent [89].

Another line of argument against the unadjusted use of historical average returns to forecast the future risk premium has recently emerged [90]. The argument is that the statistics used to estimate the risk premiums are based on markets that have survived for a long time. The US and UK markets are the only equity markets with a continuous history of returns over the last 70 years. As these are the two markets most usually analysed, it means that the most common risk premium statistics are based on markets that have shown a long period of

---

* Sometimes known as market risk premium.

survival. The basis of the argument that this leads to a bias is as follows. Suppose that it was not known at the beginning of the period that these markets would be the ones to survive. The returns often used to estimate the risk premium do not include this possibility of non-survival. At the beginning of the period, however, non-survival would have been one of the possibilities to include in the expected return. This means that the average return would be biased upwards as an estimate of the true expected return, or the true risk premium.

Although the academic debate about the risk premium has been very active, it has almost certainly not been the most influential reason for interest in this area in the UK. The behaviour of the Monopolies and Mergers Commission (MMC) and certain regulators based on simpler analysis of the issue has greatly affected perceptions of what is an allowable risk premium for the purpose of UK regulation.

The arguments used by the MMC and some regulators for a low premium are quite simple. One is that the current dividend yield on the equity market (3.8 per cent) plus a sensible estimate of the long-run real growth rate of dividends (2-3 per cent) gives the long-run expected real return on the equity market. If the long-run index-linked gilt rate (3.5 per cent) is subtracted, the result is an estimate of the long-run equity market risk-premium of about 3 per cent. An alternative is to use a current forecast of dividend growth based on investor expectations. This was used by the MMC, in the case of British Gas, to support their conclusion based on the long-run economic growth rate and gave a similar figure.

Since the British Gas ruling in 1993 the MMC has used risk premiums of between 3 per cent and 4.5 per cent. The MMC view appears to be based on evidence from the time varying risk premium literature and surveys of institutional investors in the UK. The consistent use by the MMC of such a low figure in three rulings (British Gas, Scottish Hydro and Southwest Water) has clearly influenced various regulators to also adopt a low figure.

Justification for the use of a low value for the risk premium can also be made for purely technical reasons based on the statistical procedure for averaging past returns. This perspective claims that the geometric average is more appropriate than the arithmetic average and, as the geometric average is always lower, this reduces the estimate of the equity risk premium. For instance, the arithmetic mean return on the UK stock market in the period 1919-1993 was almost 3 per cent greater than the geometric mean return [91]. However, to counter this there is the argument that the use of the geometric average of past returns as the basis of the risk premium for capital budgeting decisions (including acquisitions and divestments) is technically incorrect if no further adjustments are made. Stated simply, the rate used in capital budgeting to discount the expected cash flow is arithmetic. Thus, an arithmetic estimate of the discount rate involved is consistent with the procedure, whereas a geometric estimate is not.

As indicated in the introductory quote, academics seem to disagree with the low equity risk premium argument. For example, Dimson and Marsh estimated the excess returns on UK equities for the period 1955 to 1994 along with comparable estimates for the US and Japan [92], as being:

Country	Risk Premium (%)
UK	8.7
USA	8.4
Japan	8.3

The results obtained by Dimson and Marsh are very similar to the value of 8-9 per cent traditionally used, and they are very similar across the three countries examined.

(b) Ex ante analysis

The most common *'ex ante'* approach uses the dividend valuation model. Such a model relies on knowing the current dividend yield for shares and an estimate of the growth rate for dividends in the future. The expected growth rate to be used as an input to the dividend valuation model may be estimated in several ways. The most direct way is to conduct a survey of investors about their expectations, and this was the approach adopted by the MMC for the British Gas enquiry. There are also some regularly produced forecasts of earnings growth, which are available for both individual companies and for market indices.

An alternative way of using something like the dividend valuation model is to make less extreme assumptions than those conventionally used. For example, the assumption of a constant growth rate for dividends is unsatisfactory and one alternative draws on the discounted cash flow (DCF) approach. This starts from the current share price of the company under consideration and makes specific dividend forecasts for that company. The required rate of return is the discount rate that makes the present value of these dividends equal to the current share price [93].

The conclusion that can be drawn about the equity risk premium is that there are differing views about its calculation, each of which can be justified. Very often the basis used for its calculation in practice appears to depend to a large extent on the perspective taken. For example, in some instances where there has been a debate between the economic regulators of UK utilities and the regulated companies, as indicated earlier, the regulators have appeared to favour a low premium, while the companies' concern with shareholder interests has encouraged them to favour higher rates [*].

The appropriateness of CAPM for estimating the cost of equity

Like all models, CAPM abstracts from reality by making a series of simplifying assumptions. Many of the assumptions behind CAPM may not hold in the real world, but that does not necessarily mean that the model is not valuable. Even simple models can yield useful results with practical applications. For example, Thomas Edison understood very little of what we now know about electricity, yet he was able to harness it and produce the light bulb.

A simple test of the risk-return relationship measured by CAPM betas was performed by Sharpe and Cooper [94]. They separated all NYSE common stocks into deciles based on their betas and measured the returns that would have been achieved by holding each decile for each year during the period 1931 to 1967. The deciles were recalculated yearly to account for firms moving from one decile to another. Over the period of the study, stocks with higher betas generally produced higher future returns, as predicted by CAPM.

However, other studies have indicated that the CAPM does not adequately describe the risk-return relationship. Various researchers have identified groups of stock with some common characteristics that consistently achieve higher or lower returns than would be

---

[*] It is worth noting that the debate over the equity risk premium (and other issues) have prompted a search for alternative approaches. The substance of these is reviewed later in this chapter.

implied by CAPM. These anomalies would indicate that stocks with these characteristics have a greater or lesser exposure to systematic risk than that measured by CAPM. These characteristics are known as 'market anomalies' and the best known is the 'size' effect. Research has shown that an investor would have realised returns in excess of those predicted by CAPM (positive abnormal returns) by investing in low capitalisation (small company) stocks over the period 1936 to 1977 [95]. Both the magnitude and the statistical significance of the abnormal returns were large.

Another anomaly is known as the 'year end' or 'January' effect, which refers to the tendency for all stocks to earn excess returns in the month of January. Evidence provided has shown that this effect may also be linked to the small-firm effect and, so far, no 'satisfactory' explanation of this anomaly has been advanced [96].

In fact there has been severe criticism of the CAPM approach, with considerable doubt being expressed about the linear relationship between beta and expected returns [97]. Research has shown only a weak relationship between average return and beta over the period 1941 and 1990, and virtually no relation over the shorter period 1963 to 1990. Firm size and market-to-book ratios were found to be far more important in explaining differences, although such findings are still the subject of considerable academic debate [*, 98].

1.2 Arbitrage Pricing Theory (APT)

An alternative risk premium approach to CAPM known as Arbitrage Pricing Theory (APT for short) has been developed. The principle which underpins APT is that two assets that have identical risk characteristics must offer the same return, or an arbitrage opportunity will exist. APT attempts to measure the various dimensions of market related risk in terms of several underlying economic factors, such as inflation, monthly production and interest rates, which systematically affect the price of all shares. In a nutshell, regression techniques are used to estimate the contribution made by each APT factor to overall risk. However, this approach is more complex than CAPM and not without many difficulties in terms of its application. This is recognised in the USA where, for example, the monthly production figures published by the government are only estimates of true US industrial production. This means that they are 'noisy' (contain random errors) and inaccurate (contain biases introduced by the data-gathering procedure and the government smoothing or adjustment process). Error thus arises because high quality data in the form of share prices are regressed against lower quality data.

Arbitrage Pricing Theory (APT) requires less stringent assumptions than CAPM and it is reliant on the 'law of one price' which is used to replace the assumption that investors evaluate investments on the basis of the mean and variance of returns. The 'law of one price' simply states that in an efficient market identical products of any kind will sell for the same price. If two identical products existed at different prices, an arbitrageur could buy the cheaper product, sell it to those who wanted the more expensive product, and earn a risk-free return in the transaction. Further, this process would continue until the increased demand for the less expensive product and the decreased demand for the more expensive product caused the two prices to become the same. It is from this arbitrage condition that the APT gets its name.

---

* A more detailed review of developments associated with the cost of capital can be found in Appendix 2.

The accuracy of any implementation of the APT cannot be evaluated until factors have been chosen. Research that has been undertaken has found the following factors to be of importance [99]:

- monthly industrial production;
- interest rates;
- investor confidence (measured by the spread between low grade and high grade bonds);
- long-term inflation;
- short-term inflation.

Operational APT models have been developed in the USA using US data. As such, this means that its application outside the USA requires conversion to reflect the conditions in the market under consideration. The means by which this can be achieved are reviewed in Chapter 7.

Dividend valuation model

The Dividend Valuation Model considers that the return shareholders require (hence the cost of equity to a business), can be determined with reference to the future dividend stream they require. At its simplest, this approach takes the view that the cost of equity to a company is only the dividend it has to pay which is derived by assuming that a company's dividend per share grows at a constant rate and that the company's risk will remain unchanged. If we call K_e the cost of equity, the model is:

$$K_e \% = \frac{d(1+g) + g}{P} \times 100$$

Where,

K_e = Cost of equity;
d = Current dividend;
P = Market price;
g = Expected dividend or price growth rate provided that investors expect dividends to grow at a constant rate in perpetuity.

Thus, if a company had a current dividend per share of 4p, a market price of £1.00 and an expected growth rate of 10 per cent, its cost of equity would be:

$$K_e \% = \frac{4p(1 + 0.10) + 0.10}{100p} \times 100$$

$$= 14.4\%$$

This measure of the cost of equity is fairly popular, particularly for valuing preference shares where g reduces to zero. In this case, the calculation of a cost of equity is quite straightforward if the shares are irredeemable, that is, if the dividend is paid in perpetuity. For example, a 10 per cent irredeemable preference share with a nominal value of £1 and a market value of £2 would have a cost (K_{pref} %) using this approach of:

$$K_{pref}\% = \frac{\text{Annual dividend}}{\text{Market price}} \times 100$$

$$= \frac{10p}{200p} \times 100$$

$$= 5\%$$

If the preference share is redeemable, such that the dividend is not paid into perpetuity, then an internal rate of return calculation is required. This is necessary to find the percentage that equates all future cash flows from dividend payments and the redemption payment with the current market value of the share. This is known as the yield to redemption, yield to maturity or yield, for short. (The calculation of a yield for an irredeemable financial instrument is demonstrated shortly with reference to the cost of debt.)

However, for calculating the cost of equity relating to ordinary share capital the dividend valuation approach has to be used with care. First, the growth rate g is a long-run growth rate over an infinite horizon and as such is a difficult parameter to conceptualise. It relies on accurate estimates of growth rates that can be reliably projected into the future - a daunting task given that few businesses have a history of constant growth. Second, the long-run growth rate must, by definition, be strictly less than the cost of equity, K_e. Third, the parameters of the model are interdependent. It would seem that a higher growth rate implies a higher cost of equity. However, this is not true because the higher rate of growth will imply a higher current share value. The net effect will reduce the cost of equity but, if one estimates a higher growth rate, how much greater should P become? The answer is unclear. Finally, the model provides no obvious answer to the question - what cost of equity should be applied when the company is considering projects of different risk than its current operations? For this, approaches like CAPM are required.

It is not uncommon to find earnings being used in one form or another in cost of equity calculations. Common approaches are to calculate Earnings Yield (earnings as a percentage of the market value of equity) and Return on Equity (earnings as a percentage of the book value of equity).

2. Cost of debt

The second step in calculating the cost of capital is to calculate the cost of debt, which is the rate of return that debt-holders require to hold debt. To determine this rate the yield to maturity (YTM) has to be calculated, often by drawing on the principles of discounted cash flow analysis and particularly the internal rate of return. For example, consider a non-redeemable debenture with a nominal value of £100 that pays 10 per cent, or £10 per annum in perpetuity. What this represents as a return to the investor will depend on the value of the debenture in the stock market. If the value has fallen from £100 to £92, then the return or yield will be 10.87 per cent ([£10 ÷ £92] x 100). However, this may not tell the full story. First, the debenture may have a redemption date such that it may return £10 for a fixed number of years, at the end of which a sum of money will be paid by the company to redeem it. For example, if the debenture is to be redeemed after ten years at its face (par) value of £100, then the yield is the percentage that equates an annual interest payment of £10 up to the point of redemption together with £100 redemption payment in year ten, having its present value of £92. This percentage, represented by i in the following formula, is 11.38:

$$\frac{£10}{(1+i)} + \frac{£10}{(1+i)^2} + \frac{£10}{(1+i)^3} + \ldots + \frac{£110}{(1+i)^{10}} = £92$$

Second, the impact of taxation has to be taken into consideration as follows:

Cost of debt after tax = Cost of debt before tax x (100 − Marginal tax rate)

The marginal tax rate is the tax rate applied to the company's last earned pound of income, i.e. the rate that applies to the highest 'tax bracket' into which the company's income falls. Marginal tax rates can differ from the statutory tax rates due to different income thresholds and net operating loss carry-forwards, which act to reduce the tax rates.

The marginal tax rate should not be confused with the average tax rate, which is the company's total tax liability divided by its total taxable income. Because the tax rate changes with the amount of taxable income under current laws, the marginal tax rate is often different from the average tax rate. In any event, before the marginal tax rate for an unquoted business can be estimated, it is necessary to first estimate its taxable income. Once this is known the current tax schedule can be used to determine the appropriate tax rate.

The cost of debt generally increases with financial leverage. Therefore, a change in target capital structure will change the cost of debt. The cost of debt must also follow the matching principle. The cost of debt must match the risk of the cash flows being discounted. While the basic calculation for estimating the cost of debt has been illustrated, in practice the way to calculate the cost of debt depends on information available:

○ If the firm's capital structure is not expected to change and yields and market values of the relevant debt instruments are known, then the average yield to maturity of those instruments is used as the cost of debt.
○ This can be done in two steps:
   1. Find or calculate the current yield to maturity for each instrument.
   2. Use market values of each instrument to weight each instrument's yield and produce an average.

For public debt instruments, the yield to maturity can be found from market data because bond prices are quoted in financial journals. As indicated previously, the yield to maturity can be calculated as the interest rate that equates the present value of a bond's cash flows to its current market value. Whenever a bond's market value is less than its face value (i.e. the yield to maturity is greater than the coupon rate), the bond is said to be issued at a discount. Whenever a bond's market value is greater than its face value (i.e. its yield to maturity is less than the coupon rate), the bond is said to be issued at a premium.

When the cost of debt of non-publicly traded companies or divisions of publicly traded companies is required, peer analysis can be used in which the focus of attention is on peer instruments as distinct from peer companies. The objective is to try and find peer instruments for publicly quoted businesses where the characteristics are similar. In terms of the yield calculation we discussed previously, what is not known for a non-publicly traded company or the divisions of publicly traded companies is the market value of debt. In this situation, there are several other ways to estimate the cost of debt, such as:

- Find similar debt instruments that have known yields.
- Find similar firms and use their bond rating to estimate the cost of debt. Good peers should have similar operations and debt structures (short-term versus long term, duration etc.).
- Calculate a synthetic bond rating for the firm, identify yields on bonds of similar rating and duration and use that yield as the cost of debt.
- If similar instruments are not available, as a last resort divide interest expense by the book value of debt to estimate the cost of debt.

A problem often arises in determining the cost of debt in markets where the public trading of debt is not common practice. This is so in most emerging markets and also in some well developed markets in Western Europe. In such circumstances one method of estimating the cost of debt is to:

- Estimate the local risk free rate.
- Identify the spread for a company with a similar debt rating where debt is publicly traded, this spread being the difference between its cost of debt and the risk-free rate.
- Add the spread to the local risk-free rate.

Of course, as with any method of estimation this is not perfect and there are other issues that may need to be considered, e.g. should a premium be added for illiquidity. Nevertheless, in some circumstances it may be the only available option.

One key point to recognise is that for purposes of estimation, reality checks should be used. For example, one invaluable cross-check is reference to the views of the commercial banker.

Dealing with more than one source of debt

Typically businesses have more than one source of debt financing. In this case the overall cost of debt can be calculated by taking the weighted average of the individual instruments based on market values. This involves multiplying the yield to maturity of each instrument by the percentage of the total market value of the portfolio that each instrument represents, and summing the products. This is illustrated in Figure 6.3, where the approach was used to find the cost of debt for a large US buy out:

Figure 6.3: Calculation of weighted cost of debt

Type of debt	$millions	Weight A	Yield % B	% A x B
Short-term debt	13,600	0.5199	11.27	5.86
Existing long-term debt	5,262	0.2011	9.75	1.96
Subordinated increasing-rate notes (Class I)	1,250	0.0478	13.00	0.62
Subordinated increasing-rate notes (Class II)	3,750	0.1433	14.00	2.01
Convertible debentures	1,800	0.0688	14.50	1.00
Partnership debt securities	500	0.0191	11.20	0.21
Total	$26,162	1.0000		11.66 %

Once the weighted cost for all debt has been estimated before tax, the effect of tax needs to be considered as follows:

$$\text{Cost of debt after tax} = \text{Cost of debt before tax} \times (100 - \text{Marginal tax rate})$$
$$= 11.66\% \, (100 - 35.5)$$
$$= 7.52\%$$

It is important to note that it has been assumed there are tax advantages associated with debt. However, this may not always be the case. Where a business has large tax losses carried forward, the position may be much more complex; there is always a need to review each situation on a case by case basis *.

---

* In the case of Santos plc, it will be assumed for purposes of demonstrating the WACC calculation that the cost of debt after making allowance for tax is 8.4 per cent (see Figure 6.4).

Capital structure

The third step in the WACC calculation involves the estimation of the capital structure and to understand the issues involved here, let us consider the following formula:

$$\text{WACC} = K_e + (E \div V) + K_d (1 - T_c)(D \div V)$$

Where,

- V = debt (D) + equity (E);
- D/V = the proportion of total value (V) claimed by debt (D);
- E/V = the proportion of total value (V) claimed by equity (E);
- K_d = the required rate of return on debt capital;
- K_e = the required rate of return on equity capital;
- T_c = the marginal corporate tax rate.

The calculation of WACC can be demonstrated by drawing on the example company, Santos plc. In Figure 6.4 it can be seen that the cost of equity using the CAPM approach is 14.03 per cent and the cost of debt after tax is 8.4 per cent. These two, when weighted by the debt equity mix of 36:64 per cent produce a WACC of approximately 12 per cent that has been used in the strategic value and Strategic Value Added valuations in earlier chapters.

On the basis of earlier discussions there is scope to question the appropriateness of this calculation and in particular the debt/equity (D/E) mix which should relate to a long-term capital structure and not a single point in time mix. Often a target D/E mix will be used and the effect of using such an approach is illustrated in Figure 6.5 where an assumed D/E of 50:50 has been used. To make such a change in the D/E of the WACC calculation it is necessary to ungear (illustrated for Santos plc in Figure 6.2) and regear the beta. The target D/E would be used to regear the beta, thereby changing the cost of equity. The change in the debt to equity mix would also impact on the overall WACC calculation as the cost of equity and cost of debt are weighted accordingly.

Figure 6.4: WACC for Santos plc

	£m	%
Cost of equity (general)		14.03
Risk-free rate		6.94
Beta	1.222	
Equity risk premium		5.8
Cost of debt		12.0
Marginal rate of corporation tax		30.0
Cost of debt (after tax @ 30%)		8.4
Equity (market value)	125.33	64
Debt (book value)	70.92	36
	196.25	100

$$\text{WACC} = \left[14.03\% \times \frac{125.33}{196.25} \right] + \left[8.4\% \times \frac{70.92}{196.25} \right]$$

$$= 12.00\%$$

The effect of making such adjustments to Santos plc for an assumed 50:50 debt to equity mix is a reduction in WACC to 11.76 per cent. By ungearing the beta (Figure 6.2) and regearing it at the target D/E, the result is 1.41. This regeared beta is then used to recalculate the cost of equity of 15.12 per cent (6.94% + (1.41 x 5.8%)). Assuming no change in the cost of debt, for purposes of illustration it can be seen that the impact of the new capital structure is to increase the beta and the cost of equity. However, there is a fall in the WACC percentage because of the counterbalancing effect of proportionately more (cheaper) debt. If, as is often the case, the cost of debt increases with such a change in the capital structure, the effect may be quite the opposite – attempts to gear the business up may actually result in a higher WACC percentage.

As regards the D/E ratio used in the WACC calculation, there is the question of whether book (balance sheet) values or market values should be used. Market values are conceptually superior, despite their volatility, because the firm must yield competitive rates of return for debt-holders and shareholders based on the respective market values of debt and equity. For example, suppose shareholders invested £5 million of initial capital in a company ten years ago. Over the ten year period book value grew from £5 million to £7 million. The market value, however, increased to £20 million over the same

Figure 6.5: WACC for Santos plc with 50:50 D/E mix

Cost of equity	15.12%
Risk-free rate	6.94%
Beta published	1.222
– ungeared	0.83
– regeared	1.41
Equity risk premium	5.8%
Cost of debt	8.4%

$$\text{WACC} = \left[15.12\% \times \frac{50}{(50+50)} \right] + \left[8.4\% \times \frac{50}{(50+50)} \right]$$

$$= 11.76\%$$

period. A reasonable return in light of present market conditions is 20 per cent. Would the shareholders be satisfied with a 20 per cent return on the £7 million book value, based on the firm's historical costs, or would they expect to earn 20 per cent on the current market value of £20 million, based on current economic value? Clearly, the investors will expect returns based on current market value because they could liquidate their investment for £20 million and find other opportunities yielding 20 per cent. Thus, book value is not relevant to current investment decisions.

Despite the preference for market values, there are many difficulties associated with the determination of the market value of debt and equity. In very simple terms, the market value of equity can be determined for a quoted firm by multiplying the current stock price by the number of shares outstanding. For an unquoted business, the task is more difficult. In the case of the market value of debt, for a quoted company it is its price in the market multiplied by the volume of traded debt. In the case of an unquoted company it could be computed by discounting the future cash flows of each instrument at an estimated current yield to maturity, as described in the previous section on the cost of debt. If this information is not available, the book value of debt may have to be used as a proxy for the market value of debt. However, very often the difficulties associated with the estimation of actual market values for equity and debt encourages the use of a target capital structure, i.e. a target D/E ratio. This target will be either based on judgement or benchmarked against peer group companies. An illustration of its application is provided in Figure 6.5.

Is there an optimal capital structure?

The potential tax related benefits of debt capital and 'gearing up' on the one hand, and the disadvantages of increased risk on the other has given rise to the view of there being an optimal, or ideal, capital structure. That is, there is some mix of debt relative to equity at which the tax advantage can be maximised before the perception is reached by debt and equity providers that the risk needs to be compensated for by a higher return.

Many believe that it is difficult to determine a single truly optimal capital structure in practice but that it is more valuable to see it as corresponding with a limited range of possible debt and equity mixes. Irrespective of the exact characteristics of the capital structure, the real challenge is to locate where it potentially lies when taking a forward-looking view. This is because in terms of undertaking a valuation, the real concern is typically to find the required rate of return or cost of capital to apply in valuing a potential opportunity from a series of estimated future cash flows. This means that the cost of capital should relate to the future, which is achieved by attempting to identify the most beneficial blend of debt and equity over the planning period. Attention will have to be paid to the most appropriate debt structure, which will have to take into consideration conditions relating to both the economy and the business. For example, we know that perceptions and the reality of borrowing can change given different economic conditions. In times of recession a massive change typically occurs in views about what constitutes an acceptable level of borrowing. Individuals and corporations often see the upside of borrowing from boom-time turn into a very real downside as interest rates rise at a time when effective demand and confidence are falling.

In addition to what is regarded as an acceptable level of gearing from a broad economic perspective, there is a need to consider specific business/industry characteristics since different types of business have different types of asset and repayment structure. Those with more to offer as security, or with more robust cash flows, should be able to gain most benefit from debt financing. The same is also the case for businesses with a good track record, even though their tangible sources of collateral may be limited.

The addition of debt has two opposing effects on a firm's cost of capital. First, since the after-tax cost of debt is normally less than the cost of equity for a firm, replacing debt with equity allows the firm to use a less expensive source of financing. This acts to reduce the overall cost of capital. However, additional debt increases both the cost of equity through financial leverage and the cost of debt through increasing risk of default. This acts to increase the cost of capital.

There is some debate concerning the extent to which these two effects counterbalance each other. Some have argued that there is no 'optimal capital structure'[100]. According to this view, a firm's value is determined by its assets, and its total value does not change when the cash flows from those assets are split into streams that go to different investor groups. This is equivalent to saying that the two effects of debt cancel each other out at all ratios of debt to equity. The alternative view favours the concept of an 'optimal capital structure' *,[101]. According to this view, capital structure does make a difference because of imperfections in the capital markets, such as the tax deductibility of interest and transaction costs. If this

---

* In reality, supporters of this view hold with there being a range of desirable debt:equity mixes, rather than the more elusive concept of optimality.

is the case, the two effects will cancel only when the firm is at its 'optimal capital structure'. At that point, increasing the percentage of debt in the capital structure will increase the cost of capital, as will decreasing the percentage of debt in the capital structure. If an additional unit of debt causes the overall cost of capital to decline, the first effect predominates and the firm is below its optimal debt/equity ratio. This means that the firm can create value for its shareholders by adding more debt. If an additional unit of debt causes the cost of capital to rise, the leverage effect predominates and the firm can create value by reducing the amount of debt in its capital structure.

Figure 6.6: Two views on capital structure [102]

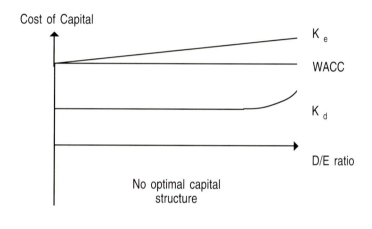

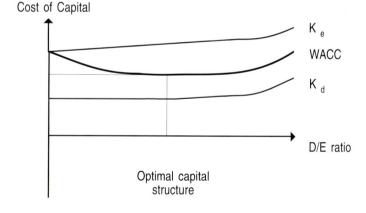

In reality, the problem lies in understanding where these most desirable blends of debt/equity are located. Optimal gearing models have been developed based on the relationship between bond ratings and ratios, like interest-coverage [169]. However, such relationships may serve as useful screening tools, but our preference is to seek the most desirable debt/equity mix by taking a business unit perspective, which is covered in the next section.

Cost of capital - a divisional business unit perspective

The approach outlined in this chapter enables a cost of capital for the whole company to be estimated, but it has some very real shortcomings. Often it is important to understand the value of the individual business units which, together, make up the whole company.

Companies can be thought of as consisting of a number of component businesses each of which has a different risk return relationship. However, the calculation of the divisional cost of capital is by no means a simple task. The cost of capital is, in fact, the weighted average of the costs of the separate sources of capital, in terms of equity and debt. In other words, when estimating the cost of capital for divisions of quoted companies, financial managers need to determine the cost of equity, the cost of debt and the capital structure for each of the divisions.

The main problem with the calculation of divisional discount rates is the availability of information. For publicly quoted companies finance theory provides an established existence of a relationship between risk and return. Risk is measured through the returns of a security, but the market data required does not exist for a non-traded firm or for a division of a publicly traded firm. However, there are two main approaches that can be used in such circumstances:

1. the analytical approach (sometimes known as the "cross-sectional" approach;
2. the analogous approach.

1. The analytical approach

Involves working from revenue, margins, asset saleability and other operating and structural characteristics. Data are developed from history or simulation and connected to market estimates of systematic risk and debt capacity via some linking mechanism. The analytical approach seeks to develop a relationship between accounting and market risk measures. If a stable relationship can be observed, divisional accounting data can be used to estimate the market risk of the division. However, although there is theoretical support for the analytical technique, there is no evidence that accounting and market linkages are stable. In other words, conflicting results from empirical studies illustrate that accounting returns fail to account for market risk.

2. The analogous approach

Involves finding firms that have market histories, as well as a restricted set of products very similar to the product line being examined. Analogous approaches differ from the analytical approach in that market data are utilised as a measure of risk. A series of analogous approaches have been developed, the most notable being the pure-play approach. This method is based on the premise that a proxy beta derived from a publicly traded firm, whose operations are as similar as possible to the division in question, is used as the measure of the division's systematic risk. The pure-play approach attempts to identify firms with publicly traded securities that are engaged solely in the same line of business as the division [103]. Once the pure-play firm is identified, its cost of equity capital is determined and then used as a proxy for the required divisional cost of equity capital. The presumption, of course, is that the systematic risk and capital structure of the pure-play are the same as those of the division.

Another analogous approach, the full-information approach, is based on the theoretical premise that a firm is simply a portfolio of projects; therefore the beta of a firm is the weighted average of the betas of its projects. This approach assumes that the beta of a division is the same, no matter which firm owns the division. The estimation of the cost of equity for a division is then a relatively simple process. Suppose a company has four business segments. The starting point would be to look for a number of quoted companies that have similar business segments in their portfolio and to calculate their equity betas. In addition, sales for each business segment are necessary to estimate the divisional betas, as these represent the weights for each business segment. Segment betas are then extrapolated by applying regression analysis assuming that the beta of a firm is the weighted average of its divisional betas.

The implication of analogous approaches varies in the degree of complexity, but the main strength of these techniques lies in the fact that market data are utilised as a measure of risk, thus validating their use in divisional cost of equity estimations.

Once cost of equity estimates have been undertaken for business units they can be fed into business unit cost of capital calculations. However, questions often arise about the appropriate debt:equity mix to use. In fact, careful consideration must be given to the question of the balance between both the parent company and the business unit's capital structures. A good case can be made for not basing the target capital structure for a business unit on the existing capital structure of the corporation as a whole, but on the debt capacity it could support as a stand-alone company. Corporate raiders have often taken advantage of managements' failure to consider this fact.

One way of estimating stand-alone debt capacity and leverage is to ask: 'What would the business unit's target capital structure be after a leveraged buyout?' This requires a thorough analysis of its financial position, the degree to which its assets are specialised (and therefore of lower collateral value in the event of bankruptcy) and its industry and competitive position. Another way of determining a business unit's target capital structure is by comparing its present structure to that of its peer group companies and adjusting the structure according to its competitive position. This method assumes that the average company in a given peer group has reached its optimal capital structure, which may not be the case.

The cost of capital in practice

How the cost of capital is estimated in practice was investigated as part of a research study undertaken during 1995 [104]. The study was directed at the Finance Directors of the top 250 companies quoted on the London International Stock Exchange. Overall, 142 companies (56.8 per cent) responded. They consisted of 101 (40.4 per cent) companies which agreed to participate and 41 (16.4 per cent) which refused for a variety of reasons.

WACC calculations in one form or another were undertaken by all respondents. As regards estimating the cost of equity the use of a single method was exceptional and many respondents reported using more than one. In follow up interviews as many as four methods were reported as being used, though not with equal importance being attached to each. The method most used by responding companies was the CAPM and in follow-up interviews considerable importance was found to be attached to it. Other methods found to be in use were the dividend yield model, earning yield model, return on equity and Gordon's growth method.

As regards estimating the cost of debt, both market value and book value were found to be used in estimating yields. For estimates of the capital structure, the proportion of debt used in a WACC calculation was typically the result of a corporate policy on gearing, rather than a figure determined with reference to the debt capacity of individual divisions.

Most respondents were found to use a company-wide WACC which supports the findings of a survey conducted in the US. This showed that roughly one third of Fortune 1,000 US companies used a single cost of capital [105]. In fact, only 21 companies in total responded that they used a divisional cost of capital.

New directions in estimating the cost of capital

In recent years the appropriateness and validity of CAPM has been questioned. This has lead to a move towards approaches that estimate a 'market derived' or 'market driven' cost of equity. Such approaches entail using today's market data (which contain the market's future oriented perspective), to derive the market's view of the forward-looking cost of equity.

Some proponents of a CFROI approach, reviewed in Chapters 4 and 5, derive the cost of capital by taking a forward looking view. They contend that the Capital Asset Pricing Model is too crude and backward looking, particularly when viewed from the perspective of the external equity investor. Their CFROI valuation models calculate a forward looking cost of capital from 'market-derived' discount rates which are maintained from a universe of companies with monitored forecasts of future cash flows. These companies are aggregated and have a known market value. The 'market' discount rate is then derived at a point in time. This is then the rate that equates a present value of these future cash flows to the known price [106]. According to this view, the firm's discount rate is the sum of the market rate plus a risk differential for size and financial leverage, similar to variables used for firms' credit ratings.

Figure 6.7: SBC Warburg Dillon Reed approach to cost of capital compared with CAPM

		Rate component		Excess equity return component
Estimated Cost of Equity (CAPM)	=	Risk free rate	+	(Market risk premium x beta)
Estimated Cost of Equity (Equity term structure)	=	Corporate bond	+	(Call option at forward strike)

As an alternative, a recent innovative approach by SBC Warburg Dillon Reed uses traded equity options of companies in conjunction with option pricing theory to derive a term structure for the cost of equity [107]. This is similar to the term structure of interest rates that exists for government debt which is used for everyday trading in the capital markets. Unlike the other approaches used to calculate the cost of equity, this approach does not assume that risk is constant over time.

In order to calculate an equity term structure, the approach begins with the term structure for the risk free rate. Unlike CAPM, SBC Warburg Dillon Reed includes credit spreads to create a term structure for the corporate debt of the firm (see Figure 6.7). Then, using the market data of the firms traded equity options, option pricing theory is used to calculate the excess equity returns that a rational investor would expect to earn above the cost of debt going out ten years. In summary, this approach first identifies the term structure of corporate debt and then overlays it with the term structure of excess equity returns.

Support for a term structure of equity is based on the argument that the use of long term historical average excess returns to estimate the market risk premium is likely to be misleading, not least because the market risk premium has been found to vary over time in predictable ways [108].

Summary checklist

- Two main valuation approaches can be used, involving discounting the valuation of free cash flows at WACC or equity cash flows at the cost of equity. Whichever cost of capital is used, it must match the cash flows which are being discounted, in terms of whether the cash flows are pre- or post-tax and real or nominal.
- WACC estimation can be thought of in terms of three steps estimating the cost of equity, the cost of debt and the target debt to equity mix.
- The most difficult step is estimation of the cost of equity for which a number of different approaches can be used, but the most popular is the CAPM.
- Within a CAPM calculation there are many judgements that have to be made relating to the selection of the risk-free rate, beta and the equity risk premium. Many adjustments may also be required, e.g. to remove financial risk from beta estimates.
- The objective in making a cost of capital estimate is to obtain a forward looking view. With this in mind, it is important to understand the distinction between the backward looking view of the cost of capital as calculated on the basis of past data and the forward looking view of the cost of capital calculated on the basis of forward looking data.
- The question of how capital structure affects the cost of capital is still the subject of much debate and there are a number of competing theories.
- The consideration of risk is essential in any discussion about what cost of capital to use. In simple terms, it is market related (systematic) risk that should be included in cost of capital estimates.
- The cost of capital can be calculated for business units as well as the corporation as a whole. This raises some additional complications because of the need to draw on peer group company information for estimating betas and the like.
- A number of alternative forward looking methods for calculating the cost of capital are under development that challenge the basic underpinnings of CAPM.

Concluding remarks

Irrespective of the valuation method adopted there has to be a yardstick against which to evaluate the outcome. In the case of the new valuation methods reviewed in Chapter 4, this yardstick is the cost of capital. In most cases this cost of capital is calculated in the manner outlined in this chapter drawing on CAPM. There are those who take the exceptional view and argue that CAPM is too crude and backward looking, particularly when viewed from the perspective of the external equity investor. Their preference is to calculate a forward looking cost of capital from 'market-derived' discount rates where, the firm's discount rate is the sum of the market rate plus a risk differential for size and financial leverage, similar to variables used for firms' credit ratings.

Irrespective of the view taken of the estimation of the cost of capital, it requires careful analysis because of its impact on a valuation, directly and through assumptions, about the length of the CAP. This analysis also requires that risk assessment is looked at carefully, particularly when assessing emerging market opportunities. This, and other issues associated with the cost of capital, like the treatment of cross-border opportunities, are dealt with in the next chapter.

Part 3: Applications

126 PART THREE

Introduction

In the first two parts of this book the fundamental principles of Strategic Value Analysis and the key issues associated with it have been discussed. Many common and recurring threads have been introduced which are well conveyed in the 'following' roadmap, which should serve as a useful guide for all kinds of valuation applications, including those reviewed in the last four chapters of this book.

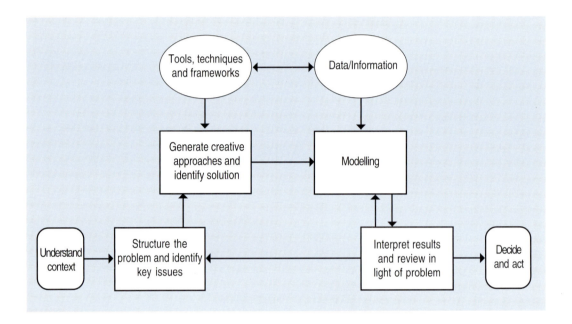

1. Starting from the left-hand side of the roadmap, it is important to understand the internal and external context within which a valuation is being carried out, i.e. before carrying out any valuation it is important to ask – 'what is the purpose of carrying out the valuation?' Is it for purposes of pricing an initial public offering, valuing an acquisition or to support an executive compensation programme. This is because some tools/techniques may be more appropriate in some applications than others.

2. Once the context is understood, it is necessary to structure the problem and identify the key issues. For example, is it a valuation situation for which terminal value issues are important, or for which the characteristics are more like a real option?

3. Following this, generating creative approaches that may help to understand how to solve the valuation problem is essential. This can be illustrated by way of a real-life example. A power distribution company recognised that the assets it used to distribute electricity could be used to carry telephone cables and support a cellular network system. In other words, its tangible assets used for its primary business had a potential value for other purposes. In simple terms, access to its assets had a value and such access could be sold as 'rights'. Such rights had a clear value to those seeking the rights, because via them a telephone business

could be operated. In fact, to such a buyer the value of these rights was seen in terms of the rental cost associated with using the power company's assets. However, from the perspective of the power company selling the rights, a completely different potential value could be seen. To this seller the value could be looked at in terms of the benefit to be derived from having the rights. How to estimate this value represents a good example of a situation where creative thinking was required and this, in turn, involved drawing on a number of valuation tools and techniques *.

4. Modelling in some form will be required, almost invariably involving the use of computer software, recognising, of course, any constraints dictated by the availability and validity of information.

5. The last step, involving the making of the decision, requires the interpretation and the review of the results of the model in light of the initial problem.

---

* This is considered later at the end of Chapter 9.

Chapter 7: Valuation in Emerging Markets and Cross-Border Valuations

If the UK or French stock market surged by 30 per cent I would take profits. But in Russia am investing on a long-term horizon and betting on the success of economic reform.

Mr Arnab Banerji, Chief Investment Officer,
Foreign and Colonial's emerging market funds

Financial Times, 31 January 1996 [109].

Chapter preview

○ The definition and significance of emerging markets.
○ The issues that have to be faced in dealing with emerging market valuations which relate to:
  1. differences in accounting practices;
  2. limited and sometimes questionable data;
  3. treatment of risk and uncertainty;
  4. estimating the cost of capital;
  5. dealing with inflation pressures;
  6. dealing with valuations in cross-border situations where different currencies are used.

Introduction

Globalisation of the world economy and international competitiveness are having a significant and far-reaching impact on all economies and all types of organisations, not least those in emerging markets. Emerging markets have been defined as:

> *... places where financial institutions and multinational companies see profitable opportunities for investment or speculation in what used to be called the Third World* [110].

Emerging geographic markets are important and cannot be ignored for many reasons, not least because they:

- cover more than three-quarters of the world's land area;
- represent more than three-quarters of the world's population;
- account for only about one-quarter of the world's GDP;
- make up less than one-tenth of global stock market capitalisation; and
- have enjoyed historically high growth rates.

In fact, the World Bank reported that private capital flows into emerging markets increased by $60 billion in 1996 to achieve a new record level. Of course, this has all changed following the recent Asian currency crisis. This crisis has had enormous implications for many markets, like Indonesia, which had been particularly attractive because of the potentially large opportunities they offer. Indonesia is one of the so-called 'Big Emerging Markets', like China, India, Brazil and Mexico [111]. However, there are many smaller markets, like those in Eastern Europe and Malaysia, where the potential opportunities have not been overlooked. Unfortunately, for the smaller and medium-sized Asian markets like Malaysia, there has been a significant change in perceptions of the potential benefits manifested in revised growth forecasts. On 12 January 1998, *Asia Business News* reported that the historically high average growth rate of 10 per cent for Malaysia had been revised downwards by the Malaysian Government to 4-5 per cent. A more pessimistic view was portrayed by the IMF (International Monetary Fund) which estimated growth of around 2.5 per cent.

The theory is that emerging markets offer higher returns than those in mature markets of the industrialised world. This is because these economies are expected to enjoy higher rates of economic growth, making the value of their stock markets tend to grow faster. As recent events have shown, there are higher risks associated with such markets so that the higher risks should be rewarded by higher returns in good times and vice versa in bad times.

In principle, the same basic techniques as outlined in preceding chapters should be applicable to such markets, but the practice is typically very different [112]. Some of the important financial issues to be faced in applying the basic technique in emerging markets include:

- differences in accounting practices;
- limited and sometimes questionable data;
- treatment of risk and uncertainty;
- estimating the cost of capital;
- dealing with inflation pressures;
- dealing with different currencies and currency fluctuations.

In this chapter we will examine the effect of these issues on valuation analysis and we will demonstrate ways in which they can be handled in practice [113].

Differences in accounting practices

Accounting practices differ substantially despite international standardisation efforts and such practices may be particularly pronounced, even in mature markets [114].

There is increasing interest in the international standardisation of accounting practices. Currently 'standardisation' goes under the banner of compliance with US GAAP set by the Federal Accounting Standards Board (FASB), or International Accounting Standards (IAS) set by the International Accounting Standards Committee (IASC). The requirements of US GAAP transparency in financial reporting are not always appealing, but have been an essential prerequisite until recently for gaining access to equity capital in the USA. A recent change in attitudes in the USA has been influential in the IASC striving to put in place a set of core standards for acceptance by the world's leading stock markets by early 1999 [115].

While the moves towards increased international standardisation are to be welcomed, major limitations of accounting data will not be removed. The basic challenges to valuation in economies that are in transition, such as those of the former Soviet bloc countries, derive from the use of socialist styled accounting data, historic under-investment and neglect, and the absence of capital markets [116]. In Russia, an important emerging market, few companies are reckoned to produce Western style accounts, preferring to use cash based accounts rather than the accruals method used in the West [117]. The plain fact of the matter is that with discounted cash flow valuation the free cash flows are the same regardless of the accounting standards used within the country under consideration. That does not mean to say that the application of this approach does not present its own problems, some of which will be reviewed briefly.

Data limitations

Transparency in financial reporting may not be an accepted or acceptable practice which means that in addition to the problems created by accounting differences, emerging markets are often characterised by a lack of relevant data. The implications of this are that time spent on developing and refining elegant mathematical models may well be more productively spent in focusing on improving the input data set. To this end, a facilitation approach undertaken with relevant individuals can be used very powerfully. This approach is intended to force thinking around the limitations imposed by having imperfect data [118]. It can be used simply and powerfully. In recognition that what is required may not be available, or what is required is not yet known, efforts are made to unravel a picture of likely outcomes, the ultimate objective being to develop a sound base case. Often the first attempts are less than perfect, but the approach encourages the results to be refined and draws heavily on 'scenario thinking'. This is particularly useful for trying to unravel a cash flow picture and also for other parts of the analysis where data may often not be available or in need of some cross-checking. So, a focus on a scenario approach (See Chapter 3), using multifunctional teams to develop the scenarios, avoids deterministic thinking.

The scenario approach has been found to be very effective for forcing clarity of thought about tough issues and it certainly helps to avoid the so-called GIGO problem of 'garbage in, garbage out', or even worse 'garbage in, gospel out'! It is also fundamental to the analysis of risk covered in the next section.

Treatment of risk and uncertainty

Risk and uncertainty represent a major problem in emerging market valuation. There are some useful principles that can be used when undertaking valuation analysis, the most important of which is to try and separate the risk into specific and market-related components. The assumption underpinning this approach, which was discussed in Chapter 3, is that:

$$\text{Total risk} \quad = \quad \text{Market risk} \quad + \quad \text{Specific risk} \quad [119]$$

Market risk, sometimes referred to as systematic risk, is non-diversifiable and unavoidable, whereas specific (or unsystematic) risk is assumed to be diversifiable or avoidable *. Market risks, like changes in the economy, tax reforms, or a change in the world energy situation cannot be diversified away, such that even the investor who holds a well-diversified portfolio will be exposed to this type of risk. This is not so for specific risks which are often unique to a particular company and are independent of economic, political and other factors which affect securities in a systematic manner. Examples are technological breakthroughs threatening product obsolescence, a new competitor producing essentially the same product, or the potential expropriation of assets by a foreign government.

Specific risks can be factored into valuation analysis by means of alternative cash flow scenarios, while market-related risks are built into the discount rate via the cost of capital. While the distinction between these two types of risk is very often difficult to make in respect of some issues, it forces appropriate questions to be asked about key issues which might otherwise not be questioned. It also helps to prevent the loading of the discount rate as being the simple and only solution to higher perceived risk. While such action may be appropriate in the case of market-related risk, it is a far less convincing argument for risks which may impact at a specific point in time. Associated with this is the advantage that not all cash flows are penalised, as would be the case if risk were built into the cost of capital by raising the percentage required.

As discussed in Chapter 3, the implication of this risk separation is that alternative cash flow scenarios can be constructed to take account of specific risks. Scenarios can be viewed as long-term 'stories' about possible future external environments, which are framed as two or three credible pathways [120]. Specific risks can be included in these stories and can be thought of as being capable of being 'managed' by company action to avoid them.

Underlying this separation of the total risk into the market risk component and the specific risk component, is the assumption that there is no interactive relationship between the two [121]. This presents a further weakness to CAPM as no explicit recognition is given for the role that the reduction of specific risk can play in reducing market risk. Examples of specific risks include:

○ changes in demand for a specific organisation's products or services;
○ the impact of competitors' practices on a specific aspect of business operations; and
○ operational problems or dislocations such as labour disputes specific to an organisation.

---

* Market related risk was discussed in Chapter 6 with reference to the CAPM and beta values.

An organisation's strategies to address issues such as these, if effective, would reduce the company specific risk, and would also be likely to influence the stability of its cash flows relative to the market and, hence, the level of market risk.

Estimating the cost of capital

Financial markets in emerging market countries are often thin or non-existent. What is more, long-term government bonds may not be quoted, such that substitutes are required. Even if there is a quoted yield, it may not be default-free, as would usually be expected for developed economies.

By way of an example, consider the task of estimating the cost of capital for an equity stake in a chemicals company in China. If it is assumed that the venture would not use any debt, how can the required return on equity be estimated in an environment where betas are not available, the equity risk premium is unknown, and there is no relevant government debt that can be used to estimate the risk-free rate? To be specific, in some markets like Indonesia, such medium-term government bonds do not exist, and in others even where they do exist there may be concern that they satisfy the technical requirements of the risk-free rate. In such circumstances a rate can be estimated by drawing on the principles of corporate finance in which one of the fundamental laws is that two investments of equal risk must have the same real return. The suggestion, therefore, is that two investments with identical cash flows and risk must also have the same net present value, otherwise an arbitrage opportunity will exist. In a perfect world it should make no difference whether an investment opportunity is evaluated from a foreign or domestic perspective, because the investment risk is identical. Thus, the domestic currency equivalent net present value of an investment analysed from a foreign perspective must be equal to what would have been calculated if the project had been analysed from the domestic perspective. If the two are not equal, then investment arbitrage has been created.

The principle of arbitrage can be used as the starting point for estimating the cost of capital in emerging markets because often the type of information required for its calculation, like the beta, may not be available. For example, by applying purchasing power parity (PPP) whereby exchange rates adjust with the experienced inflation rate differential between the domestic and foreign countries, an estimate of the cost of capital can be made [122].

Once the potential depreciation in the currency has been estimated, a principle known as the Fisher effect is applied. The Fisher effect also states that the nominal rate of interest embodies in it an inflation premium sufficient to compensate lenders for the expected loss of purchasing power associated with the receipt of future money [123]. It is typically expressed as follows:

$$(1 + m) = (1 + r) \times (1 + i)$$

Where,

m = nominal, or money, rate;
r = real rate;
i = expected rate of inflation.

134 CHAPTER SEVEN

For example, if today's $US:$HK exchange rate is 1:7.75 and let us assume that the $US:$HK exchange rate is 1:7.25 in one year's time and the US cost of capital to be converted is 12 per cent, then:

$$(1 + m) = (1 + r) \times (1 + i)$$

Where, in this case:

- m = HK cost of capital to be estimated;
- r = US cost of capital;
- i = depreciation in the $HK exchange rate assumed to be a proxy for inflation.

$$(1 + m) = (1.12) \times [1 + ((7.75 - 7.25) \div 7.75)]$$

$$(1 + m) = (1.12) \times (1.065)$$

$$m = 19.2\%$$

The result of this calculation is an estimated Hong Kong cost of capital of 19.2 per cent. An extension of this approach, known as the international Fisher effect, focuses on interest-rate parity and suggests that differences in interest rates between two countries serve as a proxy for differences in expected inflation. This can be applied in cost of capital estimates by assuming that real rates between countries are equal, otherwise an arbitrage opportunity will occur. Taking the basic Fisher effect formula:

$$(1 + m) = (1 + r) \times (1 + i)$$

Re-arranged, this can be expressed as:

$$(1 + r) = (1 + m) \div (1 + i)$$

Assuming real rate parity between two countries, say the UK and US, this can be expressed as:

$$(1 + r)_{US} = (1 + r)_{UK}$$

Or,

$$(1 + m)_{US} \div (1 + i)_{US} = (1 + m)_{UK} \div (1 + i)_{UK}$$

If the money rate for, say, the UK is required, this can be achieved with knowledge of the other three pieces of data. By way of illustration this Fisher adjustment was used as a cross-check in determining the risk-free rate for a Malaysian infrastructure project company flotation, which will be discussed more fully in the next section. Using information about the US long-bond rate and the expected levels of inflation in the USA and Malaysia, the following cross-check estimate was obtained:

$$(1 + m)_{US} \div (1 + i)_{US} = (1 + m)_{Malaysia} \div (1 + i)_{Malaysia}$$

$$(1 + m)_{Malaysia} = (1 + m)_{US} \times (1 + i)_{Malaysia} \div (1 + i)_{US}$$

$$= (1.0684)(1.04) \div (1.023)$$

$$= 8.6\%$$

It is important to stress that this type of cost of capital analysis is rarely sufficient on its own, but as we illustrate with reference to the following Malaysian example, it is useful as a starting point. To complete the picture it typically needs to be accompanied by substantial analysis that recognises the importance of a business perspective rather than just a conversion based on information about only the respective financial markets. The analysis may also be limited by unexpected events. For example, the currency crisis in Asia in late 1997 made the use of spot and forward rates in such calculations; difficult to say the least.

Lingkaran Transkota Holdings Berhad (Litrak) Public Offering of Securities in Malaysia for an infrastructure project

On 23 April 1996, Lingkaran Transkota Holdings Berhad (Litrak) was awarded a 33-year concession by the federal government of Malaysia for the privatisation of the 40km highway linking north-west Kuala Lumpur to Putra Jaya, the planned government administration centre in the south. The expressway is named Lebuh Raya Damansara-Putra Jaya (LDP). Subsequently, on 11 October 1996, Litrak Holdings received the approval of the Malaysian Securities Commission (SC) for its listing on the Main Board of the Kuala Lumpur Stock Exchange (KLSE). Litrak Holdings is the second so-called Infrastructure Project Company (IPC) approved under the Security Council's Guidelines for the Public Offerings of Securities by sizeable IPCs (IPC Guidelines). These guidelines allow qualifying IPCs seeking substantial financing to seek a listing without a track record provided that they are projected to generate sufficient income to provide a suitable rate of return to shareholders for a remaining concession period of at least 18 years.

The Concession Agreement provides that Litrak will collect and retain all traffic tolls and will have responsibility for all operating and maintenance costs for the period of the concession. The collection of toll revenue is projected to commence by March 2000. The toll rates over the concession period are specified in the Concession Agreement.

Litrak entered into a RM1.135 billion fixed price, lump sum, turnkey contract with a joint-venture formed by Gamuda (49 per cent shareholder) and Irama Duta (51 per cent shareholder), which is responsible for the detailed design and construction of the Highway.

Under the Concession Agreement, the Government will make available the land required for the project and will, subject to reimbursement by Litrak, pay up to RM98 million to acquire such land on Litrak's behalf.

The total capital cost of the construction of the highway was estimated at RM1.327 billion inclusive of capitalised interest of RM142.3 million. Litrak arranged bank and other debt facilities, on a non-recourse basis to Litrak Holdings, totalling RM1.07 billion.

The Valuation

In the prospectus, a Retail Issue Price and Institutional Issue Price of RM3.60 per share and RM5.10 per share, respectively, were arrived at based on the discounted cash flow method [124]. The discount rates deemed to be applicable for the Retail Issue Price and Institutional Issue Price were approximately 14 per cent and 12 per cent respectively. However, different views about the value of the business opportunity emerged. The reasons for these may be best understood by reference to Figure 7.1, which summarises the performance of selected Initial Public Offers (IPOs) in Malaysia.

Figure 7.1: Selected IPO price performance in Malaysia

Stock	Date listed	Offer price RM	Opening price RM	Price at 11-12-96 RM	Premium over Offer price
P&D	31-7-96	1.80	4.80	5.15	186.1
Johor Tenggara	15-8-96	1.65	3.90	2.28	38.1
Hua Joo Seng	9-8-96	3.45	8.00	6.40	85.5
Amway	30-8-96	6.00	13.70	14.80	146.7
Tekala Corporation	28-8-96	2.60	6.40	4.14	60.8
Powertek	29-8-96	3.90	7.20	4.70	20.5
Jemeh Asia	23-9-96	2.60	6.00	6.15	136.5
K&N Kenanga	7-10-96	2.50	3.82	3.38	35.2
Apollo Food	15-9-96	2.80	6.50	7.90	182.1
Johor Port	25-10-96	2.30	4.50	3.92	70.4
Saujana	29-10-96	1.85	4.00	2.31	24.9
Ramatex	12-11-96	3.60	7.00	4.82	33.9
Kumpulan Fima	15-11-96	2.10	3.30	3.40	61.9
Delloyd Ventures	18-11-96	4.00	8.00	7.95	98.6
Pica Corporation	19-11-96	1.90	3.70	3.32	74.7
MNRB	20-11-96	4.30	7.50	8.55	98.8
Suria Capital	25-11-96	1.50	2.50	2.30	53.3
Ann Joo	26-11-96	2.00	5.10	4.10	105.0
Jaya Jusco	2-12-96	4.30	7.90	6.10	41.9
BCB	3-12-96	1.85	4.90	3.92	118.9
ICP	9-12-96	3.00	4.70	5.95	98.3
ACF	11-12-96	2.90	3.90	3.68	26.9
Average					81.8

Source: South Johor Securities SDN BHD, December 1996.

To give some idea of the differences in opinion about the valuation, one analyst commented in his 'Recommendation':

> *We have arrived at a fair value for Litrak shares of RM8.05 per share, based on the Discounted Cash Flow (DCF) method. Our discount rate of 10.2% is derived from the Capital Asset Pricing Model (CAPM).*

The assumptions used in arriving at this value were:

1. risk-free rate 8.6 per cent;
2. equity risk premium 11.3 per cent;
3. beta 1.0;
4. pre-tax cost of debt approximately 10 per cent;
5. marginal tax rate 30 per cent.

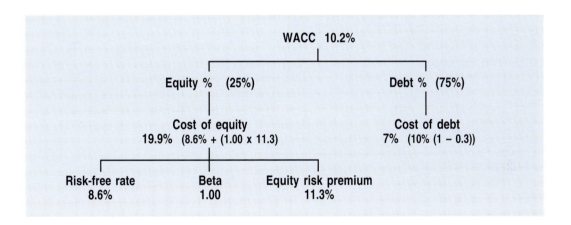

For 10.2 per cent to be the result of such a calculation the debt to equity ratio would have to be 75:25. In Malaysia, as in many parts of Asia, the aversion to high levels of debt would make this highly unlikely for companies with betas of 1. The implications of this could be seen if we were to make the assumption that a debt to equity mix of 50:50 was the norm in Malaysia for companies that move in line with the market (with betas of 1.0). By making this assumption we could estimate the beta for a company with a 75:25 mix by ungearing at an assumed 50:50, and by regearing at 75:25. The results are as follows:

$$\text{Ungeared Beta} = \text{Geared (Published) Beta} \div [1 + (1 - t)(D/E_{Current})]$$

$$= 1.0 \div [1 + (1 - 0.3)(50/50)]$$

$$= 1.0 \div 1.7$$

$$= 0.59$$

CHAPTER SEVEN

$$\text{Regeared Beta} = \text{Ungeared Beta} \times (1 + (1 - t)(D/E_{Target}))$$
$$= 0.59 \times (1 + (1 - 0.3)(^{75}/_{25}))$$
$$= 0.59 \times 3.1$$
$$= 1.82$$

The impact of a regeared beta of 1.82, other things being equal, would be a WACC of 12.55 per cent, i.e.

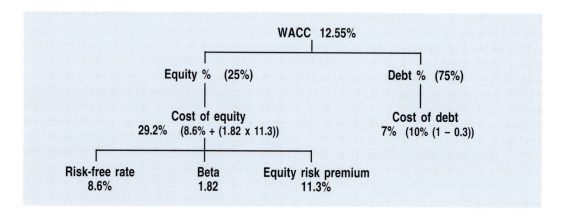

The risk associated with this project can be broken down into two components, namely the business and the financing risk, (see Figure 7.2).

Figure 7.2: Components of business and financing risk

D/E ratio	Ungeared beta	Geared beta less ungeared beta	Total beta (i.e. geared)
50:50	0.59	0.41	1.00
75:25	0.59	1.23	1.82

When the betas are broken down into their business and financing components, some key differences emerge between the two levels of gearing:

○ with a D/E ratio of 50:50 a larger proportion of the project risk arises from the risky nature of the business in which the project operates; whereas

○ with a D/E ratio of 75:25 most of the project risk is attributable to the high financial leverage employed in financing the project.

Such analysis illustrates how the principles of corporate finance can be used quite powerfully to cross-check cost of capital estimates, even in emerging market situations characterised by limited data.

Cross-checks for the cost of capital estimates might also be usefully employed, particularly for the equity risk premium. As illustrated earlier, using US data purchasing power parity (PPP) and Fisher effect calculations could be used. In the case of the latter, with knowledge of a US nominal rate and the expected rate of inflation in the USA and Malaysia, approximations for a Malaysian nominal rate could be inferred.

Dealing with inflation pressures

It is not uncommon to find emerging markets characterised by high inflation and, therefore, inflation risk. For example, the currency crisis in Asia has brought about estimates for the annual rate of inflation in Indonesia of 20 per cent and there have even been some predictions of hyper-inflation.

Inflation risk is generally characterised by highly volatile rates of inflation from one period to the next, as well as very high levels. In such situations data can be quickly distorted by inflation and forecasting can be a real nightmare. The estimation of long-term expected inflation can be extremely difficult in emerging markets, making it a real challenge to determine an appropriate discount rate. Under these circumstances, it is possible to forecast nominal cash flows and discount them at the relevant nominal rate. Alternatively, the analysis can be undertaken in real terms (rather than nominal) or in terms of a hard currency, such as the US dollar, DM, or yen.

If the analysis is conducted in real terms, expected cash flows should be forecasted using real values and discounted using a real cost of capital. The use of real terms typically involves undertaking cash flow forecasts in real terms and the use of a real risk-adjusted discount rate (adjusted using the Fisher effect). It presents a significant challenge as regards forecasting real rates of growth, but there are other challenges, not least of which is tax. If, as an alternative, a high inflation currency is translated into a stable currency by using the historical spot foreign exchange rates, the resulting stable currency free cash flows should be forecast and then discounted at a weighted average cost of capital in the stable currency. The resulting value can then be reconverted to the domestic currency of the emerging market at the spot exchange rate. It needs to be recognised that although such analysis can, in principle, be executed in any currency, it is often most expedient to do so in a stable currency, such as the US dollar, for which reliable real rates of return can be estimated.

Cross-border valuations

There are many currency related problems often associated with undertaking valuations in emerging markets. These relate to:

1. The choice of currency, foreign (local) or domestic (home), in which to execute the analysis.

2. Whether to discount foreign cash flows at the time they are earned or only as they are remitted home to the parent.

3. Whether to use foreign or domestic tax rates.

4. The proper calculation of the cost of capital used to discount the cash flows.

5. The appropriate treatment of special risks unique to cross-border investments, such as foreign exchange risk, political risk, etc.

One of the first decisions that must be made when executing valuations of cross-border investments is the choice of which currency to use in forecasting free cash flows and measuring the WACC. Of course the choice of currency in which to denominate a valuation should not drive the end result. Thus, if one discounts foreign currency cash flows at the appropriate foreign currency discount rate, and home currency cash flows at the appropriate home currency discount rate, the result should be the same. However, preferences may arise for using one method instead of another from time to time. For example, if it is thought that a project's value might be especially sensitive to future exchange rate changes, it will be helpful to forecast foreign currency cash flows and then explicitly convert them to home currency cash flows using a specific set of forecasted exchange rates. This allows one to guage easily the sensitivity of the results to alternative exchange rate outcomes. In other situations, a manager may have a reasonably good estimate of a project's foreign currency cost of capital. Under these conditions, discounting foreign currency cash flows with a foreign currency cost of capital may be more intuitive. In the following we demonstrate both foreign currency techniques.

Method 1: Discounting foreign currency cash flows

Let us assume a US company and its UK subsidiary. The UK plc has provided its US headquarters with a set of expected future cash flows denominated in pounds sterling, as illustrated in Figure 7.4. Some of the general assumptions underlying these forecasts and other pertinent data about prevailing economic conditions are provided in Figure 7.3.

Figure 7.3: Assumptions

Assumptions	US	UK
Price inflation %	3.0	3.5
Yield on government bonds %	6.5	7.0
Corporate tax rate %	34	35
Equity risk premium %	4	
Spot rate Bid	1.6000	
Ask	1.6010	
Cost of debt %	9.4	11.0
Gearing	0.4	
Beta	0.90	
Cost of equity (CAPM)% (6.5 + (0.9 x 4))	10.1	
Cost of capital %	8.54	9.05

Figure 7.4: Discounting foreign currency cash flows

Year	0	1	2	3	4	5	Terminal
Free cash flow £m	−56.00	10.40	8.90	9.73	10.94	10.43	12.23
Discount factor UK (9.05%)	1.000	0.917	0.841	0.771	0.707	0.648	
Present value £m	−56	9.54	7.48	7.50	7.73	6.76	87.57
Net present value (NPV) £m	70.58						
Spot exchange rate	1.60						
NPV $m	112.93						

In the case of the US headquarters, we have assumed that the company is owned by US investors who assess future prospects with reference to US capital market investment opportunities. Using the standard WACC formula and the data provided in Figure 7.3, the WACC is as follows:

$$8.54\% = [0.4\ (9.4\%)\ (1 - 0.34)] + [0.6\ (10.1\%)]$$

The dollar WACC of UK plc's expansion project can be converted to a sterling WACC by using the differential between long-term risk free interest rates in the UK and USA. (As illustrated earlier, expected inflation rates might also be used if suitable long-term interest rates, and/or forward exchange rates were not available.) Since in each currency the risk free rate represents the time value of money, the rationale for using the interest rate differential is that it measures the difference in the time value of money between the two currencies. Using yields on government bonds obtained from Figure 7.3, the sterling WACC is 9.05% (1.0854 × 1.07 ÷ 1.065).

$$\frac{WACC_{US}}{WACC_{UK}} = \frac{\text{Yield on Government Bonds}_{US}}{\text{Yield on Government Bonds}_{UK}}$$

Using the sterling WACC of 9.05 per cent to discount the project's earned after-tax sterling free cash flows, produces a net present value of £70.58 million (Figure 7.4). Its value in dollars can be determined by multiplying this present value by the spot exchange rate. In this instance, the correct rate to use is the spot bid rate of $1.60 per pound, which yields a dollar net present value of $112.93 million.

When calculated as shown above, discount rates for cross-border projects reflect the time value of money, the non-diversifiable risk surrounding the expected cash flows, the tax advantages associated with the use of debt to fund the project, and market-wide views about the risk and return on the foreign currency. How should foreign expropriation risk, inflation risk, and other country level risks be factored into the analysis? As we indicated earlier, managers often believe that risks such as these must be reflected in the discount rate by adding an additional risk premium to the project's estimated cost of capital. Whether or not such a procedure is valid depends on the assumptions one is willing to make about the risks in question. Specifically, if the risks of concern are non-diversifiable risks that are not adequately captured in the cross-border project's beta, then adding a premium to the discount rate is in order. However, if the risks are largely diversifiable, or if they are adequately captured in the project's beta, then it would be inappropriate to penalise the project by adding an additional risk premium to the discount rate.

As a practical matter, even if the project's beta does not reflect all non-diversifiable risks adjusting the discount rate by adding a premium can often introduce errors into the analysis that may do more to distort than clarify the true value of the project. The chief problem here is determining the correct size of the premium to be added. Too frequently managers arbitrarily add an all-purpose adjustment factor (e.g. 5 per cent) without careful regard for the true nature and extent of the risks involved. If the impact of special cross-border risks on the discount rate cannot be measured fairly accurately, it is generally advisable to search for a means of reflecting them in cash flow forecasts rather than the discount rate. The virtue of doing so is that hidden assumptions about the special risks can be made explicit and different assumptions can be tested in sensitivity analysis.

Adjustments to cash flows are often possible for non-diversifiable risks. Insurance against certain types of expropriation risk and the risk of currency inconvertibility, for example, can be purchased from Lloyd's of London, or various other national export-import banks. The premiums for this insurance can be deducted from future cash flows as a means of avoiding *ad hoc* adjustments to discount rates.

A further virtue of this approach is that the timing of exposure to, say, expropriation risk may be reflected more accurately. It may be the case, for example, that the risk of expropriation of a large new project will be greatest soon after the project has been completed and all necessary financing is in place. Increasing the discount rate to reflect expropriation risk assumes implicitly that the risk of expropriation remains constant over time. Adjusting expected cash flows by charging them with premiums for expropriation risk insurance in only those years in which the risk seems substantial may better reflect the political and economic realities impinging on the project. As indicated in Chapter 3, scenario analysis is an appropriate technique for handling specific risks, such as expropriation and other forms of political risk.

Special risks have been ignored in the case of the US group's expansion in the UK and it is assumed that country and inflation risks are low in this case.

Method 2: Discounting foreign currency cash flows converted to home currency

The second method for valuing foreign currency free cash flows involves the conversion of foreign currency amounts into home currency and the subsequent discounting of the converted cash flows at the home currency discount rate. This approach can be particularly useful if:

○ a foreign investment's home-currency value is likely to be particularly sensitive to exchange rates and managers wish to engage in sensitivity analysis with respect to exchange rate changes; or

○ future rates of exchange are, for some reason, easier to determine than a foreign currency WACC.

The same value is obtained using Method 2 as shown in Figure 7.5. The interest differential has again been used, but this time to generate the exchange rates used to convert expected foreign currency cash flows into domestic currency. Relying once again on government bond yields obtained from Figure 7.3, the factor for determining the annual change in the dollar sterling exchange rate is: $(1.065 \div 1.07) = 0.9953$. Thus, at the end of year one, the spot exchange rate is expected to be $(\$1.60/£) \times (0.9953) = \$1.5925/£$. In year two, it is expected to decline to $(\$1.60/£) \times (0.9953)^2 = 1.5850$, and so on until it reaches $\$1.5628/£$ at the end of year five.

Figure 7.5: Discounting foreign currency cash flows converted to home currency

Year	0	1	2	3	4	5	Terminal
Free cash flow £m	−56.00	10.40	8.90	9.73	10.94	10.43	12.23
Exchange rate	1.6000	1.5925	1.5850	1.5775	1.5701	1.5628	1.5628
Free cash flow $m	−89.60	16.56	14.11	15.35	17.18	16.30	211.20 *
Discount factor US (8.54%)	1.000	0.921	0.849	0.782	0.720	0.664	0.664
Present value $m	−89.60	15.25	11.98	12.00	12.37	10.82	140.24
NPV $m	113.06						

Other methods for making such conversions were also considered earlier in this chapter. For example, one might assume that the currency will change to offset the expected inflation differential between the two countries. That is, one might assume that relative PPP holds. The use of the expected inflation rates in Figure 7.3 in the application of the purchasing power parity condition yields $0.9952 = (1.03 \div 1.035)$ as the annual factor by which the spot exchange rate can be expected to change. Note that this is virtually identical to the factor obtained by applying covered interest parity. This result arises because the real risk free interest rate happens to be virtually identical in both countries at $(1.065 \div 1.03) − 1 = 0.0340$ in the case of the dollar, and $(1.07 \div 1.035) − 1 = 0.0338$ in the case of the pound.

Quoted inter-bank forward exchange rates may also be used to convert foreign currency cash flows by covered interest parity; forward rates give the same future exchange rates as do interest differentials. A common problem with using forward rates, however, is that reliable quotes for many currencies are seldom available for more than a couple of years into the future. Furthermore, very wide spreads on long-dated forward contracts may exist.

---

* Terminal Value calculation = £12.23 ÷ 0.0905 x 1.5628 = £211.20 million.

In principle, it is possible to use any independent set of exchange rates for conversion rates. For example, the impact of a real depreciation of the pound against the dollar could be modelled in the example used here by assuming the dollar-sterling exchange rate declines by a factor less than 0.9953. This would mean that the pound was expected to depreciate at a rate faster than that justified by inflation differences alone. Alternatively, an isolated exchange rate shock in one year, followed by parity movements in subsequent years, could also be modelled. Note, however, that while such scenario-based exchange rate paths may be useful for understanding risk, they must be used with caution for measuring its value. When measuring value, it is advisable to take advantage of the discipline offered by market-based prices (i.e. interest rates, forward rates, etc.) rather than allow value to be built solely on subjective guesses about future exchange rates.

Once expected foreign currency cash flows have been converted to home currency, it is then a relatively straightforward matter to discount these flows to the present using the home currency WACC of 8.54 per cent (see Method 1). The net present value of the project's free cash flow converted to dollars is estimated at $113.06 million (Figure 7.5).

Note that the two values obtained using Method 1 and Method 2 are virtually the same. This is because the only difference between the two methods is the means by which the expected rate of change and, the risk of the foreign currency are captured in the analysis. In Method 2, these currency factors were captured directly in exchange rates forecasted by interest differentials. In Method 1, they were captured in the estimated cost of capital, using the same interest differentials. See Figure 7.6 for a comparison.

Figure 7.6: Summary of foreign currency methods

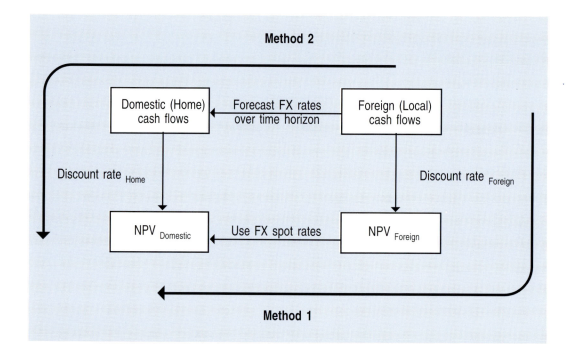

	Key Issue	Suggested Solution
Method 1	Forecasting future exchange rates over time horizon of cash flows	Apply the law of one price, i.e. use Purchasing Power Parity
Method 2	Estimating a foreign discount rate	Apply the arbitrage principle

Valuation in Parts or Adjusted Present Value (APV)

Discounting total free cash flows with WACC is a commonly used valuation technique. However, it can be problematic in many situations, particularly when dealing with some cross-border investments. The standard application of WACC is not reliable when:

○ the capital structures are expected to change over time;
○ high levels of inflation prevail or are expected;
○ subsidised sources of local financing are provided;
○ special benefits or costs related to specific methods of financing are allowed.

Also, the more complex an investment becomes, the better it is to decompose its cash flows into discrete elements, value each separately, and then invoke the principle of value additivity to produce a single estimate of value. To distinguish it from other conventional methods, this technique is often called 'valuation in parts' or 'adjusted present value'.

Valuation in parts can be represented as follows:

Total Value = Base case value + Value of all financing side effects

The first component, the base case value, measures the investment's intrinsic worth to all its capital providers as though the investment was entirely financed by equity. In effect, it is the investment's free cash flows (the same cash flows as would be used when discounting by WACC) discounted by the all-equity cost of capital.

The second component, the present value of financial costs and benefits, can also be broken down into two or more elements such as the present value of tax shields and the value of financial subsidies.

Figure 7.7 : Adjusted present value for Santos plc

Free Cash Flow Statement	1997 £m	1998 £m	1999 £m	2000 £m	2001 £m	2002 £m	Beyond £m
Free Cash Flow	12.39	15.55	15.31	14.73	13.74	12.28	30.47
Discount factor (13.45%)		0.881	0.777	0.685	0.604	0.532	
Present value		13.70	11.90	10.09	8.30	6.53	
Cumulative present value		13.70	25.60	35.69	43.99	50.52	
Value from planning period	50.52						
+ Terminal value	120.52						
Business value (A)	171.04						

Interest tax effect cash flows							
Tax shield, i.e. interest payment x tax rate *		2.38	2.46	2.60	2.85	3.20	3.00
Discount factor (12.00%)		0.893	0.797	0.712	0.636	0.567	
Present value		2.13	1.96	1.85	1.81	1.81	
Cumulative present value		2.13	4.09	5.94	7.75	9.56	
Value from planning period	9.56						
+ Terminal value	14.18						
Present value of interest tax shields (B)	23.74						

Total business value (A + B)	194.78
+ Marketable securities	0.0
Corporate value	194.78
− Market value of debt	70.92
Strategic value (£m)	123.86
Number of shares (m)	106
Strategic value per share (£)	**1.17**

---

* From Figure 2.7, 1998 Interest Paid = £7.94 million. Therefore, Tax Shield = £7.94 million x 0.3 = £2.38 million. The figure of £3.0 million for the continuing period has been taken from a spreadsheet.

Base case value

The base case value requires the calculation of an ungeared cost of equity. This calculation uses the following formula to adjust the cost of equity based on published data [125]:

$$K_e(U) = \frac{K_e(G) + [K_d(1 - T_c)(D/E)]}{1 + [(1 - T_c)(D/E)]}$$

Where,

- $K_e(U)$ = cost of ungeared equity;
- $K_e(G)$ = cost of geared equity;
- K_d = cost of debt;
- T_c = marginal rate of corporation tax;
- D = market value of debt;
- E = market value of equity.

In terms of the Santos plc example, the all equity cost of capital is:

$$K_e(U) = \frac{14.03 + [8.4 \times (70.92 \div 125.33)]}{1 + [(1 - 0.3) \times (70.92 \div 125.33)]}$$

$$= 13.45\%$$

In calculating the terminal value, the assumption is that there is no growth in the free cash flows in the continuing period. This means that a perpetuity calculation can be applied. For Santos plc (see Figure 7.6), the free cash flow for the period beyond 2002 is £30.47 million which, assuming a simple perpetuity calculation and an ungeared cost of equity of 13.45 per cent, produces a terminal value of £120.52 million (£30.47m ÷ 0.1345 x 0.532).

Valuing all financing side effects

Of the several possible financing side effects for Santos plc, only the benefit of the interest tax shields will be considered. These tax shields arise as a result of the deductibility of interest payments against corporation tax (versus the non-deductibility of dividend payments). Given the capital structure estimated for Santos plc, the interest deduction will reduce taxable profits by the amount of interest. This means that it will reduce the tax bill by the amount of interest times the tax rate. Tax shields, like any other future cash flow, should be discounted at an appropriate risk adjusted rate, i.e. a rate that reflects its riskiness. There is no consensus on how risky tax shields are. A common expedient is to use the pre-tax cost of debt as a discount rate, on the basis that tax shields are about as uncertain as principal and interest payments [126].

In calculating the terminal value of the tax shields it will be assumed that for the period beyond 2002 the gearing remains constant and there is the benefit of an interest tax shield in perpetuity. So, a simple perpetuity calculation produces a terminal value of £14.18 million (£3m ÷ 0.12 x 0.567).

The slight difference in strategic value per share of £0.01 produced by the 'valuation in parts' (£1.17) compared to discounting free cash flows at the WACC (£1.18), arises from a number of sources. First, not all the financing side effects have been taken account of in the valuation in parts. Second, the formula for calculating the ungeared cost of equity assumes that there is no growth in the free cash flows and that the capital structure is constant. As regards this latter point, if the capital structure is expected to change dramatically, a 'valuation in parts' will produce a more representative value for Santos plc [127].

Summary checklist

- Despite the recent moves towards increased international standardisation, the major limitations of accounting data will not disappear overnight. However, cash is the same regardless of the accounting standards used within a country; care is required when accounting data are used to calculate cash flow. Invariably this cash flow figure can only be a surrogate for the real cash flow.

- Not all countries have an open and transparent financial reporting regime that enables accurate data to be obtained. There is a need to recognise data limitations (GIGO problem – garbage in garbage out) and the impact this may have on a valuation.

- The separation of risk into its specific and market-related components is important and powerful in undertaking cross-border valuations, particularly where emerging market conditions prevail. This involves factoring specific risks into a valuation through alternative cash flow scenarios, while building market-related risk into the discount rate.

- Determining the cost of capital to use in emerging market and cross-border valuations is a difficult issue. Use of the arbitrage principle together with the international Fisher effect so that a cost of capital can be 'benchmarked' against that for a developed country, like the USA, is a useful starting point.

- Inflation pressures in valuations can be dealt with by forecasting cash flows in real terms and discounting by a real discount rate. Alternatively, it is possible to convert all local currency cash flows to a stable currency and then discount at a cost of capital in the stable currency.

- As regards dealing with different currencies, two choices are available. First, discount foreign cash flows at a foreign cost of capital and then convert the resultant valuation at the spot rate into home valuation or, second, convert all foreign cash flows into home cash flows using forward exchange rates, and discount these domestic cash flows at the domestic cost of capital.

- In situations where there are multiple sources of different cash flows that contribute to the valuation, value each part separately and sum these parts to arrive at the value of the whole.

Concluding remarks

Emerging market and cross-border situations represent real challenges, particularly in the context of the Asian currency crisis, which is arguably the product of market sentiment rather than fundamentals. In both good and bad times there is the need to accept that valuation in such circumstances is as much an art as a science. There is no complete and perfect analytical framework or tool-kit that can be used to provide 'the answer'.

In such markets, besides problems of volatility caused by speculation, problems of data availability or integrity often exist. In such circumstances, the approaches that have been reviewed in this chapter have been found to be useful. In particular they are useful in forcing key issues, relating to both the financial aspects of the valuation and commercial aspects surrounding the business decision at hand to be reviewed and discussed.

Chapter 8: Mergers, Acquisitions and Joint Ventures

... shareholders might sell out to any bidder prepared to take advantage of the further weakness in Redland's shares, which have under performed the market by 80 per cent in the last six years.

Financial Times, 3 October 1997, p. 21 [128].

Lafarge in hostile £1.7bn bid for Redland...

Lafarge of France, the world's second largest cement manufacturer, yesterday launched a £1.67bn hostile bid for Redland, the beleaguered UK tiles and aggregates company...

The 320p per share offer which Redland advised its shareholders to reject, comes after six years in which Redland's shares have lagged behind the market by 75 per cent...

The company's share price surged 31 per cent to 336.5p on hopes that a higher offer might emerge either from Lafarge or a rival bidder. Lafarge shares fell FFr3.2 to FFr430.1.

Financial Times, 14 October 1997, p. 1. [129].

Lafarge swoops on Redland...

Lafarge, the French building materials group, swooped into the market yesterday to buy 29.9 per cent of Redland, hours after securing its UK rival's agreement for a £1.8bn takeover.

The purchases were made just hours after Redland directors agreed to accept an increase in Lafarge's offer from 320p to 345p a share.'

Financial Times, 27 November 1997, p. 22. [130].

Chapter preview

- Why target shareholders are often most likely to gain from a merger or acquisition by way of financial returns.
- How to apply the Strategic Value Analysis framework to acquisition opportunities to assess the potential sources of benefit to the acquirer.
- How to apply the Strategic Value Analysis framework to joint venture opportunities to assess the potential sources of benefit to the different parties involved.
- How to structure the potential sources of benefit into those gained from operational changes, changes in the financial structure, and tax benefits.
- How options thinking can assist in evaluating joint venture opportunities.

Introduction

The challenge for the board of directors in a publicly quoted company is not only to ensure that the goods produced and/or the services provided satisfy the requirements of the market, but also to satisfy the other stakeholders of the business. For publicly quoted companies there is a market for corporate control which means that the share price is a key consideration and directors have to ensure value is provided. A failure to provide value to the shareholders may result in a loss of control by the board and a drastic change in the management of the business as it stands.

It is important to realise that there is no single view of value. The value of a business is what someone is prepared to pay for it, and unless their intention is to liquidate it and sell off the assets, its value will relate to what a potential acquirer is able to do with it. The value of the Rover car company to BMW was undoubtedly different to the view of value as part of British Aerospace. A means is required of evaluating any advantages (synergies) potentially available from combining two businesses.

In this chapter how the analysis of strategic value can be used to value a company's shares before and after an acquisition will be reviewed, with a view to trying to identify the existence of any substantial value gap between different perceptions based on the dynamics of business activities. How a large complex business with multiple divisions can be valued in principle using strategic value analysis, where the information about the detail of its activities is very limited, will also be illustrated.

Let us be quite clear at the outset that what follows is based on publicly available information which we have shown to be limited in its comprehensiveness. This means that any valuation might differ substantially from that based on expert knowledge of specific business segments, and information known to the company and not in the public domain.

When undertaking a valuation one should recognise that not only would the likely values of each value driver change over time, but also the composition and breakdown of each. For example, over the course of time the range of products or services produced or provided by a business are likely to change, and it is, therefore, desirable to disaggregate the sales growth rate to reflect this. Similarly, over the course of time the cost of capital may change to reflect the different expectations of the providers of funds.

The starting point in valuing a company is available published information such as the contents of its annual report and accounts, which can be used to obtain an historical picture of past value drivers. This historical picture can then be used as an important base from which to make future projections. This approach was adopted in producing the case study covered in this chapter which was developed around events in December 1992 to January 1993 and which lead to the acquisition of the Evode Group by Laporte. The case provides with an opportunity to understand some important issues surrounding the acquisition, and to view the acquisition from the seller's and buyer's perspective.

Returns to shareholders

Returns to shareholders can be looked at from both a short-term and a long-term perspective. Those UK studies which have analysed the short window surrounding a bid have shown the target shareholders to be the overwhelming winners, unlike the bidder shareholders who either lose or break even [131, 132, 133].

The evidence on long-term performance is typically viewed from the perspective of the acquirer because target companies are most often de-listed. One study found negative returns to UK bidders of around 10 per cent over the two years post-take-over [134]. Other UK studies, summarised in Figure 8.1, support this result.

Figure 8.1: Post-merger performance of UK acquirers

Study	%
Firth (1980) - 434 acquirers	0.0
Franks and Harris (1989) - 1,048 acquirers	-12.6
Limmack (1991) - 448 acquirers	-4.5
Sudarsanam et al. (1993) - 171 share offers	-2.0

US-based research findings are broadly consistent with these observations. For example, one study showed that the shareholders of an acquiring company 'suffer a statistically significant wealth loss of about 10 per cent over the five years following the merger completion' [135]. Its results suggest that acquirers do pay too much for the company they are purchasing. That companies may pay too much has been supported by a survey of the largest companies in Belgium, France, Germany, Italy, Spain, Sweden, Switzerland, UK and USA, which was undertaken in Autumn 1994 [136]. It found that companies in all countries with the notable exception of the USA, by their own assessment, overpaid for their acquisitions in over 20 per cent of the cases. This survey concluded that the fact companies overpay was not the only concern, rather that the potential for overpaying was not considered to be a problem.

On a related note, it may not be surprising that shareholders of acquiring companies suffer a loss of wealth. A study undertaken in 1997 found that companies tend to regard their merger and acquisition transactions as being successful, even though more than half were found to have no formal post-transaction review policy [137].

Shareholder Value (SV) in merger and acquisition analysis

While the evidence suggests that only target shareholders gain, it does not mean that acquisitions do not rest on sound value creation logic. The result of an acquisition may be increased cash flows for the newly combined business, as compared to the sum of the cash flows of the two pre-acquisition firms. However, if the acquiring company shareholders are overgenerous to target shareholders they may see none of the benefit.

A useful example of the application of a free cash flow approach like Strategic Value Analysis for evaluating an acquisition was provided by the Glaxo-Wellcome take-over. In a report by James Capel, analysts estimated a base case value for Glaxo with Wellcome of approximately 575p per share pre-acquisition, compared to Glaxo's existing share price of 732p [138].

The value of a company can be shown to depend on the perspective taken. The same company in the hands of another owner may be able to create substantially more value. The value to be created can be estimated using the following framework [139]:

| Value Created | = | Value of Combined Companies | − | Stand Alone Value of Acquirer | + | Stand Alone Value of Target |

The application of this framework involves valuing the acquired and target companies on a stand alone basis and then comparing the sum of the two values obtained with their estimated value as a combined entity, making due allowance for all potential synergistic benefits. To be effective, such valuations require the identification of the key value drivers so that the potential sources of benefit can be understood and analysed. Unfortunately, the research from the 1997 survey introduced previously revealed that 32 per cent of the respondents were unaware of which key performance measures financial markets use to value their organisation's shares [140].

One important technique that can be used to understand the various perspectives and sources of benefits is value mapping. Such value mapping is illustrated in Figure 8.2 [141], where the sources of synergies resulting from an acquisition were 'mapped' in conjunction with the value to acquirer and target shareholders.

Figure 8.2: Value mapping synergies

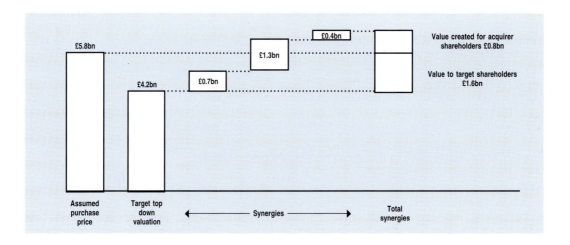

This type of analysis also gives some indication of the maximum price to pay. Clearly, the name of the game from the acquirer's perspective is to pay less than the value created, otherwise value to the acquirer's shareholders will be destroyed *.

---

* For a review of the use of valuation techniques and merger and acquisition practices, see Mills, R. W. et al., 'The use of Shareholder Value Analysis in acquisition and divestment decisions by large UK companies', Henley Management College Working Paper, 1997.

The Evode Group

Background and the sellers' perspective

In 1993, the Chairman of the Evode Group, Mr Andrew Simon, faced the prospect of having to mount a credible defence of his company against a hostile bid from the mini conglomerate Wassall. The Evode Group was a small multi-national organisation that had experienced considerable growth since the second half of the 1980's through acquisition. For example, its turnover grew from £95.8 million in 1987 to £279 million in 1991. Evode's businesses were broadly grouped in the speciality and industrial chemicals sector, and organised in five divisions:

- Adhesives and sealants;
- Industrial coatings;
- Polymer compounds;
- Plastics;
- Footwear materials and components (Chamberlain Phipps).

The Evode Group had been in some difficulty since it had announced the 1991 results at the beginning of the previous year. It had reported a turnover performance, down 6 per cent from 1990 and profit before tax down 52 per cent to £7.3 million (£15.2 million 1990) which after tax, extraordinary items and dividends payments, resulted in a loss of £1.8 million.

Evode's poor position had resulted from a number of factors:

- over exposure to the recession – white goods and construction sectors in the UK being badly affected;
- its international markets, primarily the USA and EC, were affected by the world-wide economic down turn;
- overpaying for the acquisition of Chamberlain Phipps in 1989;
- the burden created by a high level of fixed payment capital to finance the acquisition;
- poor management, which saw reasonably high gross margins reduced to an average operating margin of around 2 per cent on 1991 figures.

All this left Evode's management with little credibility. Evode's share price had slumped to a low of 43p in August 1992 but was beginning to climb again following successful rationalisation, cost cutting and marketing initiatives.

Valuation from target's perspective

This view of the company's share price can be compared alongside a valuation undertaken using strategic value analysis based on published data shown in Figure 8.3.

Figure 8.3: Strategic value of Evode's cash flows

	1992 £m	1993 £m	1994 £m	1995 £m	1996 £m	1997 £m	Beyond £m
Sales	239.90	241.34	243.27	249.35	258.08	267.63	267.63
Operating profit		20.03	23.60	23.69	24.52	25.42	25.42
− Cash taxes (33%)		6.61	7.79	7.82	8.09	8.39	8.39
+ Depreciation		7.10	7.50	7.90	8.40	8.90	9.50
Operating cash flow		20.52	23.31	23.77	24.83	25.93	26.53
− RFCI		5.00	5.50	6.10	7.30	8.70	9.50
− IFCI *		0	0	0	0	0	0
− WCI †		0.32	0.42	1.34	1.92	2.10	0
= Free cash flow		15.20	17.39	16.33	15.61	15.13	17.03
× Discount factor ‡		0.895	0.801	0.716	0.641	0.574	
Present value of free cash flows		13.60	13.93	11.69	10.01	8.68	
Cumulative present value of free cash flows		13.60	27.53	39.22	49.23	57.91	
+ Present value of residual value §						83.12	
Corporate value						141.03	
− Market value of debt and preference shares						107.51	
Strategic value						33.52	
Strategic value per share (divided by 72.71m)						£0.46	

Figure 8.4: Estimation of Evode's cost of capital pre-acquisition

Beta (B)	1.53	
Equity risk premium (ERP)	4	%
Risk free rate pre-tax (Rf)	9.26	%
Cost of equity $K_e = Rf + (B \times ERP)$	15.38	%
Cost of debt	8.14	%
Cost of preference shares	11.06	%
Weighted Average Cost of Capital (WACC)	11.76	%

---

* To calculate the incremental fixed capital investment, multiply the forecast percentage (see Figure 8.5) by incremental sales. Replacement fixed capital is required to cover the cost of maintaining the existing plant and equipment.

† To calculate the working capital investment, multiply the forecast percentage (see Figure 8.5) by incremental sales.

‡ See Figure 8.4.

§ To calculate the residual value, take the residual period free cash flow (i.e. where there is no sales growth) and divide by the cost of capital. Then use the discount factor for 1997 to calculate the present value of the residual value (17.03 ÷ 0.1176 x 0.574).

Figure 8.5: Forecast percentages

Year	1993	1994	1995	1996	1997
Sales growth (%)	0.6	0.8	2.5	3.5	3.7
Operating profit margin (%)	8.3	9.7	9.5	9.5	9.5
IFCI (%)	0	0	0	0	0
WCI (%)	22	22	22	22	22

Other than the cost of capital, the following value drivers were used in estimating the shareholder value shown in Figure 8.3: sales growth; operating profit margin; IFCI and WCI. They were calculated from information which has been summarised in Figure 8.6.

Figure 8.6: Summary of commentaries relating to value drivers

Sales Growth Forecast – 1992 figures suggests some signs of the recession lifting and in particular strong growth in the North American polymer compound sector. In general sales growth will tend to be slow to flat until the recession ends and even then the effect may be lagged until core markets themselves grow. In 1992, Evode divested its footwear components business (Chamberlain Phipps Division) thus reducing its UK originated turnover by £31.6 million.

Operating Profit Margin Forecast – average margins had improved to 5.7 per cent in 1992 results. Divisional analysis suggests that the polymer business already has margins in double figures and adhesives and sealants have high gross margins, which are being eroded. So Evode's turnaround strategy must seek to achieve a target industry average of 10-12 per cent medium term. In the industrial coatings division, Evode will be forced to keep margins low by the intense competition and depressed state of the market.

Fixed Capital Investment Forecast – fixed capital for the next five years will be only for replacement purposes and has been estimated at £5 million, £5.5 million, £6.1 million, £7.3 million and £8.7 million, respectively. Replacement capital expenditure in the continuing period has been estimated as being £9.5 million. Depreciation over the five year period has been estimated at £7.1 million, £7.5 million, £7.9 million, £8.4 million and £8.9 million, respectively. It is assumed to equal replacement capital expenditure in the continuing period.

Working Capital Forecast – this is another area which may benefit from tighter financial controls. However, the effect of new marketing initiatives and a severe competitive environment may force Evode into looser credit policies and higher than desired stock levels to maintain a good service which would force working capital expenditure up.

Sources of value creation

The objective in undertaking strategic options like mergers and acquisitions is to add value. Of course, additional value may not result immediately and it may take time to capture. This is where an approach reliant on assessing future cash flows conveys distinct advantages over more traditional measures that focus on the shorter term. However, there will still be a major challenge to meet in ensuring that the additional value actually occurs!

How is value added from a merger or acquisition? Potential synergies may result, the benefits of which can be related to their impact on the seven value drivers of the SVA approach. For example:

1. Sales growth may improve because of being able to use the distribution channels of each organisation to sell the products of both.

2. Reductions in operating profit margins may be possible because of being able to use production facilities more efficiently.

3. Cash taxes may be saved by being able to plan the tax position of the new combined organisation. This area may be particularly beneficial for certain types of cross-border deals.

4. Fixed capital requirements may be lowered by being able to use available spare capacity for increased sales activity. There may also be an impact on replacement capital requirements, a good example of this being the decision to merge by two high street clearing banks. It may be possible to provide service to both sets of customers in the new organisation by cutting the number of branches.

5. Working capital requirements can be reduced if the two businesses have a profile of cash flows opposite in effect to one another. There may also be potential benefits arising from better debtor, creditor and stock management.

6. The planning period may be lengthened because, for example, the new larger venture increases barriers to entry.

7. The cost of capital may fall if access is obtained to cheaper sources of finance.

A second, and very important, source of value may also come from stripping out some activities/businesses. In this way the costs associated with a merger or acquisition can be substantially reduced and the real benefits drastically improved. For example, the large UK conglomerate Hanson plc, after buying Imperial Tobacco for £2.5 billion and selling off the group's Courage and Golden Wonder businesses and other relatively small businesses for £2.3 billion, is reckoned to have retained businesses worth about £1.4 billion.

What makes mergers and acquisitions particularly challenging is that obtaining good quality, robust financial information may be very difficult for an acquirer. On the other hand, for the organisation being acquired, a major difficulty may arise in understanding the basis for the value placed on the organisation by an outsider whose rationale might be based on a totally different view of its future potential.

The potential acquirer's perspective: Wassall's bid

On 20 November Wassall launched a hostile bid for Evode with an offer of 80p per share (£58.2 million). Wassall was run by three ex-Hanson men under the chairman Chris Miller, and recently had successfully acquired two other companies in the sealants and adhesives sector. Wassall saw Evode as a basically sound organisation, with strong market shares in UK adhesives and coatings and US plastics, which would benefit from both being unhampered by gearing and by the introduction of a strong management team.

Analysts had forecast profits of £8.9 million and earnings of 3.2p for Evode in 1992 and this confirmed Wassall's view that the company would be in a poor position to fund new capital expenditure, meet redemption obligations, repay bank debt and pay preference and ordinary dividends. In contrast its offer valued Evode at more than 25 times earnings and left Andrew Simon with little room to mount his defence. (On the announcement of the offer, Evode's shares jumped to 91p.).

In his defence document, presented to shareholders on 4 January 1993, Mr Simon claimed that Evode was back on the mend and announced a 40 per cent rise in pre-tax profits to £10.2 million for 1992. However, many feared the worst as the document omitted to include a profit forecast for the current year. Evode's shares rose to 103p and Wassall announced that it was not willing to overpay for any acquisition. As regards views about such a bid one analyst commented:

> *A range of 100p (realistic) to 120p (maximum) would appear to be the right ball park.*

This price was determined by analysing comparable peer group companies using gross cash flow multiples (share price divided by operating profit plus depreciation, and interest received), see Figure 8.7.

Cash flow multiples for Evode's peers in the sector were estimated as ranging from 5.4 to 9.4 with a mean of 7.0 (see Figure 8.7). Given its performance it would be difficult to value Evode at the higher end of that range, particularly when its gearing was taken into consideration. As a consequence, the mean multiple was used to produce the estimated valuation of Evode's share price (shown in Figure 8.8), in which non-convertible preference share capital was treated as debt. Convertible preference share capital was not treated in the same manner. Although conversion looked a long shot it could not be ruled out and an allowance was made for its conversion by way of a sinking fund to cover the potential liability of £40.7 million in nine years hence. This served to reduce operating cash flow by £4.5 million p.a.

Figure 8.7: Peer group - Gross cash flow multiples

Allied Colloids	9.4
Brent Chemicals	5.4
British Vita	5.5
BTP	7.5
Croda International	6.0
Ellis and Everard	6.5
Hickson International	5.1
Wardle Storeys	9.0
Yorkshire Chemicals	9.0
Yule Catto	6.9
Average/mean	**7.0**

Figure 8.8: Evode gross cash flow multiple valuation

	£m	Pence
Operating profit	15.6	
+ Depreciation	6.7	
+ Interest received	0.2	
− Sinking fund	4.5	
= Gross cash flow	18.0	
= Gross cash flow per share (divided by 72.71m)		24.8
× 7 multiple (a)		173.6
Bank debt	28.5	
+ Preference stock (US)	23.9	
− Allowance for 25% gearing	8.3	
= Total debt	44.1	
= Debt per share (divided by 72.71m) (b)		60.7
Valuation (a − b)		112.9

An alternative buyer's perspective: Laporte's rival bid

On 6 January, Wassall revised its bid to 95p per share and on the same day Laporte, the UK's second largest chemical group, bought 6.1 per cent of Evode's shares at 100p and announced its intention to make a bid above 100p. Laporte's announcement effectively out-manoeuvred what many thought would be Wassall's winning bid and allowed Evode to reject the 95p offer as inadequate.

Laporte's impending bid provided Evode with the opportunity of offering shareholders a good exit route. But first Laporte had to come up with a new bid price, one that Evode would be able to recommend and which would be acceptable to Laporte's investors.

Laporte's appearance was no sudden move as CEO Ken Minton had reportedly been tracking Evode for seven years, first approaching Andrew Simon in 1986 and again in January 1992 following Evode's bad results.

Laporte had a strong management team and had experience in transforming a low margin bulk operation into a speciality chemicals company. Mr Minton and his team had a reputation for ruthless cost cutting, especially in non-core businesses and had overseen the rise in Laporte's margins from 10 to 15 per cent since 1986.

Laporte had five core businesses – organic chemicals, absorbents, metals and electronic chemicals, construction chemicals, and hygiene and process chemicals. Clear potential synergies were seen between some of these businesses and Evode. In fact, Ken Minton described the adhesive and polymer businesses as a 'classic fit'. (Figure 8.9 provides an anecdotal record of Laporte's assessment of Evode's businesses).

As a result of detailed sector knowledge, it was reckoned that the management of Laporte should be able to ensure that benefits from synergies could be achieved. Furthermore, it was believed that purchasing Evode need involve no dilution of earnings in the first year following acquisition.

Laporte offered and subsequently paid 120p per share for Evode, but was not prepared to assume any additional debt and, therefore, its offer consisted mainly of paper. Laporte's shares fell 27p to 583p on announcement of the terms of the offer, having fallen 10 per cent since the announcement of its intention to bid.

Figure 8.9: Laporte's assessment of Evode's businesses

Adhesives and polymer compounds provide 'classic fit':

Ken Minton, Laporte's CEO, was reported to have claimed that Evode's two largest business sectors provided great potential for synergies from incorporation into Laporte's businesses.

Adhesives and sealants

Evode's operations have sales of £85 million from the construction and automotive sectors. Laporte already sells different adhesives to the construction sector and uses an alternative distribution network.

Polymer compounds

Laporte had no direct experience in this area. With sales of £85 million the products all involved formulating chemicals; one of Laporte's strengths and also a good fit.

The US operations were supplying high quality plastics to the food, medical and electronics sectors at good margins. The UK and Italian operations were in lower margin markets and required repositioning.

Question marks remain over other businesses:

Powder coatings

This area was outside Laporte's expertise and its potential for margin improvement limited. Therefore it would be under immediate divestment consideration.

Mr Minton said of the business, 'When I have to compete with big boys like these (ICI and Courtaulds), I start getting nervous.'

Plastic fabrication

Five operations with sales of £20 million were also less attractive to Laporte. Three operations - in the USA, UK and Italy – provided reasonable margins, but the other two businesses required a complete turnaround.

Miscellaneous

Evode's remaining businesses, of which the vinyl coatings for wallpaper accounted for the majority of £40 million sales, provided no fit at all for Laporte.

Acquisition must enhance Laporte's earning in the first year

Ken Minton was committed to immediate returns from Evode and promised to tackle their margins as his first priority. In the 1980's Mr Minton had improved Laporte's margins from 10 per cent to today's level of nearly 15 per cent.

The improvement at Evode would probably come from:

- better pricing policies;
- extending product ranges;
- reducing raw material costs;
- improved manufacturing;
- cutting overheads;
- better marketing;
- significant job losses.

Mr Minton denied that the cost of rationalisation would affect earnings. Laporte had plenty of experience of cost-cutting and there would be few environmental costs.

Value of the acquisition to Laporte

In reviewing the potential value of Evode to Laporte it is important to recognise that benefit can be derived from a number of sources. One useful classification is under three main headings: operating, financing and tax.

Operating benefits

These can be thought of in terms of what the acquirer, Laporte in this case, can do with the operations of the business that Evode has not done. One way of understanding any potential operating benefits is by reviewing the cash flow value drivers for Evode against the potential strategic fit of the two companies. For example, using the strategic value approach and sensitivity analysis on the base case shown in Figure 8.3, reveals that the business is very margin sensitive. Given Laporte's track record for margin improvement identified in Figure 8.9, significant benefit could be unleashed if similar results could be achieved from Evode. For example, margin improvement to 10 per cent, 11 per cent, 12 per cent, 14 per cent and 15 per cent for the five years of the assumed CAP, with this margin being maintained in the period beyond, results in a strategic value of £1.37 per share. However, it must be recognised that such improvement is very unlikely to be achievable in all parts of the business. In fact, given the assessment of the fit of the Evode businesses in Figure 8.9, it might well be regarded as reasonable to assume the divestment of poorly fitting businesses with the achievement of this revised margin profile on the parts remaining. If, for the sake of illustration, we assume that businesses with revenues of £80 million are sold for £80 million after tax, the resulting share price is £1.54, although this is obviously heavily dependent on the assumed disposal value.

This line of analysis could be continued to incorporate different scenarios. The advantage it conveys lies in illustrating potential from asking 'what if' questions that can be readily analysed using a spreadsheet model. However, the potential results may be very different from reality and any such speculative analysis would need to be supported by a more rigorous interrogation.

Financing benefits

Operating benefits are not the only consideration. Some acquisitions take place simply to capture the benefits of a changed capital structure, often involving the replacement of equity funding with long-term debt. As indicated in Chapter 6, a benefit of more debt is that it may lower the WACC and increase value.

However, whether this is the result will depend on the current proportion of debt. If it is perceived as being too high the result will be that attempts to drive WACC down by substituting debt for equity will fail. This is because the demands by the providers of funds to be compensated for a higher rate of return will at least offset the benefits from the substitution of debt for equity.

Tax benefits

Our preference is to review tax benefits after operating and financing benefits have been considered. Tax is very much a specialist area, which can have an important impact on a decision. However, a major problem with tax issues is that they vary from country to country and typically require specialist expertise once the operating and financing benefits have been reviewed thoroughly.

In reality, to make a full assessment of the potential of the acquisition to the acquirer it is necessary to go beyond the simple spreadsheet screening approach considered so far. Issues relating to potential operating, financing and tax benefits would be best looked at in terms of both the acquirer and the target. In its most detailed form, pursuit of this approach would involve calculating the cash flows corresponding with each business unit for both the buyer and the seller, discounting the cash flows by the relevant cost of capital for each business, and then summing the results.

As already indicated, a significant part of Evode offered little fit with Laporte and could be disposed of. If estimated cash flows from such disposal is factored in together with the consequential potential impact on the other value drivers, the result is attractive, but that is not the end of the story. When the operational restructuring opportunities to Laporte are factored in together with the potential from refinancing the Evode business, a value in excess of £2 can be obtained per Evode share. Of course, the secret as with any acquisition is in making this actually happen!

Evaluating joint ventures

In the case of a joint venture the basic procedure is the same but there will be concern that the joint venture parties will each benefit from the newly formed enterprise. This involves a second step in terms of attributing the resulting synergies. In the case of a joint venture there are therefore two steps, each of which requires estimating:

- the benefit in the form of the value that will be created by the joint venture; and
- whether the respective sharing of any value created will meet the requirements of each partner.

The primary concern in this section is with demonstrating in principle how the analysis of strategic value can be applied in evaluating a joint venture opportunity. This is quite straightforward in principle and requires the valuation of the:

- existing organisation on a stand-alone basis; and
- newly formed joint venture.

Case study - joint venture in People's Republic of China

The Chinese partner involved in this joint venture occupied a factory within a large industrial complex owned by a municipal government. The other partner was a large Hong Kong based company with multiple share listings. The factory was one of the larger producers of lubricants for the motor industry and it enjoyed a good reputation for its brand name, especially in North China. In view of the rapid growth in the automobile industry in China, the organisation was positioned to perform exceptionally well in the foreseeable years.

The factory produced two families of products. Current demand for the new but more expensive product was about 35 per cent of the total demand for lubricants, but was expected to rise to 55 per cent by the year 2001. However, as the Chinese factory was built some 20 years ago it was not designed for manufacturing this new product which enjoyed higher profit margins than the older product. There was also the added difficulty that the facilities were outdated and the production cost was no longer competitive.

In addition to the outdated equipment and poor product mix, the factory was heavily burdened by the overhead being charged by the parent organisation. The parent organisation had been experiencing financial difficulties for the past few years, mainly because of the problems of accounts receivable ('triangle debts' *) and the demand for new capital for new infrastructure projects. This situation had been getting worse, such that the factory had no alternative but to struggle along with this burden and with its existing

---

* This is a well known phenomenon in China which became more severe after the government tightened credit in 1994. Essentially the term is used to describe the situation in which a company that cannot get cash owed because of a cash flow problem with its debtor who is unable to pay its creditors.

operational structure, unless there was an injection of fresh capital from external investors. With this view in mind, a foreign partner was invited to look at the possible opportunities and serious negotiation followed the initial investigation. The potential foreign partner understood the potential of the automobile industry in China, had experience in Chinese projects, and was interested in producing auxiliary products to serve this important and growing industry.

The existing production facilities meant that there was very limited freedom to improve the product mix or increase the production volume. Using the information relating to the existing production facilities resulted in a strategic value of approximately 1.5 RMB million. This was calculated by first estimating the free cash flows for a five-year planning period using the five value cash flow drivers. The free cash flows for these five years and beyond, together with the value drivers for the first year, are summarised in Figure 8.10.

Figure 8.10: Free cash flows for the existing factory being run by the Chinese partner

Year	RMB m	1 RMB m	2 RMB m	3 RMB m	4 RMB m	5 RMB m	Beyond RMB m
Sales receipts	14.20	14.91	15.66	16.44	17.26	18.12	18.12
Operating profit		0.15	0.31	0.66	0.69	0.72	0.72
− Cash tax		0.00	0.00	0.11	0.11	0.12	0.24
Profit after tax		0.15	0.31	0.55	0.58	0.60	0.48
+ Depreciation		0.40	0.40	0.40	0.40	0.40	0.40
Operating cash flow		0.55	0.71	0.95	0.98	1.00	0.88
− RFCI		0.40	0.40	0.40	0.40	0.40	0.40
− IFCI		0.00	0.00	0.00	0.00	0.00	0.00
− WCI		0.21	0.23	0.23	0.25	0.26	0.00
Free cash flow		−0.06	0.08	0.32	0.33	0.34	0.48

Note: At this time the exchange rate was US $1 = 8.56 RMB

In determining the cost of capital to use for valuing this joint venture, the question of risk needed to be addressed carefully. The basic principle applied to risk is that the greater its magnitude, the larger will be the reward or premium required to compensate for such risk. There are alternative approaches for estimating the premium for risk in developed financial markets, none of which are particularly helpful in China. There is one additional issue associated with risk. As we have indicated on a number of occasions in earlier chapters, financial theory urges making a distinction between that risk which is market related and that which is specific to the company. While the former should be built into the estimation of the cost of capital, specific risk should be taken into account in the estimation of annual cash flows. We know that it can often be difficult to distinguish between market and specific risks. In circumstances where it is extremely difficult to use the tools and techniques of corporate finance to estimate the risk premium to include in the cost of capital estimation, our preference is to build as many risks as possible into the cash flows using a scenario approach. Such risks include political, exchange rate, sovereign and commercial risks.

Not surprisingly, estimating the cost of capital of this Chinese organisation was a challenge. In fact, a range of values was actually used in the valuation process. Here, a cost of capital of 20 per cent after tax is assumed for purposes of illustration only.

Figure 8.11 shows the calculation of the strategic value of the Chinese organisation on a stand-alone basis assuming a five-year planning period.

Figure 8.11: Chinese organisation stand-alone value calculation

Year	1 RMB m	2 RMB m	3 RMB m	4 RMB m	5 RMB m	Beyond RMB m
Free cash flow	-0.06	0.08	0.32	0.33	0.34	0.48
Discount factor (20%)	0.833	0.694	0.579	0.482	0.402	
Present value (free cash flow)	-0.05	0.06	0.19	0.16	0.14	
Cumulative present value	-0.05	0.01	0.20	0.36	0.50	
Present value of residual value					0.96	
Strategic value					**1.46**	

For the five-year planning period we have used, 1.46 RMB million is the strategic value generated; 0.50 RMB million is the result of discounting and adding the free cash flows for the five years. The remainder, which is the major part, is referred to as the residual value. This residual value, which also must be expressed in present value terms, recognises that not all value will be captured within the time period covered by the planning period. Many businesses will generate value beyond the time period in which its management may feel comfortable in forecasting. The question which typically arises is, how can any residual value be captured in a calculation? As discussed in Chapter 6, one common method is to estimate the free cash flow beyond the planning period and then to value it in present day terms. At its simplest this involves estimating the free cash flow in the period immediately beyond the end of the planning period and then valuing it as a simple perpetuity. In the case of our stand-alone valuation, the value of the free cash flow beyond five years of 0.48 RMB million is viewed as a perpetual cash flow, the value of which is found by capitalising it (0.48 ÷ 0.20) and then converting the result to a present value by discounting it. The result is 0.96 RMB milllion. In using a simple perpetuity we are assuming that beyond the planning period the organisation can only earn returns equal to its cost of capital, hence there is no additional value creation beyond the planning period. This seems consistent with the fact that the Chinese organisation wanted to form a joint venture and then close down its existing plant.

Value of the joint venture

Having estimated the value of the organisation on a stand-alone basis, the next step required an estimation of the strategic value to be created as a result of the joint venture proposal.

With additional contact and visits to the plant, the foreign investor became convinced that the factory had a reasonably strong management team and its brand name was quite valuable. More importantly, the two partners felt comfortable working with each other. With further due diligence analysis, which included a market study, the foreign investor made the following proposal for the median scenario of market demand:

- A new joint venture to be formed with the Chinese party (Party A) holding 40 per cent of the equity and the foreign party (Party B) holding the remaining 60 per cent.

- Total investment to be 32.2 RMB million of which 13.92 RMB million would be the fixed capital with the balance (18.28 RMB million) to be the working capital.

- The capital injection to be used to build a new factory with a capacity of 10,000 tons per year as compared with the 4,000 tons per year from existing operations.

- The new factory to have a product mix to reflect the demand of the market.

- The plant is to be designed to allow flexibility to change the capital injection and, hence, the scale of the plant in response to changing market demand, for which three scenarios emerged out of the market study, namely; low, median and high product mix in response to the changing customer requirements.

- The old facility to be shut down as soon as the new plant is up and running, i.e. in approximately a year's time.

Figure 8.12 shows these strategic changes for the median scenario translated into free cash flows and value terms.

Figure 8.12: Potential strategic value created by the joint venture

Year	RMB m	1 RMB m	2 RMB m	3 RMB m	4 RMB m	5 RMB m	Beyond RMB m
Sales receipts	14.20	42.60	48.14	56.81	65.33	75.13	76.63
Operating profit		5.96	6.74	10.23	11.76	13.52	13.79
– Cash tax		0.00	0.00	1.74	2.00	2.30	4.46
Profit after tax		5.96	6.74	8.49	9.76	11.22	9.33
+ Depreciation		1.00	1.00	1.00	1.00	1.00	1.00
Operating cash flow		6.96	7.74	9.49	10.76	12.22	10.33
– RFCI		1.00	1.00	1.00	1.00	1.00	1.00
– IFCI		13.92	0.00	0.00	0.00	0.00	0.00
– WCI		8.52	1.66	2.60	2.56	2.94	0.00
Free cash flow		– 16.48	5.08	5.89	7.20	8.28	9.33
Discount factor		0.833	0.64	0.579	0.484	0.402	
Present value		– 13.73	3.53	3.41	3.47	3.33	
Cumulative present value		– 13.73	– 10.20	– 6.79	– 3.32	0.01	
PV of residual value (with 2% growth)						20.83	
Strategic value						**20.84**	

In calculating the residual value we have used the perpetuity with growth method on the assumption the joint venture will be able to earn returns in excess of the cost of capital beyond the planning period; this is in contrast to the Chinese organisation. The perpetuity with growth method takes the value of the free cash flow beyond five years of 9.33 RMB million and capitalises it by the product of the discount rate less the growth rate (0.2 – 0.02). It then converts the result to a present value by discounting it. The result is 20.83 RMB million.

The results are quite impressive with a strategic value of 20.84 RMB million being generated using a five year planning period. However, nearly all the contribution now comes from the residual value element. In fact, the residual value as a proportion of the strategic value is so high that many questions should be asked about it. Is it realistic? Could it be too large, or even too small? In fact, the valuation process would certainly not stop at this point. But the illustration shows that the value of the joint venture business may well be substantially above the stand-alone value. If we believe the calculations, the value created by the joint venture is approximately 19.37 RMB million (20.83 RMB million – 1.46 RMB million).

The fact that all the value is generated beyond the selected planning period could be taken as a fundamental flaw of the approach. However, it is important to recognise that joint ventures may take a considerable time before they are ready to be judged on traditional output measures. The need for patience is underscored by a study of Fortune 500 firms that started new (wholly owned) businesses with the intent of diversifying [142].

The median start-up took seven to eight years to show a positive return on investment or positive cash flow and no ventures had positive cash flow in the first two years. In fact, many of the start-ups that turned positive early (in return on investment terms) failed to retain their profitability. Considering that joint ventures are often used in the riskiest of circumstances, the need for patience should be even greater.

Scenarios, options and strategic value

The valuation of the lubricants plant in the emerging Chinese market, for example, is unlikely to be accomplished more efficiently by using sophisticated options pricing techniques. As we indicated in Chapter 3, in these instances, the use of scenario-based cash flows combined with strategic value analysis may be more beneficial [143].

As illustrated in Chapter 3, scenarios are a powerful tool for ordering one's perceptions about alternative future environments in which today's decisions might be played out. The point of scenarios is not so much to have one scenario that 'gets it right' as to have a number of scenarios that illuminate the major forces and trends driving the system, their interrelationships, and the critical uncertainties. The value of performing this procedure is not so much the ultimate valuation number that it produces, but the insights discovered in the process of investigating the nature and existence of the opportunities available to management.

The Chinese joint venture we have described can be evaluated in terms of a number of options using scenarios and strategic value analysis. The names of these options, together with their option characteristics, are provided in Figure 8.13 [179].

Figure 8.13: Summary of the names of real options

Name of Option	Characteristics
Timing option	A call option on the project's present value, with an exercise price equal to the cost outlay.
Growth option	A call option on the future cash flows, with an exercise price equal to the cost outlay.
Shut down option	Productive assets can be viewed as a strip of call options with one option expiring each period. Each period's call option has an underlying asset equal to the period's expected revenues and an exercise price equal to production cost.
Option to alter input/output mix	Productive assets become a compounded call option embedding an option to exchange among inputs and among outputs.
Abandonment option	A 'put' option on operating cash flows with an exercise price equal to the scrap value.

Investment opportunities with the greatest value creation potential often arise at points of discontinuity caused by technological innovation, deregulation, or shifts in consumer behaviour. Investing in these opportunities is risky since potential losses could be substantial. Companies have two obvious choices in such uncertain growth situations. Either they can commit themselves to full investment and hope it pays off (high risk approach), or they can wait and re-evaluate once market trends become clearer (low risk approach) – by which time bolder competitors may have taken the lead. However, in many markets there is a third possibility, analogous to the Chinese joint venture opportunity; that of acquiring a growth option. A growth option buys a company the ability to participate in future growth without substantial risk and involves the following four steps:

1. identifying the growth option;
2. acquiring it by paying the option price;
3. nurturing it over time through development spend; and
4. realising the value of the option by paying to exercise it and, in so doing, reaping the payoff [144].

Growth options have three distinct features: they carry no obligation to make a full investment; they are considerably cheaper than full investment; and they give the buyer a preferential position over competitors from which to make a full investment without an option. A good example of this is the use of joint ventures and strategic alliances as either an entry strategy into emerging markets, or as part of a globalisation strategy. However, it must be recognised that structuring such opportunities as a growth option may be a real challenge. This is because the option of deferring full investment may be difficult to achieve in practice.

Summary checklist

○ The value created by a merger or acquisition can be estimated using the following framework:

○ Value is contingent on perspective: the acquirer's perspective and the target's perspective will differ.

○ A key imperative is to understand where any synergies are coming from and in this regard it is useful to look at them by source, i.e. operating, financing and tax.

○ The analysis of strategic value for a joint venture requires the valuation of first, the existing organisation on a standalone basis and, second, the newly formed joint venture.

○ Scenario analysis can be used to flesh out the sources of likely future value creation in the joint venture, while an option thinking perspective provides another perspective of how value could be created in the future.

○ By using a combination of Strategic Value Analysis, scenarios and options thinking, a degree of realism can be introduced into a valuation which may not be the case when DCF is used on a standalone basis. Not all the value may be captured within a DCF calculation and major benefit may be derived by adopting an options thinking perspective.

Concluding remarks

This chapter has illustrated how the principles associated with the analysis of strategic value can be applied within the context of merger and acquisition and joint venture decisions. Furthermore, the potential application of options thinking has been demonstrated, with reference to the Chinese joint venture opportunity. In general, the right to start, stop or modify a business activity at some future time is different from the right to operate it now. It may be possible to defer a specific and important decision, like whether or not to exploit an opportunity. The right to make that decision at some time in the future - that is, to do what is best when the time comes - is valuable. This is important to recognise in today's business environment, which is volatile and unpredictable because of growing market globalisation, together with exchange rate fluctuations and more rapid technology induced changes in the market place.

Irrespective of the causes of volatility, uncertainty requires managers to become more sophisticated in the ways they look at, assess and account for risk. With this in mind, thinking in terms of options provides the means by which managers can get a better understanding of available choices or possibilities that they can create. Ultimately, options approaches create flexibility which, in an uncertain world, means that greater realism can be introduced into valuations undertaken. The bottom line is that managers will increasingly have to manage in such a way as to keep their options open.

Chapter 9: Valuing New Issues and Intangible Assets

Forget p/e ratios and learn to love DCF

Anon [145]

Chapter preview

○ The use of DCF analysis in the valuation of an initial public offering (IPO), where the business is currently making a loss and a profitable position is not expected in the near future.

○ How to estimate the cost of capital for an IPO by drawing on the principles covered in Chapter 6.

○ Issues associated with estimating the terminal value of an IPO, where considerable future growth is expected beyond the planning period.

○ The importance of assessing underlying business drivers in order to develop a cash flow picture of a business.

○ How to use a number of valuation techniques to cross-check a DCF valuation.

○ The issues and challenges to be faced in valuing intangible assets.

Introduction

In Chapter 7 some of the principles involved in valuing a new issue were introduced with reference to the Malaysian infrastructure company Litrak. Concerns associated with the estimation of the cost of capital were reviewed using internal and external data. In this chapter some of these concerns will be examined further; for example, how to estimate the cost of capital by making reference to peer group companies and the need to make adjustments for the debt to equity weighting in the capital structure. The importance of looking at valuation from the perspective of more than one valuation method will also be considered. While a DCF method like strategic value may be used, it will typically be supported by other methods, such as the traditional measures reviewed in Chapter 6 within the context of the terminal value.

In this chapter, examples drawn from the telecommunications sector will be used to illustrate valuation issues associated with new issues and intangible assets. As regards new issues, the flotation valuation of Orange™, the UK mobile telecommunications service provider, will be used to illustrate how many of the issues discussed in earlier chapters were taken into consideration in valuing a business not expected to produce any serious profits until the turn of the century. These issues included; the method to adopt, the time horizon over which to undertake the analysis, and the selection of an appropriate discount rate.

One other important challenge facing many organisations concerns the valuation of intangible assets. The evaluation of intangible assets like patents, trademarks, brands, goodwill and rights of access raises some very real conceptual issues and problems. The substance of these are discussed with reference to the valuation of rights of access to telecommunications opportunities possessed by an electricity transmission company operating in the Asia Pacific region.

Orange - background

Hutchison Telecommunications entered the UK telecommunications market in 1989, beginning operations in cellular service provision. Hutchison Telecom(UK) became involved in the Personal Communications Network (PCN) business through the acquisition in July 1991 of Microtel Communications, a venture led by BAe. As part of that agreement BAe acquired a 30 per cent interest in Hutchison Telecom (UK), joining with Barclays which retained a 5 per cent interest. The brand name Orange was adopted in March 1994, one month ahead of the official launch of the service.

The high initial costs of developing the service (in excess of £1 billion per operator) had led to considerable rationalisation in the early years. Two of the original licencees, Unitel and Mercury PCN initially undertook to share infrastructure development and subsequently merged to form Mercury One2One. The result was the emergence of two main UK PCN providers – Orange and Mercury One2One. These two faced head on competition from the two most well established mobile telecommunications service providers, Vodafone and Cellnet.

PCN strategy of Orange

While they both held PCN licenses, the approaches adopted by One2One and Orange in developing their services had little in common. One2One had exploited the mass market opportunities afforded by PCN technology to the full. As a predominately regional service offering free local off-peak calls, it differed substantially from Orange's service which aimed at coverage and selling its service on a value for money basis.

Despite launching in April 1994, some eight months later than One2One, Orange experienced a much faster monthly rate of growth. Its initial strategy was to build a very strong brand and sell it into an established market. Many of its customers were users of other mobile phone services. The knowledge that the long established operators made good margins provided Orange with an opportunity to develop a value for money service by using packaged tariffs that give a certain number of 'free minutes' for a given monthly fee per second billing and a low priced messaging service.

In competing on a head to head basis with the cellular providers, Orange had to ensure extensive geographic coverage. It adopted an aggressive strategy when launched on 28 April 1994, starting with an estimated 50 per cent population coverage. By October 1995 Orange had achieved 85 per cent of hand portable coverage.

The Orange approach was to sell direct to the customer rather than relying on an intermediate layer of service providers. This enabled the company to build close relationships with its customers and deliver an end-to-end service where all elements of the service could be closely controlled.

Opportunities in the market

Cellular telephony world-wide has been characterised by accelerating rates of growth. Cheaper handsets, an increasing range of tariffs and the introduction of digital technology bringing new services and greater capacity, have been recognised as driving growth. In fact, in most other areas of the electronics industry the employment of digital technology has almost invariably replaced analogue technology. It is only through using digital technology that cellular networks were feasible in the first case.

Cellnet and Vodafone had both constructed networks which support digital handsets but the bulk of their customers remained on their older analogue system. Orange and One2One's systems were entirely digital from the outset.

The degree to which digital technology increases the capacity compared with analogue is not a straightforward issue. However, in practice a capacity increase of between two to four times has been reckoned to have been achieved and it is believed that further significant advances will be possible with the introduction of new speech compression techniques. Ultimately the handling of the traffic volumes expected to be generated within the UK market will require the majority of the scarce frequency resource to be used with digital technology. As an indication of expected traffic some manufacturers have put the eventual penetration of mobile phones at 1.2 per person. The rationale behind such forecasts is, first, that buying the service and the handset need not be linked. For example, one view is that handsets may well be as cheap as digital watches in due course. Second, the poor track record in forecasting service requirements historically has fuelled bullish forecasts. Within the UK, historical market growth forecasts for the mobile industry have been substantially underestimated. In the advertising campaign which preceded the award of the two mobile licenses for the UK market in 1983, Cellnet's market forecast was for 100,000 subscribers while Vodafone's estimate was 250,000 for the total market! Today, the UK cellular base consists of about six million subscribers and forecasts for the market to the year 2001 range from 10 million to 18 million.

Capacity is a big issue in understanding the dynamics of the cellular business and the way in which the market will evolve. Ultimately, the company with the most capacity, which can accommodate the largest number of subscribers at given levels of usage and can offer low incremental costs and hence low tariffs will benefit most. However, because of capacity issues, cellular operators must manage the transition of high usage subscribers from the fully loaded and relatively inefficient analogue system to the under utilised digital system. Migration can be encouraged by the cellular operators through efforts to reduce the barriers to moving networks. This requires that the cellular operators and their service providers subsidise digital handset prices down close to the level of analogue handsets. This is a further cost to operators to re-win customers already acquired at some expense on the analogue network. The haste to migrate subscribers is driven by more than just the capacity problems. Both Vodafone and Cellnet have long been well aware that they must secure their highest spending users onto the digital system before either Orange or One2One present a sufficiently attractive alternative.

In fact, 'churn' and 'migration' represent major opportunities for the PCN operators. Churn can be defined as the number of customers disconnecting in a period, as a percentage of the average number of subscribers on the network during the period in question. Migration represents the movement by subscribers from one service provider to another. Churn has traditionally run at levels between 20 per cent and 30 per cent in the UK market, which implies that a customer's contract, on average, lasts for four years. In theory this means that the cellular operators have to re-win their own customers all over again and leaves them prey to the PCN operators. On a forecast of 12 million subscribers, by the end of the decade the market will grow by six million.

The cellular phone is reckoned to be the first mass-market consumer product where the bulk of the costs of ownership fall after the point at which purchase is made. While this has brought a surge of growth it has not been without its problems. As the barriers to entry have dropped, many customers have been sucked into taking service without realising the on going costs. This is particularly true of subscribers to the analogue service where substantial price reductions from the equipment manufacturers together with ongoing bonus payments from the operators have enabled the street price of handsets to fall virtually to zero. In addition, connection fees have been waived and a variety of free accessories have been included.

Without doubt the increase in the rate of growth on digital networks during 1995 and 1996 is in large part due to the scarcity of frequencies and its implications for capacity. Ultimately, handling the traffic volumes that are expected to be generated within the UK market will require the majority of the scarce frequency resource to be used with digital technology. The emergence of the PCN operators and increasing volumes of digital handsets being produced has driven down terminal prices in the retail market. This has been reflected in statistics which have shown digital taking an increasing share of the market. For example, from December 1995 to February 1996 digital connections accounted for 65 per cent of net new connections. By all accounts, Orange and One2One took a disproportionate share of these new subscribers.

The valuation

The interest in the valuation of Orange was the determination of the Initial Public Offer price for the company which sought to raise funding from a full UK listing. In keeping with requirements, an Offer for Sale document was produced and revealed a loss making company with few assets and little other than 'blue sky' forecasts with which to undertake a valuation. A number of approaches were used to value Orange which relied on:

- Discounted Cash Flow (DCF) analysis, whereby future free cash flows are discounted by the Weighted Average Cost of Capital (WACC) to arrive at an enterprise (sometimes known as business) value.

- Market Relative Analysis (MRA), whereby future earnings are estimated for the business to be valued and are related to the market multiples for a peer group set of companies. Two MRA methods were used: the multiple of EBITDA (Earnings Before Interest, Tax, Depreciation and Amortisation) and the multiple of PER (Price Earnings Ratio).

The 'blue sky' nature of the business made some form of DCF analysis necessary. However, in keeping with new issues practice, reliance on this method alone could not be supported because at the end of the day there is the need to refer the pricing to current market conditions, for which MRA methods are absolutely essential.

DCF valuation

Many analysts estimated the numbers of subscribers, churn ratios, call volumes and a variety of costs up to the year 2005 in order to make their cash flow forecasts. For example, one group of analysts used the following information to generate the free cash flow forecasts as illustrated in Figure 9.1:

Churn: assume 15 per cent ongoing.

Revenues per subscriber: 51 per cent of Orange subscribers were on the Talk 15 package; 42 per cent on Talk 60, and 7 per cent on the higher tariffs. In all cases, billable revenue exceeded the 'free allocation'. Assume that, over time, subscribers would upgrade to a higher tariff and that Orange would attempt to improve market penetration in the corporate market.

Pricing: as a price war did not look imminent in the medium term and Cellnet and Vodafone seemed likely to make subtle changes to their pricing structures to avoid erosion of market share, Orange did not need to cut its prices. Assumed price increases three per cent per annum nominal.

Incoming call revenue: calls to Orange phones from the fixed network ran at 45 per cent of total traffic and Orange were able to increase the receipts it received from BT.

Interconnection payments: these payments for calls moving from the mobile to the fixed network were assumed to fall in line with price reductions forced on fixed network providers as a consequence of the regulatory environment. The minute charge of 3p in early 1996 was assumed to fall by two per cent per annum.

Dealer incentives: assumed to fall from the 1996 level of £300 to £120 by 2005, in line with reductions in manufacturers' prices for equipment.

Capital expenditure: £530 million for 1995. This was estimated as being likely to peak in 1996 and subsequently decline. By 2001 capital expenditure should be down to a care and maintenance level.

Network costs: £23 million in l995. However, in the build phase a significant amount was foreseen as being capitalised, possibly some £20 million, five per cent per annum growth in costs were assumed.

Distribution: assumed cost rise of five per cent per annum.

Administration: assumed increase three per cent per annum.

Figure 9.1: Estimated free cash flows 1996 to 2005, £ million

1996	1997	1998	1999	2000	2001	2002	2003	2004	2005
− 397.6	− 156.0	32.9	176.9	315.2	400.4	448.8	436.8	484	498.4

The free cash flows in Figure 9.1 reflect the enterprise situation, i.e. prior to the deduction of interest servicing charges, debt repayments and dividends. The negative free cash flows in the first two years and the slow build up to positive free cash flows were a reflection of the substantial capital expenditure requirements.

While the market opportunity and Orange's resultant strategy were clear, there had to be a link between this strategy and the creation of value for the investors. In responding to investors needs, management had to create value which may be thought of as being driven by three basic strategic imperatives [146]:

1. investing to achieve a return in excess of the cost of capital (return);
2. growing the business and the investment base (growth);
3. managing and accepting appropriate business risks (risk).

In order to create and deliver value, management's focus will be on a number of key operational value drivers. Figure 9.2 shows how the high level strategic value drivers of return, growth and risk can be related to the business underlying operational value drivers via the value driver framework of strategic value analysis.

Decisions about the value drivers to generate the free cash flows for the ten year period were vital but, in this case, two other crucial decisions had to be taken.

1. How to calculate the terminal value for a business in which the cash flows are generated relatively far on and where there is potential growth in the market beyond the period over which analysts are comfortable with forecasting.
2. What discount rate to use to work out the present value of these future cash flows.

In fact, these two questions are related to one another. The determination of the terminal value is very often calculated making use of the cost of capital which, in turn, is used to calculate the discount rate. The rationale for use of the cost of capital is that beyond the period over which analysts are comfortable in forecasting, no more than the cost of capital (or normal profit) will be achievable. As will be seen, the exception to this is where it is estimated there will be further growth.

Figure 9.2 : Hierarchy of value drivers

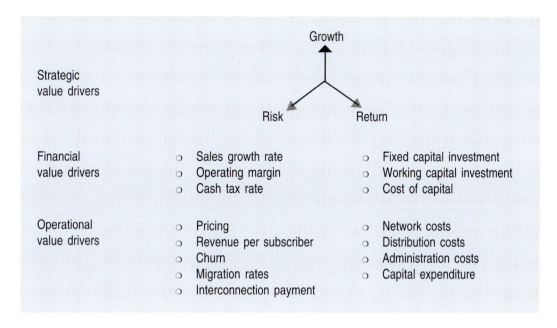

An illustration of how the weighted average cost of capital (WACC) might be estimated is shown in Figure 9.3 where it is assumed that Vodafone is a comparable company. In effect, as we demonstrated in Chapter 6, the beta for Vodafone is used as a proxy for Orange's market. Typically, a number of comparable peer group companies would be used in arriving at an estimate of the WACC for Orange, with their betas being assumed to be relevant as indicators of market risk. Where there is a difference in capital structure, an adjustment is required via an ungearing and regearing process. Quite simply, the published betas are adjusted to reflect the potential level of debt relevant to Orange. Once this adjustment had been applied to the betas and the results fed into a Capital Asset Pricing Model (CAPM) calculation, an estimate for the Orange cost of equity of approximately 14.4 per cent was obtained. This, when adjusted for the debt equity mix and an assumed post-tax cost of debt, resulted in a WACC of approximately 12 per cent.

As regards estimation of the terminal value, many analysts used the growing cash flow in perpetuity formula. This was because, as discussed earlier, within the UK market growth forecasts for the mobile industry had been shown to be underestimated substantially. Forecasts for growth were varied, but four per cent was not uncommon.

The value of a growing cash flow in perpetuity is estimated using the following formula:

$$\text{Terminal Value} = FCF \div (WACC - g)$$

Where,

FCF = free cash flow in the first year after the explicit forecast period;
WACC = the weighted average cost of capital;
g = the expected growth rate in free cash flow to perpetuity.

Figure 9.3: Cost of Capital Determination

i.e. Vodafone plc (comparable company)	
Beta (Datastream)	1.24
Marginal tax rate	33 %
Debt (£bn)	0.2
Market capitalisation (£bn) *	7.1
Unlevered beta	1.22
Orange plc	
Tax rate	33 %
Target debt:equity ratio	0.8:2.3
Levered beta	1.5 †
Risk free rate	7.6 %
Risk premium	4.5 %
Cost of equity	14.4 %
WACC assuming pre-tax cost of debt at 10%	12.4 %

As illustrated in Figure 9.4, applying a WACC of 12.4 per cent resulted in a present value of the free cash flows for the ten-year period from 1995 to 2005 of approximately £727 million. Applying a 4 per cent growth in perpetuity results in a residual value of approximately £1.857 billion and an enterprise value of approximately £2.6 billion. When the starting debt of £400 million is deducted, the result is a market value of equity of approximately £2.2 billion.

Figure 9.4: DCF valuation (£ million) - WACC 12.4 per cent, perpetuity growth rate 4 per cent

	1996	1997	1998	1999	2000	2001	2002	2003	2004	2005
Free cash flow	−397.6	−156.0	32.9	176.9	315.2	400.4	448.8	436.8	484.0	498.4
Cost of capital	12.4	12.4	12.4	12.4	12.4	12.4	12.4	12.4	12.4	12.4
Discount factor	0.890	0.792	0.704	0.627	0.557	0.496	0.441	0.393	0.349	0.311
Present value	−353.9	−123.6	23.2	110.9	175.6	198.6	197.9	171.7	168.9	155.0
Cumulative	−353.9	−477.5	−454.3	−343.4	−167.8	30.8	228.7	400.4	569.3	724.3
+ Residual value										1,845.2
Enterprise value										2,569.5
− Debt										400.0
Market value										2,169.5

---

* January 1996
† For explanation see Chapter 6

It cannot be stressed enough that the resulting market value is heavily dependent on the assumptions made and, in particular, those relating to the WACC used and the perpetuity growth rate. This is illustrated in Figures 9.5 and 9.6. A decrease in the WACC from 12.4 to 12 per cent adds almost £190 million to the market value, while a decrease in the perpetuity growth rate from four to three per cent reduces this value by almost £197 million.

Figure 9.5: DCF valuation (£ million) - WACC 12 per cent, perpetuity growth rate 4 per cent

	1996	1997	1998	1999	2000	2001	2002	2003	2004	2005
Free cash flow	−397.6	−156.0	32.9	176.9	315.2	400.4	448.8	436.8	484.0	498.4
Cost of capital	12.0	12.0	12.0	12.0	12.0	12.0	12.0	12.0	12.0	12.0
Discount factor	0.893	0.797	0.712	0.636	0.567	0.507	0.452	0.404	0.361	0.322
Present value	−355.1	−124.3	23.4	112.5	178.7	203.0	202.9	176.5	174.7	160.5
Cumulative	−355.1	−479.4	−456.0	−343.5	−164.8	38.2	241.1	417.6	592.3	752.8
+ Residual value										2,006.3
Enterprise value										2,759.1
− Debt										400.0
Market value										2,359.1

Figure 9.6: DCF valuation (£ million) - WACC 12.4 per cent, perpetuity growth rate 3 per cent

	1996	1997	1998	1999	2000	2001	2002	2003	2004	2005
Free cash flow	−397.6	−156.0	32.9	176.9	315.2	400.4	448.8	436.8	484	498.4
Cost of capital	12.4	12.4	12.4	12.4	12.4	12.4	12.4	12.4	12.4	12.4
Discount factor	0.890	0.792	0.704	0.627	0.557	0.496	0.441	0.393	0.349	0.311
Present value	−353.9	−123.6	23.2	110.9	175.6	198.6	197.9	171.7	168.9	155.0
Cumulative	−353.9	−477.5	−454.3	−343.4	−167.8	30.8	228.7	400.4	569.3	724.3
+ Residual value										1,648.9
Enterprise value										2,373.2
− Debt										400.0
Market value										1,973.2

Market relative valuations

For many reasons, not least of which is the sensitivity of DCF models to assumptions about WACC and the perpetuity value, most analysts used market relative methods. As indicated, two approaches used were the multiple of Earnings Before Interest, Tax, Depreciation and Amortisation (EBITDA) and the multiple of the Price Earnings Ratio (PER). While the PER is frequently used in new issue type valuations, earnings may be subject to a number of influences such as creative accounting. One response is to move further up the profit and loss account in search of a 'purer' measure of profit. One such purer measure is considered to be EBITDA, which represents the profit generated from a company's assets after making provision for the investment needed to maintain the value of those assets, but before distributing the money between the lenders, taxman and shareholders. This measure of profit seeks to overcome the limitation of earnings used in the PE ratio calculation because of historical cost depreciation calculations.

As indicated in Chapter 5, the way the EV: EBITDA ratio is applied for valuation purposes is that financial data of the company to be valued, Orange in this case, is used in conjunction with that for a selected peer group consisting of listed companies, ideally in the same business and same country, i.e.

$$\frac{EV_{Peer\_Group}}{EBITDA} = \frac{EV_{Target}}{EBITDA}$$

Having calculated the EV (Enterprise Value) to EBITDA ratio for the peer group and the EBITDA for the target (Orange), an estimate of the Price (market value) of the target (Orange) can be found.

The multiple of EBITDA to be applied to Orange was ascertained by looking at comparable companies already trading. Companies considered by analysts included overseas telecommunications service providers, like Telecom Italia. As with all such valuations, the question of which companies are comparable arises. An example of the determination of the multiple by one group of analysts is illustrated in Figure 9.7.

Figure 9.7: EBITDA multiples of 'comparable' companies

	Market Value	Net Debt	Enterprise Value	EBITDA Multiple 1995	EBITDA Multiple 1996
Vodafone plc (£bn)	7.1	0.2	7.3	12.6	10.4
Telecom Italia (Lbn)	21,144	1,010	22,154	10.4	8.00

In the case of Orange, a range of EBITDA multiples of between 8 and 12 were selected by many analysts. The value derived by applying these multiples to the projected EBITDA for Orange was then discounted back to present value. Any intervening positive free cash flows were also discounted to present day value and added to the discounted value of the terminal multiple. The results of these calculations are illustrated in Figure 9.8.

Figure 9.8: EBITDA valuation – enterprise value £ billion

Discount rate	14%	15%	16%
Terminal multiple:			
8 times	2.66	2.47	2.31
10 times	3.11	2.89	2.69
12 times	3.56	3.42	3.06

From this enterprise value, £400 million of opening debt must be deducted to arrive at a market value. For example, assuming a discount rate of 15 per cent and a terminal multiple of ten the implied equity value is £2.49 billion (i.e. £2.89bn – £0.46bn).

As a so-called reality check on pricing in the market place, analysts applied a Price Earnings Ratio (PER) to the anticipated level of after tax profits in the year 2005. The rationale for its use is not difficult because, ultimately as a new issue, Orange would be looked on in terms of the relationship between equity and earnings in the current market, hence the benefit in valuing it on such a basis. PER's for comparable companies for 1995 and 1996 were found to range between 12.2 and 23.8. Since most PERs were below 18.5, conservative values were taken, as illustrated in Figure 9.9. The value arrived at by applying these multiples to the earnings were discounted back using a range of discount rates.

Figure 9.9: PER valuation – enterprise value £ billion

Discount rate	10%	11%	12%
Terminal multiple:			
14 times	2.78	2.54	2.32
15 times	2.98	2.72	2.49
16 times	3.18	2.91	3.18

The advantage of the DCF method over the other methods is that rather than drawing on a PER, or the like, from the market and which may be very arbitrarily determined, value is estimated from user-based assumptions. If you disagree with such assumptions it is relatively straightforward to modify them and evaluate them within the DCF framework. The potential to have control over the valuation process may not be so obvious where dependence is placed on external observations. However, rarely will the analyst rely on one method even though it may have some potential advantages over others. As the Orange valuation shows, there is safety in numbers!

Valuing intangible assets

An important challenge facing many organisations concerns the valuation of intangible assets. The evaluation of intangible assets such as patents, trademarks, brands, goodwill and rights of access raises some very real conceptual issues and problems. The nature of these issues and problems will be considered briefly here, drawing on three different illustrations:

1. The valuation of rights of access to telecommunications opportunities possessed by a power company in the Asia Pacific Region.
2. The value of research and development expenditure for a large, multinational pharmaceuticals company.
3. The valuation of intellectual property in a global Scandinavian insurance company.

Telecommunications access rights

Globalisation and deregulation have had an important influence on the development of the telecommunications market. Such issues have provided a major potential opportunity for electricity power transmission companies, the nature of this opportunity relating to the potential granting of rights of access to companies wishing to provide services in the telecommunications market. Quite simply, the infrastructure used by the transmission companies to transmit electricity, in the form of towers from which to suspend electric cables, could be readily used by telecommunications providers. As such, these towers offer potential rights of access to two markets:

1. the mobile, Personal Communications Network (PCN), market;
2. conventional telephone services.

These two market opportunities had different implications insofar as the dynamics and competitive forces operating are different. The PCN rights of access presented far less of a monopoly opportunity for the electricity transmission company than those associated with the conventional telephone services. PCN stations were not quite so reliant on access to the electricity transmission company's towers, unlike the conventional telephone services. In the absence of obtaining the rights of access to the electricity transmission company's infrastructure assets from which fibre optic cable could be suspended, considerable effort and expenditure would have to be made in installing alternatives.

The valuation of such rights raises some interesting issues because the electricity transmission companies in such circumstances retain the title to and ownership of the infrastructure assets used to provide access. This is because the primary purpose of the assets is to support the core business; electricity transmission. The granting of rights of access therefore represent an intangible purchase, with there being no notion of any rights of possession being granted.

The retention of title and the need to support the quality of these assets for the core electricity transmission business could be interpreted as inferring a low value for the rights of access. According to this interpretation, the value of such access to assets would be viewed in terms of a rental stream for the use of the assets, which have another primary purpose. However, such a view ignores the real potential value, which may be substantially different. As a consequence of the rights of access, the telecommunications providers should be able to generate substantial financial benefits because of projected future growth within the market. This raises the key question - 'To whom should such benefit accrue?' The telecommunications providers typically see it as being the rewards due to them as a consequence of their preparedness to undertake business. However, a strong case can be made for a share of the benefit arising as a consequence of the electricity power company's right of access. The issue is, if this is agreeable in principle, what proportion is attributable to the respective parties. One way of looking at this is by comparing the value that would be generated by a telecommunications provider with and without the rights of access. This represents the benefit to the telecommunications businesses but, of course, their argument would be that this is the result of their risk-return endeavours. One response to this is to argue that the sum potentially to be looked at for purposes of sharing is the residual after their risk-return costs have been deducted.

In pulling this together from a value perspective, one part of the valuation of the two rights of access opportunities will involve an estimation of their value from the 'buyer's' perspective, i.e. desirably as low as possible. This value could be estimated by the rental stream payable from an opportunity cost perspective, i.e. what would be the cost of obtaining such rights of access from alternative sources, e.g. installing a PCN station on a tall building. Such a rental stream when converted into a present value will represent a much lower sum than the alternative 'seller's' view which involves looking at the right of access issue in terms of a full commercial opportunity value, i.e. the value potentially that can be derived as a consequence of having the rights of access and in which the electricity transmission company could stake a claim. According to this approach, the amount in which electricity transmission company might stake a claim is a proportion of the residual income, (or economic profit) left after the cost of financing both equity and debt have been met, this proportion being potentially estimated by comparing the value generated with and without rights of access. This latter approach could be assessed in value terms, i.e. by converting the residual cash flow year-on-year attributable to the electricity power company in present value terms, or according to some sharing scheme focusing on the annual division of excess cash flows. The advantage of the latter approach has been recognised in employee incentive schemes based on economic profit, whereby any division is seen to be much more palatable if it is not dependent on speculative assessments of future opportunities which may or may not transpire.

The two opportunities differed for the company in question. In the case of the granting of rights of access for conventional telephone services, the sharing of economic profit was felt to be appropriate. This was because the electricity transmission company was in a much stronger relative position than was the case for the PCN opportunity. The alternative implications for the conventional telephone service opportunity were considered to be much more onerous to those seeking rights of access. Few alternatives to the rights of access existed by comparison with the case for the PCN providers.

Research and development

The second illustration of the value of intangible assets can be seen with reference to Glaxo Wellcome, the pharmaceuticals company. At the moment Glaxo Wellcome is reckoned to be destroying shareholder value [147]. However, in five years time it could be creating more value than any of its other competitors. According to the Lex Column in the *Financial Times*, the decline of the ulcer drug Zantac will make Glaxo Wellcome hard-pushed to beat its 9.5 to 10 per cent cost of capital in 1997 and 1998 [148]. Estimates are, however, that by 2003 its return on capital will be 11 per cent higher than its WACC, this being much better than most of its rivals including SmithKline Beecham. Such a turnaround is being driven by recently launched treatments for asthma, Aids and migraine and a commitment to significant ongoing research and development expenditure.

Intellectual property

A third illustration is highlighted by Figure 9.10, which shows that most of the companies going through mergers and acquisitions in the USA during the period 1981-1993 were valued at between two to nine times their book value [149].

Figure 9.10: Financial information and acquisition values

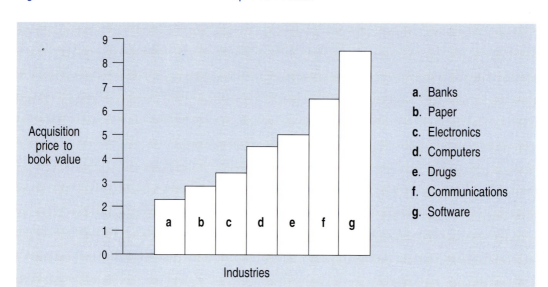

By looking at the market value versus the book value, growth companies such as Intel, Microsoft and Netscape are valued way beyond book value. The reason for this gap may arguably be attributed to the possession of what is referred to as intellectual capital [150]. The existence of this leads to a paradox. While there is a well defined and well-developed system for measuring the book value, this is not so for future growth prospects. In effect, what is needed is a way of gaining a deeper understanding of such growth prospects and it is in this regard that the issue of valuing intellectual capital becomes important [151].

Skandia, a Swedish-based global insurance company, is noteworthy for its pioneering work on defining and measuring this so called 'intellectual capital' with its own balanced business scorecard tool (see Figure 9.11)* called: 'The Business Navigator'.

Skandia views intellectual capital as represented by the sum of human, structural and customer capital. Here capital is defined as any source of profit, advantage, asset or leverage to create value. More specifically:

○   Human capital represents the capabilities of the individuals required to provide solutions to customers.

○   Structural capital represents the organisational capabilities needed to meet market requirements.

○   Customer capital represents the value of an organisation's relationships with the people with whom it does business. This may be thought of as the penetration, coverage, loyalty and profitability of a business franchise.

---

*   The Balanced Business Scorecard is considered in more detail in Chapter 10

Figure 9.11: Intellectual capital at Skandia

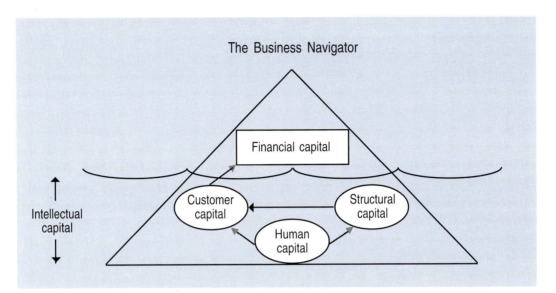

Skandia views value creation as being driven by the interaction of these three key components, with the result being financial capital which is monitored using the 'Business Navigator', see Figure 9.11 [180]. This navigator is intended to bring a balanced view of financial and intellectual capital, internal and external focus, leading and lagging indicators and past, present and future perspectives. It is contended that this framework can be used to identify the value drivers of the business and hence its sources of value creation.

This framework can be viewed as being useful for generating the right questions to ask about the potential sources of value creation within a business or from a given investment opportunity.

Summary checklist

○   The valuation of Orange demonstrated how valuation results can be assessed by calculating value in several different ways, using a number of different methods.

○   This is best supplemented by cross-checking, using market relative methods wherever possible to test and validate assumptions.

○   There is no unique formula or approach to valuation. It is important to understand that it is based on a good deal of user judgement and that, as such, valuations are as much an art as they are a science.

○   One of the biggest valuation challenges relates to intangible assets and business opportunities of a highly speculative nature. This is likely to be an area of increasing interest in the near future, particularly in the case of intellectual property.

Concluding remarks

In this chapter opportunities in telecommunications services have been used to demonstrate some interesting and important valuation issues that often need to be addressed. In the case of Orange, the approach(es) used to assess the opportunities have been shown to draw on the same core skills and concepts that have been reviewed in the preceding chapters of the book. The need to identify and estimate the value drivers in order to generate cash flow forecasts, the determination of the planning period, estimation of the terminal value and the derivation of a proxy cost of capital, all represented issues that had to be addressed. The practical reality was that the core principles outlined in earlier chapters of the book were essential.

Orange represented the 'blue sky' situation and a real challenge for valuation purposes, but it was much more straightforward than some of the other issues that have been highlighted relating to intangible assets and intellectual property. These represent the prospective valuation challenges, for which considerable developments are under way and about which more is certain to be heard.

Chapter 10: Strategic Value Management

In sum, we have the tools to manage our company better from a strategic and financial standpoint.

Sir Brian Pitman, Chairman, Lloyds TSB Group [152].

Chapter preview

- Introduction of critical value analysis and value mapping for judging whether a particular strategic management change will result in financial benefits.
- Critical value analysis as a process involving calculation of:
    1. the current market value of the business;
    2. business value as is;
    3. business value with improvements.
- Review of the experiences of organisations like ICL and the Lloyds TSB Group in applying Strategic Value Management.
- Review of key issues associated with the implementation of Strategic Value Analysis.
- Consideration of how Strategic Value Analysis can be linked with two other business initiatives, namely, the Balanced Scorecard and the Business Excellence model of the European Foundation for Quality Management, to assist in its implementation as a management tool.

190 CHAPTER TEN

Introduction

In earlier chapters Strategic Value Analysis has been shown to be an essential tool in assisting strategic decision making issues associated with mergers and acquisitions, joint ventures and new issues. However, the approaches associated with it can also be used in managing a business. In this chapter the application of the tool for such purposes is reviewed under the heading of Strategic Value Management (also known as Value Based Management).

The impetus to adopt an approach like Strategic Value Management for managing the business is often associated with some external threat, like being a potential acquisition target. For example, Ronnie Hempel the Chief Executive of ICI was reported as saying that the demerger into ICI and Zenecca was intended to allow ICI executives to concentrate on a narrower range of businesses, and to release what he referred to as 'creative management energies' [153]. By all accounts the company's focus on profitability in the past was not as good as it should have been. A second illustration of the impetus to adopt value based approaches in managing the business can be related to one of the most noteworthy adopters of the approach in the UK: Lloyds TSB Group. A major stimulus for focusing on value came from poor past performance and prospects for the future if no corrective action was taken. For example, in the early 1980s before Lloyds embarked on a shareholder value oriented approach, its shares were selling at less than book value. At the end of 1992 they were selling at 533p, or more than 240 per cent of book value.

An important early first step in developing Strategic Value Management as a tool for managing the business involves using the approach to assess the projected future of the business according to a proposed strategy. In very simple terms, the strategic plan of the business needs to be valued to identify potential value creation. While this may be undertaken at a consolidated level, the reality is that for purposes of implementation any value based approach needs to be exercised at least at business unit level if it is to have a real chance of success. At this point it has to be recognised that the multi-business nature of many organisations introduces a major challenge – the need to measure the cost of capital and value below the corporate level. The issues associated with such measurement that were introduced in earlier chapters, will be reviewed. Thereafter some of the critical implementation issues will be considered. These will extend beyond the initial focus of the chapter on issues associated with the financial perspective and recognise that a value based approach for managing the business will be dependent on people to implement it.

Value mapping and critical value analysis

Assume that a trigger for a potential change has occurred. Some means is required of being able to judge whether, in financial terms, any benefit might result. A value map, illustrated in Figure 10.1, can be used to help understand value creating potential. How the financial benefits associated with a potential restructuring can be measured may be related to the following three steps of critical value analysis which require the calculation of:

1. current market value;
2. business value as is;
3. business value with improvements.

Figure 10.1: Value map

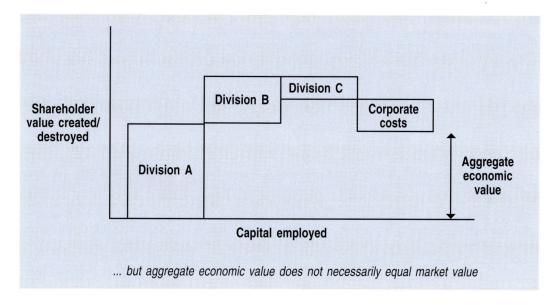

Step 1. Current market value

The key purpose of this step is to establish the current market value of the business. It is calculated for a quoted company by calculating the market capitalisation of the equity shares in issue, i.e. the product of the number of shares issued and the quoted market price of each share. However, it should be recognised that the value of the business as a whole may be greater than just this simple multiplication. The current share price would typically represent that for the average number of shares trading and a premium would typically have to be paid to gain control.

For private companies and other organisations the process of determining current market value is even less precise. Peer group analysis of comparable quoted companies or companies with comparable characteristics may be necessary and a number of different valuation approaches would typically be used in recognition of the uncertainty caused by there being no stock market price. The types of approaches that might be used for this purpose were discussed in the previous chapter with reference to Orange.

Step 2. Business value 'as is'

We illustrated how this step could be undertaken for a company as a whole with reference to Santos plc in Chapter 2 and Evode plc in Chapter 8, but the method used was very simple. In fact, calculating business value below the corporate level is very difficult in reality because different business activities may be associated with different levels of risk, such that different costs of capital should be used to establish the values of individual business units. Despite this and other complicating factors which we will review, valuing a multi-business business 'as is' involves the same basic principles that we have discussed in earlier chapters in relation to the business as a whole. The only difference is that, as illustrated in Figure 10.1, a number of individual valuations for each business unit are required, which then have to be consolidated. In this case it can be seen that Divisions A and B are creating value. However, for the capital employed, Division A is creating relatively more value than Division B. By comparison, Division C is destroying value. That is, it is providing a return on capital lower than the cost of capital.

The result of undertaking a valuation of individual business units and corporate headquarters will be a number of values which can be analysed and compared to provide an understanding of whether there would be any potential benefits from restructuring the business as a whole.

The most useful analysis will typically treat corporate headquarters in the same way as individual business units. Differentiating between business units and headquarters can be very useful, as we will show in the identification of potential improvements for Step Three. Both the business units and headquarters can be thought of as being contributors to total business value. Both can be fine-tuned via operating improvements and potentially sold for a premium to new owners who may be able to put them to a better alternative use or to manage them better, or combine them with business units of another organisation in an acquisition.

Value mapping steps at business unit level

Once the company valuation has been undertaken along the lines discussed in the example of Evode plc, a more detailed approach is required at the business unit level. This involves the following steps:

- Definition of the main business activities to be measured.
- Collection of data relevant to these activities.
- Undertaking of individual activity valuations.
- Aggregation of individual activity valuations.

Defining business activities

There are differing views about how to define business activities. One useful starting point is to look for the most practicable level of aggregation, i.e. the smallest collective unit that can be separated and viewed on a stand-alone basis. The definition of business activities may not be a problem if there are strategic business units (SBUs). However, this is not always the case and it is preferable to look at a business in terms of its strategic risk, paying attention to those parts of the business that have distinct business risk characteristics. How can these be identified? First, identify the firm's SBUs, the guiding criterion for these being that each should ideally be a full competitor in an external market. Second, analyse each SBU to see if all the operations share the same or different business risk characteristics. For example, in terms of demographic and geographic segments and operating gearing, there is the same tendency for net profit to vary disproportionately with sales. (Operating gearing increases as the ratio of fixed costs to total costs increases since variations in sales then produce much larger variations in net profit.)

One other important issue concerns the treatment of headquarters costs which can be thought of as falling into two categories; those necessary to support business units and hence attributable to those activities, and those which relate specifically to the headquarters. Those costs attributable to business units, e.g. providing services centrally that would otherwise have to be provided by the units, should be treated as business unit costs and not as headquarters costs. This distinction has important implications for the next step.

Collecting business activity data

The accounting system should be a good starting point for data, although it may often be necessary to reclassify it to correspond with the requirements of the analysis. For example, the business activities defined for strategic analysis may not correspond exactly with the definitions used in the accounting system. A classic area of difficulty concerns costs, which may well be allocated and apportioned across the business in very arbitrary ways. In fact, some of the data costs relevant for accounting purposes may often be totally irrelevant in a future oriented business valuation.

Undertaking business activity valuations

This is often the most difficult part of the process and involves:

1. Identifying the relevant cash flows for individual business activities

This can be difficult because various business activities may supply to one another and/or be supplied with goods from one another. Therefore, transfer pricing problems may represent a potential source of cash flow distortion. Where possible, transfer prices should be set as closely as possible to the market prices of any close substitutes. This reinforces the principle of viewing each activity on a stand-alone basis. Related to this, corporate overheads must be dealt with carefully. Any overheads that would be incurred with the activity operating on a stand-alone basis must be estimated and deducted in arriving at the relevant cash flow, e.g. accounting and computing costs incurred by headquarters on behalf of business units. However, those that would not be borne if the activities were separate should not be allocated.

2. Determining the cash flow costs and benefits of corporate headquarters

Those costs not easily allocable to business activities are those requiring close scrutiny at this stage. They have to be viewed in conjunction with the benefits to be obtained so that a position can be reached whereby the corporate headquarters are not seen to be either an ineffective burden relative to their cost, or too lean to perform the role required of them. What is currently being spent on headquarters? As a guide, research undertaken on headquarters costs which was based on 107 UK companies with between 2,000 and 20,000 employees suggested that headquarters cost more than 1 per cent of sales, which often represents more than 10 per cent of pre-tax profits [154]. With this in mind, it is hardly surprising that companies have made major efforts to reduce headquarters costs.

It is all too easy to focus on cost-cutting when reviewing headquarters, but the aim should be more ambitious and should focus on increasing the value which the centre adds to the company as a whole. This means tailoring headquarters activities more effectively to the company's particular strategy, structure, business portfolio, and top management style. In many cases that might mean cutbacks, but in others it may involve a cost increase.

3. Determination of relevant tax rates

The relevant tax rate for valuing independent business activities is that which would apply without the corporate umbrella. The procedure to follow is to determine the taxable income of the stand-alone entity (including the headquarters) over the foreseeable future and then seek specialist help to ascertain relevant allowances and ultimately the rate to apply.

4. Determining the relevant cost of capital

The key issues associated with estimating the cost of capital were considered in Chapter 6. Here, the issues raised in that chapter will be considered within the context of a multi-business valuation. The main problem in estimating the cost of capital for parts of an overall business is that there is no market price for the shares of each division, thereby preventing a CAPM cost of equity from being calculated. In such circumstances a cost of equity can be estimated by using peer group analysis, as illustrated in Chapter 9 with reference to Orange.

Peer group analysis

To apply peer group analysis to estimate the cost of equity, the following three-step process can be used [*]:

1. Identify the parts of a business which require separate estimates of the cost of equity.

2. For each identify several peer group firms and calculate each of their costs of equity and gearing.

3. Ungear and regear the peer group average to the desired target debt/equity ratio.

For steps 1 and 2, the starting point will often be the identification of the firm's strategic business units, the guiding criterion for these being that each SBU should ideally be a full competitor in an external market. Each of these should then be analysed to see if all the operations share the same operating characteristics [155]. For example do they have the same:

---

[*] Often referred to as the analogous approach.

- product lines;
- end markets, defined by user attributes such as age, wealth and geographic location [156];
- market share;
- total capitalisation;
- distribution network (direct selling, number of intermediaries, and so on [157]);
- cost structure (percentage of revenue spent on materials, labour and overheads);
- business strategy [158].

There is one simple message – try to find as many peers as possible, even though you may ultimately only select a few for purposes of comparison. A firm's competitors often make the best peers, but within such competitors attention should be directed in particular towards identifying the sorts of similarities in operating characteristics we have outlined.

As illustrated in Chapter 9 with reference to Orange, once a peer group has been established from publicly quoted companies, the cost of equity for each of its members can be calculated using CAPM. This will typically contain debt and hence financial risk. In recognition of the distinction between business and financial risk, the beta and hence the cost of equity, must be ungeared for each peer group member to find the ungeared peer group average. This peer group average then needs to be regeared to the target debt/equity ratio of the unquoted business. This regeared value represents the estimated cost of equity for the unquoted business.

Cross-sectional analysis

Peer group analysis can be employed only when there are a number of publicly traded firms in the same industry. For firms in new lines of business this may not be possible. If a peer group is not available, then the only recourse is a cross-sectional analysis. By contrast, cross-sectional analysis produces estimates of betas from underlying accounting information drawn primarily from the main financial statements of the business. This approach is reckoned to be less dependable for determining a cost of equity than CAPM, unless the business entity has recently changed its risk profile. However, it really does come into its own where the business is not publicly traded and particularly when no peer group is available.

Cross-sectional models are also called 'analytical', 'accounting' or 'fundamental models'. They produce estimates of CAPM betas called 'fundamental betas' based on underlying accounting information. A proxy for the CAPM cost of equity is then calculated using the CAPM equation below:

$$\text{Cost of equity} = \text{Risk free rate} + (\text{Beta} \times \text{Equity risk premium})$$

The bases for calculating this fundamental beta are accounting variables measuring profitability, turnover, operating characteristics, risk and size. In addition, a link between the accounting data and economic factors may be provided by including a cash flow coefficient in the form of the covariance of the company's cash flows with the cash flows of its economic sector.

Accounting variables that may be used in a cross-sectional model include:

- Total assets.
- Cash flow.
- Mean sales ÷ total assets.
- Mean cash flow ÷ total assets.
- Mean sales growth.
- Mean dividends ÷ shareholders' funds.
- Mean depreciation ÷ sales.
- Mean inventories ÷ sales.
- Debt ÷ equity ratio.

The predictive power of this approach varies widely from industry to industry and from company to company. It is likely to be far more accurate for companies where accounting data closely represent the value of the company than for companies where the economic value of certain assets is not represented by financial statements. For example, in industries like oil and petrochemicals many aspects are not well represented in their financial statements and the model is likely to be less accurate. For example, the discovery of an oilfield may cause large swings in the value of a company's equity but does not show up in the financial statements until the potential value is realised.

Overall, a cost of equity determined by a cross-sectional model is reckoned to be less dependable than one determined using CAPM, unless the business entity has recently changed its risk profile. However, the cross-sectional model offers an alternative when no obvious peer group is available.

Calculating the cost of capital

Once the cost of equity has been estimated for each unit, a similar calculation is required for the cost of debt. How this can be estimated we reviewed in Chapter 6. The estimates for the cost of debt and the cost of equity can then brought together to estimate the Weighted Average Cost of Capital (WACC) for each unit using the formula outlined in Chapter 6:

$$WACC = (\%Debt \times Cost\ of\ debt\ after\ tax) + (\%Equity \times Cost\ of\ equity)$$

Aggregation of individual business activity valuations

By using cost of capital estimates for individual SBUs together with their forecast free cash flows, a number of values for all the business units can be calculated (see Figure 10.1). The sum of the values of these SBUs represents total business value.

There is enormous potential for error in undertaking the individual valuations which needs to be recognised. It is therefore wise to undertake some cross-checking by asking questions such as the following:

- Does the sum of the debts for individual business units equal total corporate debt?
- Does the sum of individual business unit cash flows during the historical period approximate to corporate cash flows?

At this point it is important to recognise that it is all too easy to build a model that is flawed. Multi-business valuation is complex and will typically be undertaken using some sort of computer support, whether this is a spreadsheet or specialist business valuation software. It is wise to remember 'garbage in, garbage out' at this stage, because the aggregate value represents the base case or reference point for identifying potential areas of improvement.

Step 3. Business value with improvements

By now three areas for potential improvement opportunities (see Figure 10.2) should be apparent:

1. strategic and operating;
2. acquisition and disposal;
3. financial engineering.

The value of these needs to be estimated, together with any relationships that may exist between them, see Figure 10.2.

Figure 10.2: Three general areas for improvement opportunities

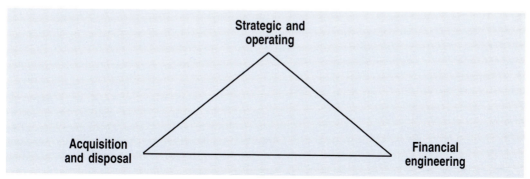

Strategic and operating opportunities

For example, the potential benefits from cutting the costs of corporate headquarters is one obvious source. However, there may be many others involving the value drivers highlighted (as in Chapter 8 with Evode plc), which may range from fine tuning on the one hand, to drastic action such as a change in strategic direction, on the other.

Acquisition and disposal opportunities

As a result of extensive analysis it may be apparent that total business value cannot be improved sufficiently from internal action alone. Disposing of parts of the business may be appropriate. In some cases, this may help to remove what has been referred to as conglomerate discount in the share price. This is where the extent of a business' diversification is seen as being almost a risk. The risk is that it may not be managed as effectively because of the breadth and often apparent lack of complementarity of activities.

A disposal should only be undertaken if it will create greater value, i.e. to get tomorrow's price today. While an obvious point, it can sometimes be very difficult to ensure that this is so. Measurement of the value to be gained starts from the base case 'as is' which was discussed earlier. To this should be added the gain from its disposal; that is the difference between its market value as a stand-alone entity as operated by its current parent, and the market price when disposed of. From this value the tax liabilities created by its sale and any expected loss of benefits, must be deducted. Some of these benefits may be difficult to measure accurately. For example, disposing of one business unit may impact on all sorts of economies previously received such as deals with suppliers and the management of operations.

It is important to search for all the benefits and if it can be guessed who might be the potential purchaser, a valuation should be undertaken from its perspective. As indicated with reference to the take-over of Evode by Laporte in Chapter 8, potential synergistic benefits can be very important.

Last, but by no means least, external improvements may warrant an acquisition. In this case establishing the benefits by way of synergies is crucial to success (see Chapter 8).

Financial engineering opportunities

A company with spare debt capacity can alter its capital structure by raising debt to reap the tax advantage of debt and such action may also possibly lower the cost of capital (see Chapter 6). The proceeds raised could be used to buy back shares, pay a special dividend or be used for investment purposes such as an acquisition. Financial engineering also has a part to play in advancing corporate strategy by allowing risk to be borne that customers, employees or counterparties seek [159]. The key message is to try and quantify all benefits as far as possible using the approach described.

Having gone through these three steps, the real underlying value of the business should be measurable. The difference between this and the market determined value for a quoted company, the 'value gap', represents what could be attained by a raider, or even by current management if it has the foresight and determination to make changes in good time. The best defence against a take-over is to ensure that the value gap between existing and restructured activities is so small that no outsider could reasonably gain from taking control.

Applying Strategic Value Management in practice

Companies with opportunities for involvement with Strategic Value Management are those that:

1. Do not appear to have experimented at all.

2. Claim to be value oriented companies but whose actions do not support this impression.

3. Have adopted various value analytical techniques but not yet the broader managerial implications of the approach.

4. Have embraced the underlying principles of a value-based approach and have also embarked on implementation.

There appear to be many companies which fall into group 1 above and which do not appear to have experimented at all. There also seem to be many companies espousing the pursuit of maximising shareholder value in their annual reports but whose apparent interpretation of this would appear to be focused towards accounting based measures like earnings per share. A number of companies fall into the third category, but all indications point to there being relatively few in the last group which have embarked on any broad based implementation. However, there is one good illustration of a company's experience with its implementation that has been recently documented and which we will review shortly.

Companies recognised as having moved substantially towards full-scale implementation include a number of US companies like Coca-Cola, AT&T, Quaker Oats, Briggs & Stratton, and CSX. For example, AT&T's decision in 1993 to buy McCaw Cellular for $12.6 billion was reported as having been influenced significantly by valuation principles[159]. In the UK, ICL is a good example of a company that has expended considerable effort in implementing a value based approach for managing the business via its business value programme.

Relatively little has reached the public domain about companies' experiences in moving further forwards than the adoption of such analytical techniques and the broader based management implications of such approaches. However, one noteworthy exception is provided by Pitman, Chief Executive of the Lloyds TSB Group. In 1981 shares in Lloyds TSB Group were selling at 66p or 40 per cent of book value. By the end of 1992 the shares were selling at 533p, or more than 240 per cent of book value. This ten-year turnaround involved a number of steps which, when taken together, illustrated what can be achieved if the shareholder value concept is embraced. What Lloyds seemingly did was to:

○ Rank its businesses on the basis of the shareholder value they had created. Each activity was viewed either as a creator or destroyer of value and businesses with a permanent negative cash flow became a target for divestment.

○ Make provisions of about £3 billion for problem country debt. This produced accounting losses but no movement in cash and as a result the share price went up, not down.

○ Adopt higher value strategies such as expansion into life assurance and private banking which reduced the group's risk profile and increased its cash flow.

○ Recognise that in measuring performance, 'cash is king'. Earnings per share and other accounting variables should not be used exclusively to assess performance because they ignore the time value of money and exclude risk. This approach involved the inherent assumption that long term cash flows are what determines market value.

- Introduce performance-related remuneration, thus linking the interest of its people more closely with those of the owners. Many employees now own shares in the company and senior management have serious money at stake in shareholdings in the company and/or shareholder options.

The Lloyds TSB experience indicates that attention to shareholder value gave it a clear discipline. The company's goal has been to analyse every strategic decision in terms of its impact on shareholder wealth. It also focuses on shareholder value to evaluate acquisitions, divestments, capital investment projects, and to assess alternative strategies. It recognises that it now has the tools to manage its companies better from a strategic and financial standpoint. Furthermore it has made some serious attempts in implementing the approach, but it also does recognise that it has a long way to go. Nevertheless, Lloyds TSB has taken the approach very seriously and sees it as having an important part to play in the bank's future.

Key issues to consider in implementing Strategic Value Management

There are four main phases in implementing Strategic Value Management:

1. Introduction of concepts and gaining of corporate commitment.
2. Establishment of policies and procedures.
3. Integration of concepts into practice.
4. Development and refinement of the approach.

Phase 1, the introduction of concepts and the gaining of commitment, can take some time. We would expect it to take a minimum of six months. It will involve:

- Presentations to senior corporate and divisional management of the concepts and the potential benefits to the company.
- Discussing key concerns and issues, e.g. value based executive compensation.
- Obtaining commitment of the managing director and key corporate and divisional management.
- Establish a pilot to identify key issues and benefits and foster commitment through demonstrated application of the concepts.

Phase 2, establishing policies and procedures, will often require considerable time and effort. In our experience quite how much time is often dependent on the size of the organisation, but as a rough guide six months is manageable if ambitious. More specifically, this phase will involve the following steps:

- Formation of a 'task force', e.g. drawn from senior central management and divisions.
- Identification of specific obstacles and issues, e.g. how to relate the approach to the corporate financial management and reporting culture, adequacy of existing MIS etc.
- Determination of appropriate divisional costs of capital, residual value frameworks, and planning periods.
- Development of appropriate applications at corporate and divisional level.
- Development of application guidelines.

- Identification of education requirements of those employees who will perform or need to understand the approach.
- Development of education programmes.

Phase 3, the integration of concepts into practice, is the longest and probably the most critical part of the implementation process. Nine months is a rough and ready guideline, the actual length of time is heavily linked to the size of the organisation and how extensively the approach is to be introduced. In particular, it typically involves the development of a framework that makes explicit recognition of the need to ensure a strong customer focus. While the first two phases are important, the reality is that without explicit attempts to integrate principles with practice, the only deliverable will be a valuation shell. Achieving a strong customer focus may sound straightforward in principle, but the practice is more difficult. The aspiration to be customer oriented may be easily thwarted without recognition that it may have broader organisational ramifications. It is one thing to have the aspirations to be customer focused, but it is quite another to be able to meet such requirements. This will be particularly so in turbulent market conditions when the areas in which internal excellence is required to achieve customer satisfaction may be difficult to say the least. The ways in which such customer orientation will be attempted differ, but approaches we will review in the next section are the 'balanced scorecard' and the 'business excellence model'. Once these issues have been considered carefully, other initiatives that need to be undertaken include:

- incorporation of the approach into performance measurement;
- delivery of education programmes on the approach and how it links to current practices;
- use of the approach for evaluating capital expenditure plans, acquisitions, research and development expenditure, and so on;
- provision of expert assistance when needed.

The last phase, Phase 4, is very much an open book as regards the time involved. It is likely to involve the:

- refinement of the approach and performance measurement;
- linking of the approach to incentive compensation schemes;
- development of the approach for investor communications.

Balanced scorecard

There has been increasing concern in many organisations about the way that performance is currently measured. The development of global markets accompanied by intense competition has necessitated a drive for quality and a search for continuous cost improvement. Accompanying this drive has been the questioning of whether established methods of measurement and analysis are still wholly appropriate.

In all areas of business it has become clear that the needs of both customers and shareholders have to be satisfied and that an emphasis on one to the exclusion of the other will not be accepted. The challenge to meet these needs in a turbulent business environment means that businesses have to be able to respond to customer requirements with their internal delivery mechanisms and also be able to update and change them as necessary. The implications of this are profound. To be successful, companies will need a broad set of performance indicators not just a set focusing on financial indicators of performance. What is more these indicators will have to be appropriate and relevant. To take a personal health example, the benefits of prevention via diagnosis are well known. However, we require an understanding of those things that really matter to our future well being. Dwelling on the past or what has happened is only relevant insofar as it helps us make future decisions.

An approach referred to as 'scorecarding', and often known under the banner of the balanced scorecard has been developed to broaden the scope of performance indicators away from a preoccupation with financial performance [160]. This approach includes some financial measures, which are complemented by operational measures like customer satisfaction, internal process measurement and the organisational innovations and improvement to activities. All the latter require operational measures of strategy and represent the drivers of future financial performance.

As illustrated in Figure 10.3, the balanced scorecard allows managers to look at the business from four important perspectives:

❍ How do customers see us? (customer perspective).
❍ At what processes must we excel? (internal business processes perspective).
❍ Can we continue to improve and create value? (learning and growth perspective).
❍ How do we look to our shareholders? (financial).

These four perspectives are not mutually exclusive but part of a more integrated whole.

Figure 10.3: The balanced scorecard

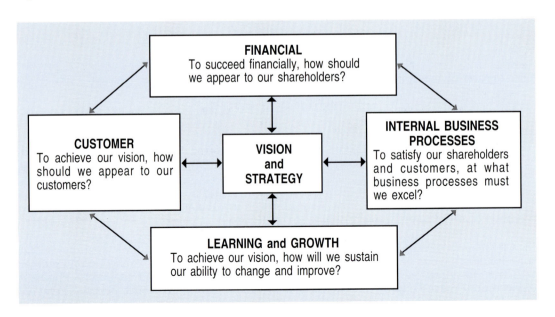

However, each perspective will deal with important performance related issues in their own right. For example, the customer perspective recognises that products incur costs, but it is customers who provide profits. This being the case they deserve attention in their own right. This means that performance indicators can usefully be developed which focus on the ability to meet customer requirements in terms of time, quality, performance and service, and cost.

Meeting customer requirements has clear implications for the organisation's delivery mechanisms and the internal business process perspective focuses on the processes and actions that need to be undertaken within the organisation. Measurement in the form of the resulting performance indicators will stem from the analysis of those features, which will have an impact on customer satisfaction.

The innovation and learning perspective has a slightly different emphasis. While the first three perspectives identify key objectives that need to be measured in determining success, this perspective focuses on the dynamics of change. The nature of global competitiveness recognises that targets have to keep changing and need to be redefined: e.g. by making continuous improvements to products and processes. This perspective therefore identifies those challenges and measures them in terms of innovation, improvements and the learning curve.

Last, but by no means least, the financial perspective, as it relates to shareholders, addresses at least two key concerns:

- How much has my investment earned and is value being created for me?
- Is my investment secure?

To this end key indicators are typically adopted which cover profitability, liquidity and increasingly, value creation.

British Telecommunications plc (BT) introduced the balanced scorecard in 1994 to help strengthen the connection between its corporate strategy and operational activities [161]. The need for a connecting mechanism was identified during Project Breakout, a group wide improvement and process reengineering drive that involved more than 1,000 teams between 1993 and 1994. As part of Project Breakout, BT focused on the strategy and planning process, and although there was a high understanding of and commitment to, strategic objectives, there was some concern as to how effectively these were being linked to operational activities. So the strategy and planning team identified the scorecard as a powerful tool for making strategic objectives come alive in operational terms.

Focusing on a handful of measures that are the most critical components of the desired objectives is a feature of the approach. As a result of this, its implementation by organisations has been shown to have two major benefits:

- It brings together in a single management report many of the disparate elements of a company's competitive agenda.
- It helps to prevent decisions being made that are not in the interests of the whole organisation, even though it may benefit one particular part of the business. By forcing senior managers to consider all-important operational measures together, the balanced scorecard lets them see whether improvement in one area may be achieved only at the expense of another.

Business excellence

Many organisations that have adopted or are adopting the principles of value, which we have discussed in connection with Strategic Value Analysis, have focused on achieving excellence. An example of such a company referred to earlier, is ICL. However, adopters also include those which have utilised the balanced scorecard approach. For example, BT's vision is to be the most successful world-wide telecommunications group and to achieve this requires excellence in everything it does.

A standard European model has been developed which companies are using to measure their 'level' of excellence. This 'business excellence' model is based on the principle that in order for an organisation or team to succeed, there are a number of key 'enablers' on which it should concentrate its efforts, and it should measure its success through a number of key 'results' areas.

Figure 10.4: The business excellence model

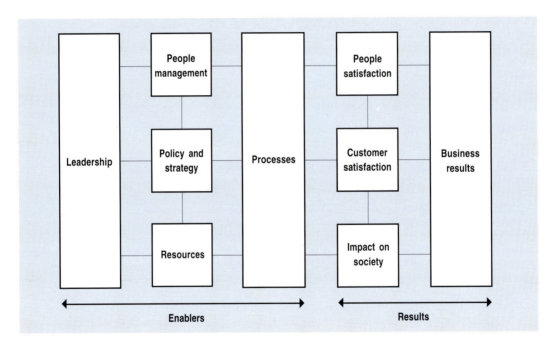

The key enablers by which companies judge themselves are:

○ How well the organisation is led.
○ How well its people are managed.
○ How far its policy and strategy are developed and implemented by its leaders and people.
○ How well it manages its resources and develops and manages its processes.

The key results areas by which the model then measures successes are those identified with reference to the balanced scorecard:

- How far it satisfies its customers.
- How well motivated and committed is its workforce.
- How the local and national community outside the organisation views its activities in terms of its contribution to society.
- Its key business results - profit, return on capital employed, shareholder earnings, achieving budgets etc.

Summary checklist

- The three driving forces of globalisation, corporate governance and the increasing use of cash flow measures by investors have been a major impetus for the adoption of Strategic Value Management/VBM by companies.
- Critical value appraisal and value mapping can be used effectively to gain an understanding of how the stock market values a company by comparing the current market valuation with an internal valuation. Looking at the internal valuation to see how the performance of the business could be realistically improved and the resultant impact of these improvements on the value of the business is a powerful source of insight. The difference between the current market value and the business value with improvements represents the value gap to be closed by management.
- Several companies have already started on the value journey. The next step is to identify where the company is in terms of the four stages identified in this chapter and to understand what needs to be done to implement Strategic Value Management/VBM.
- Other business initiatives such as the Balanced Scorecard and the Business Excellence model of the European Foundation for Quality Management are powerful in assisting with the implementation of Strategic Value Management/VBM programmes.

Challenges for the future

Value metrics and the tools associated with Strategic Value Analysis are vital for measuring whether value to all stakeholders will be created or destroyed. However, there are many challenges to be faced by the potential user of the various value-based approaches. The question of which method to use has to be resolved and, as we have indicated, there is no easy answer to this. Some approaches are more suited to particular applications than others but, as with many things in life, personal preferences and prejudices cannot be ignored.

Irrespective of the method adopted there are some important technical issues that are still in need of research and which can present significant difficulties in practice. For example, the cost of capital for reasons we have already outlined, is a major consideration because of its potential influence on value creation or destruction. The second and equally, if not more significant challenge, relates to issues associated with determining an appropriate planning period. Organisations create value by having distinctive capabilities and it is from these that strategies can be developed meaningfully. How to identify and translate them realistically into valuation models is a real challenge.

It must be acknowledged that the creation of value comes from the strategies selected and actions to implement them, not from the method of analysis adopted.

> *The three most important things you need to measure in a business are: Customer satisfaction, Employee satisfaction and Cash flow. If you are growing customer satisfaction, your market share is sure to grow too. Employee satisfaction gets you productivity, quality, pride and creativity. Cash flow is the pulse - the vital sign of a company* [1].

References

1. *Fortune Magazine*, 25 January 1993

2. Brigham, E., *Fundamentals of Financial Management*, The Dryden Press 1992.

3. 'Shareholder revolt: Europe', *Business Week*, 18 September 1995.

4. 'Valuing companies – a star to sail by', *The Economist*, 2 August 1997, p.61.

5. Ohmae K., *The Mind Of The Strategist: Business Planning for Competitive Advantage*, McGraw Hill, 1983.

6. Bachman, J.E., Black, A., & Wright, P., *In Search of Shareholder Value*, Price Waterhouse, Pitman, 1998, p.13.

7. Bachman, J.E., Black, A., & Wright, P., *In Search of Shareholder Value*, Price Waterhouse, Pitman, 1997, p.76.

8. *The Antidote – An Independent Commentary on the Theory and Practice of Management*, The Centre for Strategic Business Studies', Issue 3, 1996.

   Thomson R., 'Who needs earnings?', *Management Today*, June 1995.

   Houlder V., 'A value system for shareholders', *Financial Times*, 20th March 1995, page 11.

   Price Waterhouse announces ValueBuilder – increasing shareholder value, Press release, 2 February 1995.

9. Gomes, M. T., 'Sua Empressa Da Dinheiro?', *Exame*, Edition 613, 3 July 1996, pp. 60-61.

10. Mills R.W. and Parker D.R., *The Use of The use of Shareholder Value Analysis in Acquisition and Divestment Decisions by Large UK Companies*, Chartered Institute of Management Accountants, November 1995.

11. Mills R.W and Chen G., 'Evaluating Chinese joint venture opportunities using Strategic Value Analysis', *Journal of General Management*, January 1996.

12. 'A serving of added value', *Financial Times*, 13 January 1997.

13. Rappaport A., *Creating Shareholder Value: The new standard for business performance*, The Free Press, 1986.

14. Mills R.W., *Finance, Strategy and Strategic Value Analysis: Linking Two Key Business Issues*, Mars Business Associates Ltd., 1994, p.49.

15. Mills R.W. and Weinstein W.L., 'Calculating Shareholder Value in a Turbulent Environment', *Long Range Planning*, Vol.29, No.1, 1996, pp.76–83.

16. Mills R W. and Print C., Strategic value analysis, shareholder value and economic value added - what's the difference?, *Management Accounting*, February 1995, p.35-37.

17. Black A.,Wright P., and Bachman J. E., *In Search of Shareholder Value: Managing the Drivers of Performance*, Pitman Publishing, 1999, p.13.

18. 'Valuing companies – a star to sail by', *The Economist*, 2 August 1997, p.63.

19. Marsh P., *Short-termism on Trial*, Institutional Fund Managers' Association, 1990.

20 Valuing companies – a star to sail by, *The Economist*, 2 August 1997, p.62.

21 Griffith I., *Creative Accounting: How To Make Your Profits What You Want Them To Be*, Unwin Hyman, 1986.

22 Smith T., *Accounting for Growth: Stripping the Camouflage from Company Accounts*, Century Business, 1992.

23 Pijper T., *Creative Accounting: The Effectiveness of Financial Reporting in the UK*, MacMillan, 1994.

24 Jack A., 'Accounting tricks 'fool City analysts'', *Financial Times*, December 8, 1993, p. 24.

25 Terazono, E., 'JBA hit by world according to GAAP', *Financial Times*, 26 September 1997, p.20.

26 Valuing companies – a star to sail by, *The Economist*, 2 August 1997, p.62.

27 Simmonds, A. and Azieres O., *Accounting for Europe: success by 2,000 AD?*, Touche Ross, 1989.

28 Roberts, C.B., Salter, S. B. and Kantor, T.J., 'The IASC comparability project and current financial reporting reality: an empirical study of reporting in Europe', *British Accounting Review*, Vol.28, 1996, pp. 1–22.

29 Nobes, C.W., 'Classification of Financial Reporting Practices', *Advances in International Accounting*, Vol.1, 1987, pp. 1–2.

30 Doupnik, T. and Salter, S.B., 'An Empirical Test of a Judgmental International Classification of Financial Reporting Practices', *Journal of International Business Studies*, No. 1, 1993, pp. 41–60.

31 Nobes. C., *International Guide to Interpreting Company Accounts 1996-1997*.

32 Beresford, D., 'US should import UK improvements', *Financial Times*, op. cit.

33 Wright, P.D. and Keegan, D.P., 'One foot in the future', *Financial Times*, 24 April 1997.

34 Wright, P. D. and Keegan, D. P., *Pursuing Value: The Emerging Art of Reporting on the Future*, PW Papers, Price Waterhouse LLP, 1997.

35 Barron, M. and Lawless, J., 'Growth of no account', *Business Magazine*, September 1988.

Henry, D. and Smith, G., 'Letter to Financial Times', *Financial Times*, 27 June 1991.

36 Bowen, R. M., Burgstahler, D. and Daley, L. A., 'Evidence on the relationships between earnings and various measures of cash flow', *The Accounting Review*, Vol.LXI No.4, 1986, pp.713–725.

Gombola, M. J. and Ketz, J. E., 'A note on cash flow and classification patterns of financial ratios', *The Accounting Review*, Vol.LVIII, No.1, 1983, pp.105–115.

Rayburn, J., 'The association of operating cash flow and accruals with security returns', *Journal of Accounting Research*, Vol.24, 1986, Supplement, pp. 112–133.

Wilson, G. P., 'The relative information content of accruals and cash flows: combined evidence at the earnings announcement and annual report release date', *Journal of Accounting Research*, 1986, Vol.24, Supplement, pp. 165–200.

Wilson, G.P., 'The incremental information content of the accrual and funds components of earnings after controlling for earnings', *The Accounting Review*, Vol.LXII, No.2, 1987, pp.293–322.

Bowen, R.M., Burgstahler, D. and Daley, L. A., 'The incremental information content of accrual versus cash flows', *The Accounting Review*, Vol.LXII, No.4, 1987,pp.723–747.

Bernard, V. L. and Stober, T. L., 'The nature and amount of information in cash flow and accruals', *The Accounting Review*, Vol.LXIV, No.4, 1989, pp.624–652.

Charitou, A. G. and Ketz, E., 'An empirical examination of cash flow measures', *ABACUS*, Vol.27, No.1, 1991, pp.51–64.

Arnold, A. J., Clubb, C. D. B., Manson, S. and Wearing, R. T., 'The relationship between earnings, funds flows and cash flows: evidence for the UK', Accounting and Business Research, Vol.22, No.85, pp.13–19,1991.

Simmonds, A. and Azieres, O., *Accounting for Europe: success by 2001AD?*, Touche Ross, 1989.

Nobes, C. 'Accounting for differences in the Far East: are they inscrutable?', *Management Accounting*, October 1994, p.36.

Solomon, E., 'Return on investment: the relation of book yield to true yield,' in *Research in Accounting Measurement*, R. J. Jaedicke, Y. Ijiri, and O. Nielson, (Eds.) American Accounting Association, Chicago, 1966), pp.232–244.

37 Madani, H. H., 'An empirical examination of the explanatory power of accrual earnings versus cash flows: UK industrial sector', Ph.D.Thesis – Henley Management College/Brunel University, 1996.

38 Lukasik, T., 'What drives asia pacific valuations? evidence from the markets', *CPS Global Review*, Vol.111, No.VII, October 1997, p.5.

39 Copeland T., Mueller and Murrin, *Valuation*, McKinsey & Co., 1994.

40 Mahoney, W. F., 'Monsanto focusing on new metrics to improve business valuation', *Valuation Issues*, Vol.2, No.3, May/June 1996.

41 Mauboussin, M. and Johnson, P., 'Competitive advantage period 'CAP': the neglected value driver', *Frontiers of Finance*, Credit Suisse First Boston, 14 January 1997, p.10.

42 Rappaport, A, ' CFOs and strategists: forging a common framework', *Harvard Business Review*, May-June, 1992.

43 Miller, M. and Modigliani, F., 'Dividend olicy, growth and the valuation of shares', *The Journal of Business*, October 1961.

44 Bennett-Stewart III, G., *The Quest for Value*, Harper Collins, New York 1991, pp. 289-298.

45 Miller, M. and Modigliani, F., 'Dividend policy, growth and the valuation of shares', *The Journal of Business*, October 1961.

46 Porter, M. E., *Competitive Strategy: Techniques for Analysing Industries and Competitors*, The Free Press, 1980.

47 Rumelt, R. P., 'How much does industry matter?', *Strategic Management Journal*, Vol., No.3, March 1991, pp.167-186.

48 Rumelt, R. P., 'How much does industry matter?', *Strategic Management Journal*, Vol., No.3, March 1991, pp.167-186.

49 Porter, M.E., *Competitive Advantage*, The Free Press, 1985.

50 Kay, J., *Foundations of Corporate Success: How Business Strategies add value*, Oxford University Press, 1993.

51 Prahalad, C. K. and Hamel, G., 'The core competence of the corporation', *Harvard Business Review*, Vol.68, No.3, May/June 1990, pp.79–93.

52 Aaker, D.A., 'Managing assets and skills; the key to a sustainable competitive advantage', *California Management Review*, Winter 1989.

53 Source, Aaker, op.cit.

54 Williams, J.R., 'A new way to understand business competition', Working Paper, Graduate school of Industrial Administration, Carnegie-Mellon University, May 1985

55 Ansoff, H. I., *Implanting Strategic Management*, Prentice Hall, New Jersey, 1984.

56 Slywotzky, A.J., *Value Migration*, Harvard Buisness School Press, 1996

57 Mills, R. W. et al.,'*The Use of Shareholder Value Analysis in Acquisition and Divestment Decisions*, Chartered Institute of Management Accountants, 1997.

58 Rappaport, A., *Creating Shareholder Value*, Free Press, New York, 1986, p.85.

59 Mauboussin, M. and Johnson, P., 'Competitive advantage period 'CAP': the neglected value driver', *Frontiers of Finance*, Credit Suisse First Boston, op.cit., p.9.

60 Mills, R.W. and Weinstein, W.L., 'Calculating shareholder value in a turbulent environment', *Long Range Planning*, Vol.29, No.1, 1996, pp.76–83.

61 Ogilvy, J., *Probabilities: Help or Hindrance in Scenario Planning*, GBN Publication on Internet ,June 1996.

62 Hayes, R. and Garvin, D., 'Managing as if tomorrow mattered', *Harvard Business Review*, Vol.60, May/June 1992, pp.70–79.

63 Clemons, E. and Webber, B., 'Strategic information technology investments: guidelines for decision making' *Journal of Management Information Systems*, Vol.7, Fall 1990, pp.9–28.

64 Kaplan, R., 'Must CIM be justified by faith alone?', *Harvard Business Review*, Vol. 64, March/April 1986, pp.87–95.

65 Naj, A., 'In R & D, the next best thing to a gut feeling', *The Wall Street Journal*, May 21,1990.

66 Polakoff,J., 'Computer integrated manufacturing: a new look at cost justification', *Journal of Accountancy*, Vol.169, March 1990, pp 24-29.

67 Dixit, A. K. and Pindyck, R. S., 'The Options Approach to Capital Investment', *Harvard Business Review*, May/June 1995.

68 Bachman, J.E., Black, A., and Wright, P., *In Search of Shareholder Value*, Price Waterhouse, Pitman, 1998, p.171.

69 Cheung, J. K., 'Managerial flexibility in capital investment decisions: insights from the real – options literature', Vol.12, 1993, pp.29–66.

70 Newton ,D., 'Opting for the right value for R&D', *Financial Times*, 28 June 1996, p.17.

Newton, D.P. and Pearson, A.W., 'Application of option pricing theory to R&D', *R&D Management*, Vol.24, No.1, 1994, p.83.

71 Sender, G. L., 'The new pharmaceutical paradigm: option analysis at Merck', *Harvard Business Review*, January/February, 1994.

72 Black, F. and Scholes, M., 'Application of Options and Corporate Liabilities', *Journal of Political Economy*, Vol.81, 1973, p.637.

73 Nichols, N. A., 'The New Pharmaceutical Paradigm: Scientific Management at Merck', *Harvard Business Review*, January/February, 1994.

74 Mills, R. W. and Weinstein, W. L., 'Calculating Shareholder Value in a Turbulent Environment', *Long Range Planning*, Vol.29, No.1, 1996, pp.76–83.

75 *CPS Alcar Global Review, Special EVA™ Edition*, Vol.111, No.V, Spring 1997, p.1.

76 McConville, D. J., 'All about EVA', *Industry Week*, 13–14 April, 1994, pp.1–3.

77 Madden, B. J., 'Valuation: the need for a common language', *Director's Monthly (US)*, Vol.20, No.1, January 1996.

78 Lex Column, *Financial Times*, 12 March 1997.

79 *Ionica: Air Costs Less than Cables and Wires*, SBC Warburg, June 1997, page 4.

80 Copeland, T., Koller T. and Murrin J., *Valuation*, McKinsey & Co., 2nd Edition, 1995, p.276.

81 Mills, R.W. et al., 'The use of shareholder value analysis in acquisition and divestment decisions by large UK companies', The Henley Research Centre Working Paper Series (HWP 9641), 1996.

82 *The EV Guide*, SBC Warburg, November 1996.

83 'Cash flow', Lex column, *Financial Times*, 13 November 1995.

84 Lex Column, *Financial Times*, 23 June 1997.

85 Marsh P., *Financial Times*, 7 October 1996.

86 Hamada, R.S., 'Portfolio analysis, market equilibrium, and corporate finance', *Journal of Finance*, Vol.24, 1969.

87 Blanchard, O.J., Movements in the equity premium, *Brookings Papers on Economic Activity*, Vol.2, 1993, pp.75–138.

   Blanchard, O.J., The vanishing equity premium, Working Paper, MIT, October, 1992.

   Jenkinson, T., The equity risk premium and the cost of capital debate in the UK regulated utilities, Working Paper, Keble College, Oxford, 1993.

   Scott, M.F., 'The cost of capital and the risk premium on equities', *Applied Financial Economics 2*, 1992, pp.21–32.

   Siegel, J.J., 'The equity premium: stock and bond returns since 1802', *Financial Analysts' Journal*, January-February, 1992, pp. 28–38.

88 Blanchard, O.J., *Movements in the Equity Premium, Brookings Papers on Economic Activity 2*, 1993, pp. 75–138.

   Blanchard, O.J., The Vanishing Equity Premium, Working Paper, MIT, October, 1992.

   Chan, K.C., Karolyi, A. and Stulz, R.M., 'Global Financial Markets and the Risk Premium on U.S. Equity', *Journal of Financial Economics*, Vol.32, 1992, pp.137–167.

   Fama, E. F. and French, K., 'Business conditions and expected returns on stocks and bonds', *Journal of Financial Economics*, Vol.25, pp.23-49.

89   Jenkinson, T., 'The Equity Risk Premium and the Cost of Capital Debate in the UK Regulated Utilities', Working Paper, Keble College, Oxford, 1993.

Jenkinson, T., 'The cost of equity finance: conventional wisdom reconsidered', *Stock Exchange Quarterly*, Autumn 1993, pp.23–27.

90   Brown, S. J., Goetzmann, W.N. and Ross, S.A., 'Survival', *Journal of Finance* Vol.50, 1995, pp.853–873.

91   *BZW Equity-Gilt Study*, BZW Strategy, London, 1994.

92   Dimson, E. and Marsh, P., 'UK financial market returns 1955-94', Working Paper, London Business School, 1995.

93   Myers, S.C. and Borucki, L.S., 'Discounted Cash Flow Estimates of the Cost of Equity Capital - A Case Study', *Financial markets, Institutions and Instruments*, Vol.33, 1994, pp.945.

94   Sharpe and Cooper, G.M., 'Risk, return class of New York Stock Exchange common Stocks, 1931-1967;' *Financial Analysts Journal*, Vol.28, March/April, 1972, pp.46–52.

95   Banz, R.W., 'The relationship between return and market value of common stock;' *Journal of Financial Economics*, Vol.9, 1981, pp.3–18.

96   Keim, D.B., 'Size related anomalies and stock return seasonality, *Journal of Portfolio Management*, 1982.

Roll, R., 'The turn of the year effect and the return premium of small firms, *Journal of Portfolio Management*, 1982.

97   Fama, E. F. and French, K.R., 'The cross-section of expected stock returns', *Journal of Finance*, Vol.47, June, 1992.

98   Kim, D., 'The errors in the variable problem in the cross-section of expected stock returns', *Journal of Finance*, Vol.50, No.5, December 1995.

99   Chen, N., Roll, R. and Ross, S., 'Economic forces and the stock Mmarket,' *Journal of Business*, Vol.59, 1986.

100 Modigliani, F. and Miller, M.H. 'The cost of capital, corporation finance and the theory of investment, *American Economic Review*, June 1958, pp.261–297

101 Brealey, R. and Myers, S., *Principles of Corporate Finance*, McGraw Hill, New York, 1984. See the excellent, simple discussion of the Modigliani-Miller propositions on pp.359–370.

Ellsworth, R.R., 'Subordinate financial policy to corporate strategy', *Harvard Business Review*, November/December, 1983.

Hong, H. and Rappaport, A., 'Debt capacity, optimal capital structure, and capital budgeting analysis', *Financial Management*, Autumn, 1978.

Miller, M. H. 'Debt and taxes', *Journal of Finance*, May 1977.

Modigliani, F., and Miller, M. H. 'The cost of capital, corporation finance and the theory of investment', *American Economic Review*, June 1958.

'Complete income taxes and the cost of capital: a correction', *American Economic Review*, June 1963.

Piper, T.R. and Weinhold, W.A., 'How much debt is right for your company?', *Harvard Business Review*, July/August 1982.

102 Brealey, R.A. and Myers, S.C., *Principles of Corporate Finance*, Fourth edition, McGrawHill, 1991.

103 Fuller, R. and Kerr, H., 'Estimating the divisional cost of capital: an analysis of the pure play technique', *Journal of Finance*, December 1981, pp.997-1009.

104 Mills, R.W., et al., The Use of Shareholder Value Analysis in Acquisitions and Divestment Decisions by Large UK Companies, Chartered Institute of Management Accountants, 1997.

105 Gitman, L.J. and Mercurio, V. A., 'Cost of capital techniques used by major US firms: A survey and analysis of Fortune's 1000', *Financial Management*, Winter, 1982.

106 Madden, B. J. and Eddins, S., 'Different approaches to measuring the spread of return on capital in relation to the cost of capital', *Valuation Issues*, Vol.2, No.4, July/August 1996.

107 McNulty, J.J.and Yeh, D.Y., 'New directions in estimating the cost of capital', SBCWarburg Dillon Reed internal paper, September 1997

108 Brennan, M.J., 'The term structure of discount rates', *Financial Management*, Spring, 1997

109 'Analysts grapple with Russian valuations', *Financial Times*, 31 January 1996, p.24.

110 Fidler, S., 'Guide to emerging markets', *Financial Times*, 8 September 1997, p.15.

111 Garten, J. E., 'The big emerging markets', *Columbia Journal of World Business*, Summer 1996, p.8.

112 Matyszczyk, R. and McCreanor, P., Coping with valuations in emerging markets, *Acquisitions Monthly*, July 1997, pp.72–73.

113 Mills, R.W., 'Valuing in emerging markets', *Euromoney Guide to Asian Corporate Finance and Treasury*, 1997, pp. 30-32.

114 Simmonds, A. and Azieres, O., 'Accounting for Europe; success by 2001AD?', Touche Ross, 1989.

115 Adams, J., 'US Exchange open for new business', *Corporate Finance*, July, 1996, pp. 14–16.

116 'Analysts grapple with Russian valuations', *Financial Times*, 31 January 1997.

117 Ferris, S., Joshi, Y. and Makhija, A., 'Valuing an eastern european company', *Long Range Planning*, Vol.28, No.6, 1995, pp. 48–60

118 Mills, R.W. and Weinstein, W.L., 'Calculating shareholder value in a turbulent environment', *Long Range Planning*, Vol.29, No.1, 1996, pp.76–83.

119 Van Horne, J. C., *Financial Management and Policy*, 10th edition, Prentice Hall, 1995, p.69.

120 Mills, R.W. and Weinstein, W.L., 'Calculating shareholder value in a turbulent environment', *Long Range Planning*, Vol.29, No.1, 1996, p.79

121 Ritchie, B. and Marshall, D., *Business Risk Management*, Chapman and Hall, 1993.

122 Miyamoto, Arnold (1996), 'How to evaluate foreign investments', *Corporate Finance*, March, pp. 40 to 43.

123 Van Horne, J. C., *Financial Management and Policy*, 10th Edition, Prentice Hall, 1995, p.495.

124 Arab-Malaysian Merchant Bank Berhad, 12 November 1996.

125 Benninga, S.Z. and Sarig, O.H., *Corporate Finance: A valuation approach*, McGrawHill, 1997.

126 Luehrman, T.A., 'Using APV: a better tool for valuing operations', *Harvard Business Review*, May/June 1997.

127 Inselbag, I. and Kaufold, H., 'Two approaches for valuing companies under alternative financing stratgeies (and how to choose between them)', *Journal of Applied Corporate Finance*, Vol.10, No.1, Spring 1997.

128 *Financial Times*, 3 October 1997, p.21.

129 *Financial Times*, 14 October 1997, p.1.

130 *Financial Times*, 27 November 1997, p.22.

131 Firth, M., 'Takeovers, shareholder returns and the theory of the firm', *Quarterly Journal of Economics*, Vol.94, 1980, pp.235–60.

132 Franks, J. and Harris, R., 'Shareholder wealth effects of corporate takeovers: the UK experience 1955–85', *Journal of Financial Economics*, Vol.23, 1989, pp.225–49.

133 Sudarsanam, P. S., Holl, P. and Salami, A., 'Shareholder wealth gains in mergers: empirical test of the synergy and agency effects', paper presented to the Midwest Finance Association, USA, April 1993.

134 Higson, C. and J. Elliot., 'Returns to takeovers – the evidence', IFA Working Paper 173-93, London Business School, Spring 1993.

135 Agrawal, A., Jaffe, J.K. and Mandelker, G.N., 'The post-merger performance of acquiring firms: a re-examination of an anomaly', *Journal of Finance*, Vol.47, September 1992, p.1618.

136 Coopers and Lybrand, *Corporate Finance: Survey of Critical Valuation Issues in Mergers and Acquisitions*, 1994.

137 'Colouring in the map', *Mergers and Acquisitions in Europe Research Report*, KPMG Management Consulting, 1997.

138 James Capel Equity Research, *Pharmaceuticals: In search of Shareholder Value*, May 1995.

139 Banks, S. and Pape, J-P., 'Putting a Price on Success', Acquisitions Monthly, February 1994.

140 'Colouring in the map', *Mergers and Acquisitions in Europe Research Report*, KPMG Management Consulting, 1997.

141 Wislon, T., 'Evaluating Mergers and Acquisitions', Advanced Strategies for Company Valuation Conference, Euromoney, 1997.

142 Biggadike, 'The risky business of diversification', *Harvard Business Review*, May/June 1979, pp.103–111.

143 Mills, R.W. and Weinstein, W.L., 'Calculating shareholder value in a turbulent environment', *Long Range Planning*, Vol.29, No.1, 1996, pp.76–83.

144 Allas, P., McDonald, D. and Venkataraman, R., 'Managing growth options', *McKinsey Quarterly Bulletin*, No.2, 1996.

145 O'Connor, G., 'How the experts value blue sky forecasts', *Financial Times*, 24/25 February, p. 7.

146 Bachman, J.A., Black, A., & Wright, P., *In serach of Shareholder Value*, Pitman, 1997

147 Lex Column, *Financial Times*, 1 August 1997.

148 Lex Column, *Financial Times*, 1 August 1997.

149 SEC Workshop on 'The Reporting of Intangible Assets', Washington, 11-12 April 1996.

150 Edvinsson, L., 'Developing intellectual capital at Skandia', *Long Range Planning*, Vol.30, No.3.

151 Stewart, T., *Intellectual Capital: The New Wealth of Organisations*, Nicholas Brealey, 1997.

152 Pitman, B., 'Shareholder value analysis in action', *The Treasurer*, Special issue, March, 1993, pp.14–17.

153 Abrahams, P., 'Relaunch into more enterprising culture', *Financial Times*, 29 July 1993, pp.20.

154 Lorenz, C., 'Size isn't everything', *Financial Times*, 29 November 1993, p.13.

155 Hergert, M., 'Strategic resource allocation using divisional hurdle rates', *Planning Review*, January/February, 1987.

156 For example, the cyclicality and competitive structure of say the ice cream business will differ for companies operating in very different climates, e.g. Alaska versus Florida.

157 Kotler, P., *Marketing Management*, 3rd edition, Prentice Hall, New York, 1976, pp.275-302.

158 Porter, M. E., *Competitive Strategy*, The Free Press, New York, 1980.

159 Tufano, P., 'How financial engineering can advance corporate strategy', *Harvard Business Review*, January/February, 1996.

160 Kaplan, R.S. and Norton, D.P., 'The balance scorecard measures that drive performance', *Harvard Business Review*, January/February, 1992, pp.71–79.

Kaplan, R.S. and Norton, D.P., Putting the balanced scorecard to work, *Harvard Business Review*, September/October, 1993, pp.l34–137.

161 *Measuring Business Excellence* – Vol.1, No.1., 1997.

162 Frankfurter, G.M. and McGoun, E.G., 'Toward finance of meaning: what finance is, and what is could be', *The Journal of Investing*, Fall 1996.

163 Fisher, I., *Theory of Interest*, Macmillan, New York, 1930.

Hirshleifer, J., 'On the theory of optimal investment decisions', *Journal of Political Economy*, 1958, pp.329–372.

164 Fama, E. F., 'The behaviour of stock market prices', *Journal of Business*, January 1965, pp.34–105.

165 Markowitz, H., *Portfolio Selection*, Yale University Press, New Haven, 1959.

166 Sharpe, W. F., 'Capital asset prices: a theory of market equilibrium under conditions of risk', *Journal of Finance*, September 1964, pp.425–442.

167 Ross, S. A., 'The Arbitrage Theory of Capital Pricing', *Journal of Economic Theory*, Dec. 1976, pp. 343–362.

168 Fama, E. F. and French, K.R., 'The cross-section of expected stock returns', University of Chicago Centre for Research in Security Prices, 1991.

Fama, E. F. and French, K.R., "The cross-section of expected stock returns', *The Journal of Finance*, June 1992, pp.427-465.

169 Damodaran, A., *Corporate Finance: Theory and Practice*, Wiley, 1997.

170 Roll, R. and Ross, S. A., 'On the cross-sectional relation between expected returns and betas', Working Paper #21, Yale School of Management, 1992.

171 Modigliani, F. and Miller, M.H., 'The cost of capital, corporation finance and the theory of investment', *American Economic Review*, Vol.48, June 1958.

172 Miller, M., 'The Modigliani-Miller Propositions after Thirty Years', 1988.

173 Brealey, R.A. and Myers, S.C., *Principles of Corporate Finance*, 4th edition, McGrawHill, 1991.

174 Barclay, M.J., Smith, C.W. and Watts, R.L., 'The determinants of corporate leverage and dividend policies', *Bank of America Journal of Applied Corporate Finance*, Vol.7, No.4, Winter 1995.

175 Opler, T. and Titman, S., 'The debt-equity choice: an empirical analysis', Ohio State University working paper, December 1995.

176 Bernstein, P., *Against the Gods: The Remarkable Story of Risk*, Wiley, 1996.

177 Black, F. and Scholes, M., 'The pricing of options and corporate liabilities', *Journal of Political Economy*, No.81, May/June 1973.

178 Merton, R.C., 'Theory of rational option pricing', *Bell Journal of Economics and Management Science*, No.4, Spring 1973.

179 Cheung, J.K., 'Managing flexibility in capital investment decisions: insights from the real options literature', Vol.12, 1993, pp.29-66.

180 Saint-Onge, H., et al., 'Measuring and Managing Intellectual Capital', Business Intelligence BPM 96 Conference, 23-24 April 1996.

181 Grundy, T., Corporate Strategy and Financial Decisions, *Kogan Page*, 1992.

Present Value of £1

%	1	2	3	4	5	6	7	8	9	10
Period										
1	0.990	0.980	0.971	0.962	0.952	0.943	0.935	0.926	0.917	0.909
2	0.980	0.961	0.943	0.925	0.907	0.890	0.873	0.857	0.842	0.826
3	0.971	0.942	0.915	0.889	0.864	0.840	0.816	0.794	0.772	0.751
4	0.961	0.924	0.888	0.855	0.823	0.792	0.763	0.735	0.708	0.683
5	0.951	0.906	0.863	0.822	0.784	0.747	0.713	0.681	0.650	0.621
6	0.942	0.888	0.837	0.790	0.746	0.705	0.666	0.630	0.596	0.564
7	0.933	0.871	0.813	0.760	0.711	0.665	0.623	0.583	0.547	0.513
8	0.923	0.853	0.789	0.731	0.677	0.627	0.582	0.540	0.502	0.467
9	0.914	0.837	0.766	0.703	0.645	0.592	0.544	0.500	0.460	0.424
10	0.905	0.820	0.744	0.676	0.614	0.558	0.508	0.463	0.422	0.386
11	0.896	0.804	0.722	0.650	0.585	0.527	0.475	0.429	0.388	0.350
12	0.887	0.788	0.701	0.625	0.557	0.497	0.444	0.397	0.356	0.319
13	0.879	0.773	0.681	0.601	0.530	0.469	0.415	0.368	0.326	0.290
14	0.870	0.758	0.661	0.577	0.505	0.442	0.388	0.340	0.299	0.263
15	0.861	0.743	0.642	0.555	0.481	0.417	0.362	0.315	0.275	0.239
16	0.853	0.728	0.623	0.534	0.458	0.394	0.339	0.292	0.252	0.218
17	0.844	0.714	0.605	0.513	0.436	0.371	0.317	0.270	0.231	0.198
18	0.836	0.700	0.587	0.494	0.416	0.350	0.296	0.250	0.212	0.180
19	0.828	0.686	0.570	0.475	0.396	0.331	0.277	0.232	0.194	0.164
20	0.820	0.673	0.554	0.456	0.377	0.312	0.258	0.215	0.178	0.149

%	11	12	13	14	15	16	17	18	19	20
Period										
1	0.901	0.893	0.885	0.877	0.870	0.862	0.855	0.847	0.840	0.833
2	0.812	0.797	0.783	0.769	0.756	0.743	0.731	0.718	0.706	0.694
3	0.731	0.712	0.693	0.675	0.658	0.641	0.624	0.609	0.593	0.579
4	0.659	0.636	0.613	0.592	0.572	0.552	0.534	0.516	0.499	0.482
5	0.593	0.567	0.543	0.519	0.497	0.476	0.456	0.437	0.419	0.402
6	0.535	0.507	0.480	0.456	0.432	0.410	0.390	0.370	0.352	0.335
7	0.482	0.452	0.425	0.400	0.376	0.354	0.333	0.314	0.296	0.279
8	0.434	0.404	0.376	0.351	0.327	0.305	0.285	0.266	0.249	0.233
9	0.391	0.361	0.333	0.308	0.284	0.263	0.243	0.225	0.209	0.194
10	0.352	0.322	0.295	0.270	0.247	0.227	0.208	0.191	0.176	0.162
11	0.317	0.287	0.261	0.237	0.215	0.195	0.178	0.162	0.148	0.135
12	0.286	0.257	0.231	0.208	0.187	0.168	0.152	0.137	0.124	0.112
13	0.258	0.229	0.204	0.182	0.163	0.145	0.130	0.116	0.104	0.093
14	0.232	0.205	0.181	0.160	0.141	0.125	0.111	0.099	0.088	0.078
15	0.209	0.183	0.160	0.140	0.123	0.108	0.095	0.084	0.074	0.065
16	0.188	0.163	0.141	0.123	0.107	0.093	0.081	0.071	0.062	0.054
17	0.170	0.146	0.125	0.108	0.093	0.080	0.069	0.060	0.052	0.045
18	0.153	0.130	0.111	0.095	0.081	0.069	0.059	0.051	0.044	0.038
19	0.138	0.116	0.098	0.083	0.070	0.060	0.051	0.043	0.037	0.031
20	0.124	0.104	0.087	0.073	0.061	0.051	0.043	0.037	0.031	0.026

PRESENT VALUE OF £1

% Period	21	22	23	24	25	26	27	28	29	30
1	0.826	0.820	0.813	0.806	0.800	0.794	0.787	0.781	0.775	0.769
2	0.683	0.672	0.661	0.650	0.640	0.630	0.620	0.610	0.601	0.592
3	0.564	0.551	0.537	0.524	0.512	0.500	0.488	0.477	0.466	0.455
4	0.467	0.451	0.437	0.423	0.410	0.397	0.384	0.373	0.361	0.350
5	0.386	0.370	0.355	0.341	0.328	0.315	0.303	0.291	0.280	0.269
6	0.319	0.303	0.289	0.275	0.262	0.250	0.238	0.227	0.217	0.207
7	0.263	0.249	0.235	0.222	0.210	0.198	0.188	0.178	0.168	0.159
8	0.218	0.204	0.191	0.179	0.168	0.157	0.148	0.139	0.130	0.123
9	0.180	0.167	0.155	0.144	0.134	0.125	0.116	0.108	0.101	0.094
10	0.149	0.137	0.126	0.116	0.107	0.099	0.092	0.085	0.078	0.073
11	0.123	0.112	0.103	0.094	0.086	0.079	0.072	0.066	0.061	0.056
12	0.102	0.092	0.083	0.076	0.069	0.062	0.057	0.052	0.047	0.043
13	0.084	0.075	0.068	0.061	0.055	0.050	0.045	0.040	0.037	0.033
14	0.069	0.062	0.055	0.049	0.044	0.039	0.035	0.032	0.028	0.025
15	0.057	0.051	0.045	0.040	0.035	0.031	0.028	0.025	0.022	0.020
16	0.047	0.042	0.036	0.032	0.028	0.025	0.022	0.019	0.017	0.015
17	0.039	0.034	0.030	0.026	0.023	0.020	0.017	0.015	0.013	0.012
18	0.032	0.028	0.024	0.021	0.018	0.016	0.014	0.012	0.010	0.009
19	0.027	0.023	0.020	0.017	0.014	0.012	0.011	0.009	0.008	0.007
20	0.022	0.019	0.016	0.014	0.012	0.010	0.008	0.007	0.006	0.005

% Period	31	32	33	34	35	36	37	38	39	40
1	0.763	0.758	0.752	0.746	0.741	0.735	0.730	0.725	0.719	0.714
2	0.583	0.574	0.565	0.557	0.549	0.541	0.533	0.525	0.518	0.510
3	0.445	0.435	0.425	0.416	0.406	0.398	0.389	0.381	0.372	0.364
4	0.340	0.329	0.320	0.310	0.301	0.292	0.284	0.276	0.268	0.260
5	0.259	0.250	0.240	0.231	0.223	0.215	0.207	0.200	0.193	0.186
6	0.198	0.189	0.181	0.173	0.165	0.158	0.151	0.145	0.139	0.133
7	0.151	0.143	0.136	0.129	0.122	0.116	0.110	0.105	0.100	0.095
8	0.115	0.108	0.102	0.096	0.091	0.085	0.081	0.076	0.072	0.068
9	0.088	0.082	0.077	0.072	0.067	0.063	0.059	0.055	0.052	0.048
10	0.067	0.062	0.058	0.054	0.050	0.046	0.043	0.040	0.037	0.035
11	0.051	0.047	0.043	0.040	0.037	0.034	0.031	0.029	0.027	0.025
12	0.039	0.036	0.033	0.030	0.027	0.025	0.023	0.021	0.019	0.018
13	0.030	0.027	0.025	0.022	0.020	0.018	0.017	0.015	0.014	0.013
14	0.023	0.021	0.018	0.017	0.015	0.014	0.012	0.011	0.010	0.009
15	0.017	0.016	0.014	0.012	0.011	0.010	0.009	0.008	0.007	0.006
16	0.013	0.012	0.010	0.009	0.008	0.007	0.006	0.006	0.005	0.005
17	0.010	0.009	0.008	0.007	0.006	0.005	0.005	0.004	0.004	0.003
18	0.008	0.007	0.006	0.005	0.005	0.004	0.003	0.003	0.003	0.002
19	0.006	0.005	0.004	0.004	0.003	0.003	0.003	0.002	0.002	0.002
20	0.005	0.004	0.003	0.003	0.002	0.002	0.002	0.002	0.001	0.001

Annuity of £1

%	1	2	3	4	5	6	7	8	9	10
Period										
1	0.990	0.980	0.971	0.962	0.952	0.943	0.935	0.926	0.917	0.909
2	1.970	1.942	1.913	1.886	1.859	1.833	1.808	1.783	1.759	1.736
3	2.941	2.884	2.829	2.775	2.723	2.673	2.624	2.577	2.531	2.487
4	3.902	3.808	3.717	3.630	3.546	3.465	3.387	3.312	3.240	3.170
5	4.853	4.713	4.580	4.452	4.329	4.212	4.100	3.993	3.890	3.791
6	5.795	5.601	5.417	5.242	5.076	4.917	4.767	4.623	4.486	4.355
7	6.728	6.472	6.230	6.002	5.786	5.582	5.389	5.206	5.033	4.868
8	7.652	7.325	7.020	6.733	6.463	6.210	5.971	5.747	5.535	5.335
9	8.566	8.162	7.786	7.435	7.108	6.802	6.515	6.247	5.995	5.759
10	9.471	8.983	8.530	8.111	7.722	7.360	7.024	6.710	6.418	6.145
11	10.368	9.787	9.253	8.760	8.306	7.887	7.499	7.139	6.805	6.495
12	11.255	10.575	9.954	9.385	8.863	8.384	7.943	7.536	7.161	6.814
13	12.134	11.348	10.635	9.986	9.394	8.853	8.358	7.904	7.487	7.103
14	13.004	12.106	11.296	10.563	9.899	9.295	8.745	8.244	7.786	7.367
15	13.865	12.849	11.938	11.118	10.380	9.712	9.108	8.559	8.061	7.606
16	14.718	13.578	12.561	11.652	10.838	10.106	9.447	8.851	8.313	7.824
17	15.562	14.292	13.166	12.166	11.274	10.477	9.763	9.122	8.544	8.022
18	16.398	14.992	13.754	12.659	11.690	10.828	10.059	9.372	8.756	8.201
19	17.226	15.678	14.324	13.134	12.085	11.158	10.336	9.604	8.950	8.365
20	18.046	16.351	14.877	13.590	12.462	11.470	10.594	9.818	9.129	8.514

%	11	12	13	14	15	16	17	18	19	20
Period										
1	0.901	0.893	0.885	0.877	0.870	0.862	0.855	0.847	0.840	0.833
2	1.713	1.690	1.668	1.647	1.626	1.605	1.585	1.566	1.547	1.528
3	2.444	2.402	2.361	2.322	2.283	2.246	2.210	2.174	2.140	2.106
4	3.102	3.037	2.974	2.914	2.855	2.798	2.743	2.690	2.639	2.589
5	3.696	3.605	3.517	3.433	3.352	3.274	3.199	3.127	3.058	2.991
6	4.231	4.111	3.998	3.889	3.784	3.685	3.589	3.498	3.410	3.326
7	4.712	4.564	4.423	4.288	4.160	4.039	3.922	3.812	3.706	3.605
8	5.146	4.968	4.799	4.639	4.487	4.344	4.207	4.078	3.954	3.837
9	5.537	5.328	5.132	4.946	4.772	4.607	4.451	4.303	4.163	4.031
10	5.889	5.650	5.426	5.216	5.019	4.833	4.659	4.494	4.339	4.192
11	6.207	5.938	5.687	5.453	5.234	5.029	4.836	4.656	4.487	4.327
12	6.492	6.194	5.918	5.660	5.421	5.197	4.988	4.793	4.611	4.439
13	6.750	6.424	6.122	5.842	5.583	5.342	5.118	4.910	4.715	4.533
14	6.982	6.628	6.302	6.002	5.724	5.468	5.229	5.008	4.802	4.611
15	7.191	6.811	6.462	6.142	5.847	5.575	5.324	5.092	4.876	4.675
16	7.379	6.974	6.604	6.265	5.954	5.668	5.405	5.162	4.938	4.730
17	7.549	7.120	6.729	6.373	6.047	5.749	5.475	5.222	4.990	4.775
18	7.702	7.250	6.840	6.467	6.128	5.818	5.534	5.273	5.033	4.812
19	7.839	7.366	6.938	6.550	6.198	5.877	5.584	5.316	5.070	4.843
20	7.963	7.469	7.025	6.623	6.259	5.929	5.628	5.353	5.101	4.870

Annuity of £1

Period	21%	22	23	24	25	26	27	28	29	30
1	0.826	0.820	0.813	0.806	0.800	0.794	0.787	0.781	0.775	0.769
2	1.509	1.492	1.474	1.457	1.440	1.424	1.407	1.392	1.376	1.361
3	2.074	2.042	2.011	1.981	1.952	1.923	1.896	1.868	1.842	1.816
4	2.540	2.494	2.448	2.404	2.362	2.320	2.280	2.241	2.203	2.166
5	2.926	2.864	2.803	2.745	2.689	2.635	2.583	2.532	2.483	2.436
6	3.245	3.167	3.092	3.020	2.951	2.885	2.821	2.759	2.700	2.643
7	3.508	3.416	3.327	3.242	3.161	3.083	3.009	2.937	2.868	2.802
8	3.726	3.619	3.518	3.421	3.329	3.241	3.156	3.076	2.999	2.925
9	3.905	3.786	3.673	3.566	3.463	3.366	3.273	3.184	3.100	3.019
10	4.054	3.923	3.799	3.682	3.571	3.465	3.364	3.269	3.178	3.092
11	4.177	4.035	3.902	3.776	3.656	3.543	3.437	3.335	3.239	3.147
12	4.278	4.127	3.985	3.851	3.725	3.606	3.493	3.387	3.286	3.190
13	4.362	4.203	4.053	3.912	3.780	3.656	3.538	3.427	3.322	3.223
14	4.432	4.265	4.108	3.962	3.824	3.695	3.573	3.459	3.351	3.249
15	4.489	4.315	4.153	4.001	3.859	3.726	3.601	3.483	3.373	3.268
16	4.536	4.357	4.189	4.033	3.887	3.751	3.623	3.503	3.390	3.283
17	4.576	4.391	4.219	4.059	3.910	3.771	3.640	3.518	3.403	3.295
18	4.608	4.419	4.243	4.080	3.928	3.786	3.654	3.529	3.413	3.304
19	4.635	4.442	4.263	4.097	3.942	3.799	3.664	3.539	3.421	3.311
20	4.657	4.460	4.279	4.110	3.954	3.808	3.673	3.546	3.427	3.316

Period	31%	32	33	34	35	36	37	38	39	40
1	0.763	0.758	0.752	0.746	0.741	0.735	0.730	0.725	0.719	0.714
2	1.346	1.331	1.317	1.303	1.289	1.276	1.263	1.250	1.237	1.224
3	1.791	1.766	1.742	1.719	1.696	1.673	1.652	1.630	1.609	1.589
4	2.130	2.096	2.062	2.029	1.997	1.966	1.935	1.906	1.877	1.849
5	2.390	2.345	2.302	2.260	2.220	2.181	2.143	2.106	2.070	2.035
6	2.588	2.534	2.483	2.433	2.385	2.339	2.294	2.251	2.209	2.168
7	2.739	2.677	2.619	2.562	2.508	2.455	2.404	2.355	2.308	2.263
8	2.854	2.786	2.721	2.658	2.598	2.540	2.485	2.432	2.380	2.331
9	2.942	2.868	2.798	2.730	2.665	2.603	2.544	2.487	2.432	2.379
10	3.009	2.930	2.855	2.784	2.715	2.649	2.587	2.527	2.469	2.414
11	3.060	2.978	2.899	2.824	2.752	2.683	2.618	2.555	2.496	2.438
12	3.100	3.013	2.931	2.853	2.779	2.708	2.641	2.576	2.515	2.456
13	3.129	3.040	2.956	2.876	2.799	2.727	2.658	2.592	2.529	2.469
14	3.152	3.061	2.974	2.892	2.814	2.740	2.670	2.603	2.539	2.477
15	3.170	3.076	2.988	2.905	2.825	2.750	2.679	2.611	2.546	2.484
16	3.183	3.088	2.999	2.914	2.834	2.757	2.685	2.616	2.551	2.489
17	3.193	3.097	3.007	2.921	2.840	2.763	2.690	2.621	2.555	2.492
18	3.201	3.104	3.012	2.926	2.844	2.767	2.693	2.624	2.557	2.494
19	3.207	3.109	3.017	2.930	2.848	2.770	2.696	2.626	2.559	2.496
20	3.211	3.113	3.020	2.933	2.850	2.772	2.698	2.627	2.561	2.497

Appendix 1

Santos plc

Consolidated profit and loss accounts for the years ended 31 December

		1997 £m	1996 £m	1995 £m
Turnover		285.02	247.84	215.51
- Cost of sales		122.94	111.76	101.60
Gross profit		162.08	136.08	113.91
- Operating expenses		125.75	104.79	95.26
Operating profit		36.33	31.29	18.65
- Interest payable	1	8.51	8.43	7.54
Profit before tax		27.82	22.86	11.11
- Taxation		8.35	6.86	3.33
Profit attributable to shareholders		19.47	16.00	7.78
- Dividends		5.30	5.85	6.50
Transfer to reserves		14.17	10.15	1.28
Earnings per share		18.37	13.68	5.98

Santos plc

Consolidated balance sheets for the years ended 31 December

		1997 £m	1996 £m	1995 £m
Fixed assets				
Tangible fixed assets		104.20	101.40	92.50
Current assets				
Stocks		71.25	61.96	53.88
Debtors	2	47.50	41.31	35.92
Cash		0.80	0.70	0.50
		119.55	103.97	90.30
Creditors: amounts falling due within one year	3	54.63	49.96	43.70
Net current assets		64.92	54.01	46.60
Total assets less current liabilities		169.12	155.41	139.10
Creditors: amounts falling due after one year	3	70.92	70.28	62.82
		98.20	85.13	76.28
Capital and reserves				
Called up share capital (10p shares)	4	10.60	11.70	13.00
Share premium account		38.70	38.70	38.70
Revaluation reserve		2.10	2.10	2.10
Profit and loss account		46.80	32.63	22.48
Shareholders' funds		98.20	85.13	76.28

Santos plc

Notes to the accounts

		1997 £m	1996 £m	1995 £m
1.	Interest payable			
	Loans repayable after one year	8.51	8.43	7.54
2.	Debtors: amounts falling due within one year:			
	Trade debtors	47.50	41.31	35.92
3.	Creditors: amounts falling due within one year:			
	Trade creditors	40.98	37.25	33.87
	Taxation	8.35	6.86	3.33
	Proposed dividend	5.30	5.85	6.50
		54.63	49.96	43.70
	Creditors: amounts falling due after one year:			
	Loans	65.02	64.98	60.02
	Finance leases	5.90	5.30	2.80
		70.92	70.28	62.82

4. Called up share capital

   Ordinary shares 10p each: 1997, 106 million (1996, 117 million and 1995, 130 million)

5. Other relevant information

   Current share price in the market £1

Appendix 2

Key concepts of Modern Financial Theory

The impression one gets after forty years of effort, generating over 50,000 articles, is that there are just seven accomplishments

Frankfurter, G.M and McGoun, E.G. [162].

The seven accomplishments referred to by Frankfurter and McGoun comprise:

1. Present value rule.
2. Fama's efficient markets hypothesis.
3. Markowitz and portfolio theory.
4. Sharpe's capital asset pricing model.
5. Ross's arbitrage pricing theory.
6. Modigliani and Miller's models of capital structure and dividend choice.
7. Black and Scholes' option pricing formula.

The present value rule (see Exhibit 1.1) has become increasingly important in recent years with the emphasis upon discounted cash flow analysis for purposes of company valuation.

Exhibit 1.1 Present value rule

- Fisher-Hirshleifer Model – Fisher (1930) and Hirshleifer (1958) [163].
- The rule proved why, in a world of certainty, accepting all projects with a positive NPV maximises the wealth of shareholders.

Rules like the present value rule often give the impression that the whole subject area is akin to a natural science. It is true that the subject area may be approached by many scientifically, but the testing process is far more exacting than other subjects because of the number and complexity of variables involved. One analogy sometimes made is between the weather and finance, but there is one vital difference. The causes of the weather are the same now as they were yesterday and even hundreds of years ago: humidity, pressure differentials, sea-surface temperatures, and so on. While depressions cause rain and are considered as having always done so, financial markets change all the time. As regards finance, the world is in a state of perpetual change. This can be illustrated with reference to three key concepts that underpin numerous contemporary financial applications, and which represent the next three accomplishments identified by Frankfurter and McGoun – the efficient market hypothesis, portfolio theory, and the Capital Asset Pricing Model.

The first of these concepts, the efficient market hypothesis, gave quite a clear message – there is no way to beat the market [164]. Anyone who was lucky enough to do so would not be able to sustain the advantage over the long term because information flows swiftly into the market where it reaches investors who react immediately. Decisions to buy or sell will drive prices quickly to a point where shares are fully valued and only unforeseen events can affect those prices. Such unforeseen events can affect share prices both positively and negatively which means that there are no clear trends in the movement of shares.

Exhibit 1.2 Efficient Market Hypothesis

- Attributable to Eugene Fama, 1965.
- The main implication of market efficiency is that, as far as we can tell, share prices can be trusted; given the existing stock of publicly available information, shares will neither be over, nor under valued.
- There is no way to beat the market other than by getting information faster.
- Current prices reflect all information about a security.
- Only unpredictable news can cause a change in prices; old news has already been discounted.
- Because unpredictable news is unpredictable, price changes are unpredictable and follow a 'random walk'.

Key within the efficient market hypothesis are two important ideas; the first being that investors are rational and second, that rational investors trade only on new information, not on intuition. Such a belief that investors are rational gave rise to a pillar of modern finance to which we will make extensive reference, the Capital Asset Pricing Model, otherwise known as CAPM. This presumes that rational investors will seek a premium from risky investments and sets out to define the risk premium of a share in relation to the market. The model attempts both to predict market behaviour and to serve as a tool to help corporate managers invest in those projects that the market will value positively.

CAPM was developed from portfolio theory which quite simply suggests that an investor who diversifies will do better than one who does not. This simple observation helped to stimulate the development of a whole new wave of investment products – including the investment index funds – which seen in conjunction with the efficient market hypothesis reinforced the message to investors that there was no way to beat the market. Quite simply, if it is not possible to beat the market, then a sensible investor will simply hold the market in the form of a basket of shares that in some way represents all the markets upside potential while trying to diversify all the downside risks.

Exhibit 1.3 Portfolio Theory

- Attributable to Markowitz [165].
- There are two important assumptions:
    1. Risk in investment appraisal is defined by the amount of variation of returns over time.
    2. Overall risk may be reduced (relative to return) if assets are combined into portfolios.

228   APPENDIX 2

From portfolio theory it became a logical step to develop a model to judge the risk of any one share in relation to the market as a whole. This is achieved by a measure of the volatility of one share in relation to the market as a whole, known as a beta. The beta forms a part of the CAPM which is a statistical model developed in the mid-1960s and which is based on the observation that some shares are more volatile than others. This means that when stock markets rise these shares rise faster and higher than the markets and when the stock markets fall they fall faster and further. If markets use information efficiently such that share prices are adjusted quickly and continue to reflect new information about a company's risks and prospects, the fact that some shares are riskier than the average is considered a reflection of the riskiness of their underlying business. Armed with this it is possible to measure the sensitivity of a share's price to market movements by calculating its beta. The market as a whole has a beta of one. Any share moving in line with the market would also have a beta of one. A share twice as volatile as the market (that is when the market climbs 10 per cent it climbs 20 per cent) would have a beta of two; one that is half as volatile would have a beta of one-half.

Exhibit 1.4 Capital Asset Pricing Model (CAPM)

- Attributable to Sharpe, 1964 [166].

- The return on any risky asset is the risk free interest rate plus a risk premium, which is a multiple of the beta and the premium on the market as a whole.

- Security prices include discounts for certain sorts of risks, which alone explain consistently higher returns by some investors.

- The more volatile a portfolio of securities, the lower its price for a given return. Therefore, the only way to get higher returns on a portfolio in the long run is to accept higher risks.

Concerns about measuring risk using a beta have been raised by a number of academics resulting in the development of a multi-factor model known as Arbitrage Pricing Theory (APT) which is claimed to be far more effective in predicting the markets.

Exhibit 1.5 Arbitrage Pricing Theory (APT)

- Attributable to Ross, 1976 [167].

- The principle of APT is that two assets that have identical risk characteristics must offer the same return or an arbitrage opportunity will exist.

- APT attempts to measure the various dimensions of market related risk in terms of several underlying economic factors such as inflation, monthly production and interest rates, which systematically affect the price of all shares.

- In a nutshell, regression techniques are used to estimate the contribution made by each APT factor to overall risk.

However, even this approach has been questioned and a number of problems have been identified. These are summarised in Exhibit 1.6:

Exhibit 1.6 Problems with APT

○   The approach is more complex than CAPM and has difficulties in its application.

○   This has been recognised in its application in the USA where, for example, the monthly production figures published by the government are only estimates of true US industrial production.

○   This means that they are "noisy" (contain random errors) and inaccurate (contain biases introduced by the data-gathering procedure and the government smoothing or adjustment process).

○   Error thus arises because high quality data in the form of share prices are regressed against lower quality data.

However, it is worth noting that means have been devised to overcome such problems and to operationalise the approach. A significant improvement in the explanatory power of APT over CAPM has been demonstrated. What really brought the whole issue to a head was that Eugene Fama, whose efficient market work underpinned much of what is considered to be 'modern finance', concluded that beta was the wrong measure of risk. Fama, in conjunction with his colleague Kenneth French, concluded that the CAPM does not describe the last 50 years of average share returns [168]. Their observations are summarised in Exhibit 1.7.

Exhibit 1.7 Beta as a measure of risk

○   CAPM does not explain why returns on shares differ, quite simply beta is not a good guide.

○   All financial shares traded on NYSE, AMEX and NASDAQ between 1963 and 1990 were analysed and were grouped into portfolios.

○   When grouped on the basis of size (market capitalisation), CAPM provided an explanation of differences in returns, but each portfolio contained a wide range of betas.

○   Shares were also grouped by firm size and the ratio of book value to market value which provided a better explanation of differences in returns than betas.

○   Conclusion - size and market to book ratios are better indicators of likely returns.

The results of Fama and French have been contested on two fronts [169]. First, Amihud, Christensen and Mendelson, using the same data, performed different statistical tests and showed that betas did, in fact, explain returns during the time period. Second, Chan and Lakonishok examined a much longer time series of returns from 1926 to 1992 and found that the positive relationship between betas and returns broke down only in the period after 1982. They attribute this breakdown to indexing, which they argue has allowed the larger, lower beta stocks in the S&P 500 to outperform smaller, higher beta stocks. They also find that betas are a useful guide to risk in extreme market conditions, with the riskiest firms (the 10 per cent with highest beta) performing far worse than the market as a whole, in the ten worst months for the market between 1926 and 1991.

In spite of the work by Fama and French, others believe the results can be explained without discarding beta, because:

1. Investors may irrationally favour big firms.
2. They may lack the cash to buy enough shares to spread risk completely, so that risk and return are not perfectly matched in the market.
3. There may be "noise" in the CAPM beta.

However, the direct implications of the work by Fama and French are that if beta is not the appropriate predictor of risk then perhaps risk is not related to return in the way financial theorists have predicted for the past two decades. This would mean that either the markets are not efficient in the way that we have understood them to be, or that the Capital Asset Pricing Model is the wrong model, or both.

The current situation is that these controversial empirical findings, when combined with a good deal of criticism of the Capital Asset Pricing Model, leave financial theory in turmoil. However, there is a view that it may be possible to understand what is happening using chaos theory. Like earlier market theorists, the chaos school begins with science, drawing on 'cutting-edge' work in physics, maths and computing. Those involved are using new mathematical techniques to view the markets as complex and evolving systems. At the heart of their search is a belief that the secrets of any situation can be unlocked if the right perspective is taken. An analogy with a simple traffic accident can be used to illustrate the chaos perspective. If you get in your car and follow your normal route to work but then turn a corner and collide with another car, the accident seems random to you. However, if you are watching the two cars from a helicopter overhead, the collision may well seem to be inevitable. The chaos school with its focus of attention on physics and mathematics believes that properly observed, apparently random events like the movement of stock prices will show themselves to be, if not predictable, then at least decipherable.

While the chaos school seems rather far afield from traditional finance, it is attracting much attention, but unfortunately those involved have tended to develop multidimensional market models which only a privileged few can understand. The plain fact of the matter is that because of their complexity, the models are simply useless to senior management. For this reason, the death of the Capital Asset Pricing Model or the efficient markets hypothesis is unlikely. Quite simply, no one has come up with a workable alternative. Instead of throwing out the old financial models in favour of new ones, senior managers are likely to find it more helpful to use the new concepts to understand the assumptions and limitations that are built into the models they have been using all along. However, the chaos theorists may well be able to help managers think about investments in new ways and to question some of the assumptions of the old ones.

Some believe that the Capital Asset Pricing Model and Arbitrage Pricing Theory can still be applied. For example, Roll and Ross argue on the basis of their work that one cannot conclude that Capital Asset Pricing Theory is dead [170]. Although CAPM and APT are limited they can be improved operationally using a robust peer group or industry average return as a measure of market related risk. This will also help overcome some of the acknowledged problems of the two approaches, which may be summarised as:

○ Both assume that the past is a good representation of the future, a view that is clearly flawed for businesses undergoing, or which have undergone, a period of substantial structural change.

- Since beta is measured by regressing returns over a long period of time (usually five years), the effect of the change on the company's beta will be slow to appear.

- Thus, the historical beta of a company that has recently changed its exposure to risk may not be a good estimate of its future beta.

- Changes in gearing over the historical time period used may have a significant distorting effect on market related risk in calculating beta.

- Last, neither approach can be used directly for firms, divisions or other business entities which do not have publicly traded shares.

The last but one point above raises one very important question: Does capital structure matter? A firm's basic resource is the stream of cash flows produced by its assets. When the firm is financed entirely by equity, all those cash flows belong to the shareholders. When it issues both debt and equity, it undertakes to split up the cash flows into two streams, a relatively safe stream goes to the debt holders and a more risky one goes to the shareholders. The firms mix of equity and debt is known as its capital structure. In principle, secured debt financing is cheaper than equity financing because debt holders, since they have first call on the cash flows of the firm bear lower risk and therefore demand lower return. A superficial analysis would therefore suggest that management can decrease the average cost of capital by financing operations through debt rather than equity. Modigliani and Miller were among the first to try to provide an answer to the question: Is there an optimal capital structure that maximizes the value of a firm? (see Exhibit 1.8).

Exhibit 1.8 Capital structure and Modigliani and Miller

- Modigliani and Miller (MM) irrelevancy theorem [171] was put forward in two propositions (1958) that held under certain assumptions, notably the absence of taxes.

- MM proposition I: the market value of a firm is independent of capital structure.

- MM proposition II: the average cost of capital cost is independent of capital structure, i.e. as the level of debt in the capital structure increases, equity holders will demand higher returns to compensate for higher risk, which increase linearly with the level of gearing, resulting in a constant average cost of capital.

This 'irrelevancy' rests on numerous theoretical and impractical assumptions. MM always recognised the nature of these assumptions, a fact supported by their publication of subsequent papers attempting to account for real world situations [172].

Adjusting the MM propositions for taxes and other real world implications implies that capital structure does indeed have a bearing on the value of the firm. The tax deductibility of interest payments (the tax shield) on debt further emphasises the cost benefit of debt over equity. If a firm is unlikely to gain the full benefits of an interest tax shield due to insufficient profits, debt will carry less of an advantage. As the proportion of debt in the capital structure increases, the relative expected realisable tax advantage of debt will tend to decrease. This marginal reduction in the tax advantage of debt forms the basis for the traditional theory of capital structure (see Exhibit 1.9).

Exhibit 1.9 Capital structure and the Traditional Theory [173]

○ As gearing increases the cost of capital decreases due to the increasing proportion of cheaper debt, all other things being equal.

○ However, there comes a point at which debt holders begin to demand higher returns due to increased default risk (i.e. higher probability of financial distress) and the associated costs (direct and indirect costs of bankruptcy, e.g. legal fees, opportunity costs of passing up positive NPV projects due to monitoring and agency costs).

○ Also, equity holders begin to demand higher returns as gearing increases to compensate for the higher risk inherent in holding highly geared shares.

○ Thus, the Traditional Theory suggests that there is some optimal capital structure at which point the average cost of capital is minimized and the value of the firm is maximized.

Other theories assume that management does not always act with an economic rationale, that is they assume that management does not always aim to maximise shareholder returns. (see Exhibit 1.10 for a summary of the Pecking Order Theory).

Exhibit 1.10 Capital structure and the Pecking Order Theory

○ The Pecking Order Theory hypothesises that managers rank funds in order of preference: internal equity (retained profit) is the preferred choice, followed by the issuance of debt as their second preference and, lastly, external equity.

○ These rankings are ascribed according to the issuance costs of the various types of finance and with reference to the levels of scrutiny and disciplinary influences which the market applies to each type of finance.

Put simply, the Pecking Order Theory suggests that management will first attempt to use any internal 'slack' it has built up. However if additional external finance is required, the first preference is for debt rather than equity financing. Although this choice for debt rather than equity seems rational, it is made for behavioural rather than economic reasons.

Throughout our review of the capital structure issue, one of the assumptions is that there was no impact on the firm's investment and dividend policy decisions. There have been attempts to analyse the gearing and dividend choices of companies, much of which has been undertaken in the USA. Barclay *et al.* reviewed more than 6,700 industrial corporations over a 30 year period and their main finding was that the most important determinant of a company's gearing ratio and dividend yield appears to be the extent of its investment opportunities [174]. Companies whose value consists largely of intangible growth options (as measured by high market to book and R&D to value ratios) had significantly lower leverage ratios and dividend yield, on average than companies whose value is represented primarily by tangible assets (as indicated by low market to book and high depreciation to value ratios). This pattern of financing and dividend choices can be explained as follows. For high growth firms, the under-investment problem associated with heavy debt financing and the costs of high dividends make both policies potentially very costly. But, for mature firms with limited growth opportunities, high leverage and dividends can have substantial benefits in controlling the free cash flow problem – the temptation of managers to over-invest in mature businesses or make diversifying acquisitions.

However, just to provide a counter balance to these results, Opler and Titman compared US firms which issued equity between 1976 and 1993 to those that issued debt, with an emphasis on determining the relative importance of each [175]. Their results suggest that pecking order explanations of capital structure are useful in explaining firm behaviour. They found that firms which have less debt than predicted were most likely to issue debt. Moreover, profitable firms which enjoy significant gains from gearing are the most likely to issue debt. At the same time, they confirmed previous studies which show that firms are much more likely to issue equity after experiencing a rise in their share price.

Recently a Nobel prize for economics was awarded to Robert Merton and Myron Scholes for their work on valuing options which lead to an explosive growth in derivatives, e.g. options, futures, forwards and swaps. They are referred to as derivatives because their value depends on the value of another asset. They can be viewed more specifically as side bets on the value of the underlying asset [176]. Derivatives cannot reduce the risks that go with owning volatile assets, but they can determine who takes on the speculation and who avoids it.

Of particular note within the context of valuation are options, which can be described as follows. A call (or put) option gives the buyer (or seller) the right, but not the obligation to:

❍ buy (or sell) a prescribed asset, known as the underlying asset for a prescribed amount, known as the exercise price;

❍ on (European option) or before (American option) a prescribed time in the future, known as the expiration date.

❍ They bear a strong resemblance to insurance policies and are often bought and sold for the same reasons, e.g. portfolio insurance whereby a put option is purchased to protect an underlying portfolio of assets.

The value of an option is determined by a number of variables as illustrated in Exhibit 1.11:

Exhibit 1.11 Determinants of an Options Value [169]

Variables relating to the underlying asset:

❍ Its current value;
❍ Variance in its value;
❍ Dividends paid on the underlying asset.

Variables relating to the options characteristics:

❍ Its exercise price;
❍ The time to expiration.

Variables relating to the financial markets:

❍ Risk free rate of interest corresponding to life of option.

What is so notable from Exhibit 1.11 is that the probability that the price of the underlying asset might go up or down is irrelevant to the value of an option – this really is counterintuitive. The thing that matters is how far the asset price might move (i.e. variance), not the direction in which it moves.

Exhibit 1.12 Option Pricing theory

- Attributable to Fischer Black 1973 [177] and Myron Scholes 1973 [178].
- Developed a model for valuing dividend protected European options using the idea of a replicating portfolio – a portfolio composed of the underlying asset and the risk free asset that had the same cash flows as the option being valued – to come up with their formula.
- Based on the fundamental insight that in effect, by breaking down assets into their constituent parts, it is possible to remove those risks not required and to take on those that are.

In essence the model provided a means of valuing risk so that it can be traded.

Adjusted present value (APV)

An approach that captures the interaction of the financing and investment decisions. APV analysis starts with an estimate of the business base case net present value (NPV) assuming all equity financing. To this base case NPV the value of financing decisions is added, i.e.:

$$\text{APV} = \text{Base case NPV of an all equity financed firm} + \text{NPV of financing decisions}$$

Accounting policies

These are disclosed in the annual reports published by quoted companies and represent the interpretation of accounting principles and requirements adopted by the board of directors.

Accounting principles

A number of generally accepted accounting principles (GAAP) are used in preparing financial statements. They are only generally accepted and do not have the force of law. Sometimes they are referred to as accounting concepts and conventions.

Accounting rate of return

A method used to evaluate an investment opportunity that ignores the time value of money. The return generated by an investment opportunity is expressed as a percentage of the capital outlay.

Amortisation

The writing-off of a fixed asset over a time period. It is typically used in conjunction with intangible assets, e.g. goodwill. See depreciation.

Annual report

A report issued to shareholders and other interested parties which normally includes a chairman's statement, report of the directors, review of operations, financial statements and associated notes.

Annuity

A series of payments of an equal, or constant, amount of money at fixed intervals for a specified number of periods.

Arbitrage

A purchase in one market with the intention of immediate resale in another market, in order to profit from the price difference.

Arbitrage Pricing Theory (APT)

The principle which underpins APT is that two assets that have identical risk characteristics must offer the same return or an arbitrage opportunity will exist. APT attempts to measure the various dimensions of market related risk in terms of several underlying economic factors, such as inflation or monthly production and interest rates, which systematically affect the price of all shares.

Asset value analysis (AVA)

AVA methods measure the economic value of assets as if they are sold.

Balanced scorecard

An integrated and holistic approach which translates a business vision and strategy into objectives and measures which are viewed from four perspectives:

1. How do customers see us? (customer perspective).
2. At what processes must we excel? (internal perspective).
3. Can we continue to improve and create value? (innovation and learning perspective).
4. How do we look to our shareholders? (financial).

Balance sheet

A statement showing the financial position of a company in terms of its assets and liabilities at a specific point in time.

Beta

Beta is a relative measure of volatility that is determined by comparing the return on a share (stock) to the return on the stock market. In simple terms, the greater the volatility, the more risky the share, which will be reflected in a higher beta.

The type of risk that beta in the CAPM measures is called systematic, market, or non-diversifiable risk. This risk is caused by macroeconomic factors like inflation or political events, which affect the returns of all companies. If a company is affected by these macroeconomic factors in the same way as the market is, then the company will have a beta of one and will be expected to have returns equal to the market. Similarly, if a company's systematic risk is greater than the market, then a relative measure of volatility is determined by comparing a share's returns to the market's returns. The greater the volatility, the higher the beta.

Bond rating

Bond rating is the most widely used measure of a firm's default risk and is generally assigned by an independent ratings agency using a mix of private and public information.

Business excellence model

Developed in the early 1990s by the European Foundation for Quality Management (EFQM), the model is based on the simple premise that processes are the means by which a company harnesses and releases the talents and potential of its people to produce results. The logic is simply: by improving the 'how' of a company's operations (the enablers of leadership, policy and strategy, people management, resources and processes), improved results will follow for each of its key stakeholders (financial, customers, people and society).

Business value

The present value generated by the free cash flows over a planning period in which *all* providers of funds have a claim. It is the value generated from business activities and excludes the value of any external investments (marketable securities).

Capital Asset Pricing Model (CAPM)

Modern financial theory suggests that the cost of equity can be estimated from analysing what return investors require when buying a share. Their requirement can be estimated using the Capital Asset Pricing Model, known as CAPM. The underlying premise of the approach is the more risk an investor is required to take on, the higher the rate of return that will be expected. It is in a class of market models called risk-premium models which rely on the assumption that every individual holding a risky security will demand a return in excess of the return they would receive from a risk-free security. This excess return is the premium to compensate the investor for risk that cannot be diversified away.

The CAPM cost of equity can be estimated using the following formula:

Cost of equity = Risk-free rate + (Beta x Equity risk premium)

Capital investment appraisal

The evaluation of proposed capital projects. Sometimes referred to as project appraisal.

Capital structure

The composition of a company's sources of long-term funds, e.g. equity and debt.

Cash flow return on investment (CFROI)

CFROI is an economic measure of a company's performance and is analogous to the IRR used to measure the economic return from an investment project, but is applied to a business as a whole rather than an individual project. In place of the initial investment used in a project appraisal internal rate of return (IRR) calculation, the firm's gross operating assets are used. The firm's cash earnings are taken as the annual cash flows and the asset life is substituted for project life.

Cash flow statement

A statement that UK and US companies are required to include in their published accounts. Such statements analyse cash flows under three types of activity: Investing activities, Financial activities and Operating activities.

Chaos theory

New mathematical techniques used in finance to view the markets as complex and evolving systems.

Competitive advantage period (CAP)

The CAP is the time period during which a company is expected to generate returns on incremental investment that exceed its cost of capital.

Compounding

A technique for determining a future value given a present value, a time period and an interest rate.

Continuing period

Time horizon beyond the planning period.

Continuing value

See terminal value.

Core competences

Resources, processes or skills, which provide competitive advantage.

Corporate value

The sum of business value and marketable securities, i.e. when a business holds investments in other businesses, the benefits of which are not captured in the business valuation process, any such benefits have to be added to business value to determine corporate value.

Cost of capital
The cost of long-term funds to a company.

Cost of equity
The cost of shareholders' funds to a company.

Creative accounting
The name given to a number of approaches by which companies could use (and have used) considerable judgement to produce results which put them in the best possible light, while staying within the letter of the law.

Critical value appraisal
A method of appraisal used to judge whether in financial terms any benefit might result from an organisational change. It requires the calculation of:
- current market value;
- business value 'as is';
- business value with improvements.

Cross-sectional analysis
Method of estimating the cost of equity for an unquoted business entity. Cross-sectional models are also called analytical, accounting, or fundamental methods.

Current assets
Those assets of a company that are reasonably expected to be realised in cash, or sold, or consumed during the normal operating cycle of the business. They include stock, debtors, short-term investments, bank and cash balances.

Current liabilities
Those liabilities which a company may rely on to finance short-term activities. They include creditors, bank overdraft, proposed final dividend, and current taxation.

Debtors
Amounts owed to a company by its customers.

Deferred tax
The provision for deferred tax is caused by the tax effect of timing differences on tax payable between the period they are recognised for accounting purposes and the period they are assessable for income tax purposes.

Depreciation
An accounting adjustment to take account of the diminution in value of a fixed asset over its economic life.

Discount rate
Rate used to discount future cash flows in order to calculate their present value.

Discounted Cash Flow (DCF)
A technique for calculating whether a sum receivable at some time in the future is worthwhile in terms of value today. It involves discounting, or scaling-down, future cash flows.

Distinctive capability
The features of a firm's position or organisation which cannot readily be reproduced by competitors and so represent a firms competitive advantage when applied to specific markets. Generally based on architecture, innovation, reputation, or the ownership of strategic assets.

Diversifiable risk
That part of total risk that can be eliminated in a diversified portfolio. (Also called unsystematic or specific risk.)

Dividend
The proportion of the profits of a company distributed to shareholders.

Dividend Valuation Model
A valuation model used for calculating the cost of equity, which is based on the future dividend stream.

Dividend yield
A ratio showing the relationship between the ordinary dividend and the market price of an ordinary share.

Earnings per share
Profit attributable to shareholders (which is often the same as profit after taxation) divided by the weighted average number of ordinary shares in issue during the period. The calculation and result is shown by way of a note in a company's annual report.

Earnings before tax, interest, depreciation and amortisation (EBITDA)
EBITDA is a proxy for gross operating cash flow and is calculated before financing and investment requirements.

Economic profit
Economic profit measures the amount of value created by a business in a single year and is defined as NOPAT less a capital charge. See Strategic Value Added.

Economic Value Added (EVA)
See Strategic Value Added.

Efficient Market Hypothesis
A hypothesis which postulates that because of market efficiency there is no way to beat the stock market. Efficient means that share prices react quickly and unambiguously to new information.

Equity
The sum of issued share capital, capital reserves and revenue reserves, which is also known as shareholders' funds, or net worth.

Equity risk premium
The excess return above the risk-free rate that investors demand for holding risky securities.

Equity share capital
The share capital of a company attributable to ordinary shareholders.

Financial risk
The risk that results from a significant dependency on capital funded by debt and which typically requires to be serviced by non-discretionary interest payments.

Fisher effect
The Fisher effect states that the nominal rate of interest embodies in it an inflation premium sufficient to compensate lenders for the expected loss of purchasing power associated with the receipt of future money. It is typically expressed as follows:

$$(1 + m) = (1 + r) \times (1 + i)$$

Where,
- m = nominal, or money, rate;
- r = real rate;
- i = expected rate of inflation.

Fixed assets
Those assets which an organisation holds for use within the business and not for resale. They consist of tangible assets such as land and buildings, plant and machinery, vehicles, fixtures and fittings, and intangible assets such as goodwill.

Floating charge
A charge against assets as security for a debt. It is a general claim against any available asset of the company.

Flow through accounting
A system of bookkeeping that forces all transactions through both the profit and loss account and the balance sheet. With a few notable exceptions, in the USA and UK, GAAP are largely a 'flow through' method of accounting. However, not all countries follow this type of accounting system.

Forecast horizon
The last year of the planning period.

Free cash flow
The cash available to the providers of finance.

Gearing
Expresses the relationship between some measure of interest-bearing capital and some measure of equity capital or the total capital employed.

Goodwill
The difference between the amount paid for a company as a whole and the net value of the assets and liabilities acquired.

Income statement
The term used for the profit and loss account in the USA.

Incremental Fixed Capital Investment (IFCI)
Investment in new assets to enable intended sales growth to occur.

Incremental Working Capital Investment (IWCI)
Investment in working capital, such as stocks of materials, to enable intended sales growth to occur.

Intangible assets

Assets the value of which does not relate to their physical properties, e.g. goodwill and brands.

Internal rate of return (IRR)

The rate of discount at which the present value of the future cash flows is equal to the initial outlay, i.e. at the IRR the net present value is zero.

Interest payable

Money payable (but not necessary paid) on interest bearing debt.

International Fisher effect

The proposition that the currency of a country with high interest rates will depreciate over time, relative to currencies of countries with low inflation rates.

Law of one price

One of the fundamental laws of finance is that two investments of equal risk must have the same return. This suggests that investments with identical cash flows and risk must also have the same net present value (NPV). If the two investments do not have the same value, then an arbitrage opportunity exists.

Leverage

A US term for gearing.

Liabilities

The financial obligations owed by a company to shareholders, other providers of debt, trade creditors and other creditors.

Loan capital

Finance that has been borrowed and not obtained from the shareholders.

Long-term liabilities

Liabilities which are not due for repayment within one year.

Market value of equity

The product of the market value of shares and the number of shares issued. Often referred to as market capitalisation.

Market implied capital advantage period

Using the seven value driver framework, market estimates are made of all the value drivers except the length of the forecast horizon which is stretched as many years as necessary to achieve the current share price. This time period is the company's market implied capital advantage period (CAP).

Market relative analysis (MRA)

See relative valuation models.

Market risk

Market risks, like changes in the economy, tax reform or a change in the world energy situation cannot be diversified away, such that even the investor who holds a well diversified portfolio will be exposed to this type of risk.

Market value add (MVA)

The difference between the market value of capital (debt and equity) minus the book value of invested capital. Invested capital can be calculated from an operating perspective as the sum of fixed assets and working capital or from a financing perspective as the sum of all equity and interest bearing debt.

Marketable securities

Marketable securities are short-term cash and investments that a company holds over and above its target cash balances to support operations. The returns on marketable securities just compensate for their risk and so they are zero NPV investments. Marketable securities are often referred to as non-core or peripheral assets.

MB ratio

The relationship between market value (market capitalisation) and shareholders' funds.

Minority interest

The proportion of shares in subsidiary companies which is not held by a holding company. Profit attributable to minority interests and accumulated balances are shown in the consolidated financial statements.

Net assets

See net capital employed.

Net capital employed

The sum of fixed assets, investments, current assets, but minus current liabilities.

Net current assets

See working capital.

Net operating profit after taxes (NOPAT)

The after tax operating profits of a business which are unaffected by financing issues.

Net present value (NPV)

The difference between the discounted value of future net cash inflows and the initial outlay.

Peer group analysis

An approach involving the analysis of peer group companies which can be used in conjunction with financial information relating to a company to estimate its value. Sometimes referred to under the heading of the analogous approach.

PE ratio

One of the most significant indicators of corporate performance which is widely quoted in the financial press. It is calculated by dividing the market price of a share by the earnings per share (or the total market value by the total profit attributable to shareholders), i.e.

$$\text{PE ratio} = \frac{\text{Market price of a share}}{\text{Earnings per share}}$$

PE relative

A means of comparing a company's PE ratio with the market as a whole:

$$\text{PE relative} = \frac{\text{PE of the company}}{\text{PE of the market}}$$

Performance spread

The difference between the return on capital and the cost of capital expressed as a percentage.

Perpetuity

A special case of an annuity in which the cash flows are assumed to be received forever, i.e. in perpetuity.

Planning period

The period over which a business forecasts its future financials for purposes of undertaking a free cash flow valuation. Also known as the forecast period.

Portfolio theory

A theory which suggests that an investor who diversifies will do better than one who does not.

Present value rule

A rule which explains why in a world of certainty accepting all projects with a positive NPV maximises the wealth of shareholders.

Profit and loss account

A statement showing what profit has been made over a period and the uses to which the profit has been put.

Purchasing power parity (PPP)

According to PPP the exchange rate adjusts to keep purchasing power constant among currencies.

Real option

An option on a non-traded asset, such as an investment project, R&D, joint ventures etc.

Realisable value

An estimate of the value that is likely to be derived from the sale of an asset of the business to a third party.

Reducing balance depreciation

A method of depreciation whereby the periodic amount written off is a percentage of the reduced balance (i.e. cost less accumulated depreciation). This results in higher charges for depreciation during the earlier life of the asset and correspondingly lower charges each year.

Relative valuation models

Relative valuation models enable the value of a business to be derived from the pricing of comparable businesses, using earnings, cash flow, book value or revenues.

Replacement Fixed Capital Investment (RFCI)
Investment in fixed assets to maintain the existing revenue base.

Replacement value
The cost of replacing an asset.

Reserves - capital
That portion of total equity which is regarded as not being available for withdrawal by proprietors/shareholders, e.g. share premium and revaluation surplus.

Reserves - revenue (profit and loss account)
That portion of total equity representing retained earnings which is available for withdrawal by proprietors/shareholders.

Residual value
Value generated beyond the planning period. Also known as the terminal value.

Risk-free rate
The most secure return that can be achieved.

Sales
Income derived from the principal activities of a company, net of value added tax (VAT).

Scenarios
Scenarios can be viewed as long term stories about possible future external environments, which provide two or three credible pathways. Scenarios are a tool for clarifying perceptions about alternative future environments in which decisions might be played out.

Sensitivity analysis
A commonly used approach for assessing risk whereby input variables are changed to determine their effect on financial results.

Share capital (issued)
The product of the total number of shares issued and the nominal value of the shares.

Shareholder's funds
Another name for equity.

Shareholder Value Analysis
A valuation approach which considers in broad terms that the value of a business to a shareholder can be determined by discounting its future cash flows using an appropriate cost of capital.

Share premium
The excess paid for a share, to a company, over its nominal value.

Short-termism
A term associated with managing for today rather than tomorrow and beyond.

Specific (unsystematic) risk

Refers to the risk that is isolated to a particular firm, group of firms, or an industry, which can be reduced, if not eliminated, by holding a well diversified portfolio.

Straight-line depreciation

A method of depreciation whereby an equal amount is written-off the value of a fixed asset over its estimated economic life.

Strategic business unit (SBU)

Strategic business unit means a unit within the overall corporate entity for which there is an external market for its goods and services and which is distinct from that of other SBUs.

Strategic value

A measure of value calculated as follows:

	Business value
+	Marketable securities or investments
=	Corporate value
−	Market value of debt and obligations
=	Strategic value

Sometimes known as shareholder value.

Strategic value added (SVA)

The relationship between the return on capital, the cost of capital and the capital employed, which can be calculated in two ways, both of which produce the same result:

Method 1: The 'spread' approach, where for a particular period, SVA represents the amount of capital invested in a business multiplied by the 'performance spread', (i.e. the difference between the return achieved on invested capital and the WACC):

$$SVA = \text{Invested capital} \times \text{performance spread}$$

Method 2: The total profits less total capital charge approach, where SVA is calculated as NOPAT less a charge on the capital invested in the business:

$$SVA = NOPAT - \text{Capital charge}$$

SVA is also known as economic profit and EVA®.

Strategic value management

A term associated with the implementation of the principles of strategic value as a management tool for running the business.

Synergies

Synergies occur in situations where two or more activities or processes complement each other to the extent that their combined effect is greater than the sum of the parts.

Tangible assets

Assets having a physical identity such as land and buildings, plant and machinery, vehicles etc.

Terminal value

The terminal value is the value of cash flows generated by a business beyond the forecast period. In applying the principles of strategic value, a company's future free cash flows can be separated into two time periods and the value generated can be identified as:

$$\text{Value} = \text{Present value of cash flows during explicit forecast period} + \text{Present value of cash flows after explicit forecast period}$$

The present value of cash flows after the explicit forecast period is known as the terminal value.

The term structure of interest rates

The discounted present value of an extended series of cash flows is:

$$\text{Present value} = \frac{CF_1}{(1 + r_1)} + \frac{CF_2}{(1 + r_1)^2} + \frac{CF_3}{(1 + r_1)^3} + \ldots$$

In principle there can be a different rate of interest for each future period. This relationship between the interest rate and the maturity of the cash flow is called the term structure of interest rates. This term structure can be seen in the capital markets where government securities maturing at different dates offer different rates of interest.

Time value of money

A concept that is an integral part of the discounted cash flow technique used in strategic value analysis. It recognises that cash flows received from a later years opportunity cannot be compared with cash flows received from the earlier years. Other things being equal, there would be a preference for the same sum of money received sooner rather than later, because it could be invested to earn a return.

Total assets

The sum of fixed assets, investments and current assets. Also known as invested capital which may be viewed from either an operating perspective or a financing perspective.

Total business return (TBR)

Total business return is the internal rate of return that equates the estimated future value of a business plus its free cash flow generated over a period with the estimated initial value of the business. TBR is often calculated as an annualised percentage.

Total shareholder return (TSR)

A widely accepted measure in the investment community for measuring wealth creation for shareholders. This measure represents the internal rate of return that equates the original purchase price of a share, the dividend stream received by the investor and the market price of the share at the end of its holding period. TSR is often calculated as an annualised percentage.

Value drivers

Determinants of future business value:
1. Sales growth rate.
2. Operating profit margin.
3. Cash tax rate.
4. Fixed capital investment.
5. Working capital investment.
6. Planning period.
7. Cost of capital.

Value drivers one to five above are called the cash flow drivers as they are the means by which free cash flow estimates can be generated.

Value mapping

Value mapping is achieved by plotting the value it generated by each strategic business unit against the level of investment needed to generate it. The value map that results gives a vivid picture of which business units create and which consume value.

Weighted Average Cost of Capital (WACC)

A principle associated with the view that the benefits from debt financing can be interpreted in terms of an optimal or ideal capital structure. WACC is calculated as follows:

$$\text{Weighted average cost of capital} = \%\text{Debt } K_d + \%\text{Equity } K_e$$

Where,
K_d = Cost of debt;
K_e = Cost of equity.

Working capital

The excess of current assets (stock, debtors and cash) over current liabilities (creditors, bank overdraft etc.).

Yield to redemption (maturity)

The percentage which equates all future cash flows and any redemption payment with current market value.

Index

A

Accounting policies 235
Accounting principles 235
Accounting rate of return 235
Accounting Standards Board 11
Acquisitions 15, 19, 153, 158, 162, 186, 190, 198
Adjusted present value 235
Amortisation 79, 235
Analytical approach 120
Analogous approach 120
Annuity 87, 235
APV 235
Arbitrage 235
Arbitrage Pricing Theory (APT) 101, 109, 227, 235
Architecture 43
Asset beta 103
Asset value analysis 96, 97, 235

B

Balance sheet 9, 10, 66, 71, 96, 236
Balanced scorecard 186, 201-203, 236
Base case value 145, 147
Beta 102, 105, 109, 115-121, 133, 137, 138, 180, 195, 229, 236
Bond rating 236
Brands 13, 96, 183
Business excellence model 204, 236
Business units 71
Business value 35, 191, 236
Business navigator 186, 187

C

Capital Asset Pricing Model (CAPM) 19, 101-109, 115, 121, 122, 132, 194-196, 227, 236
Capital charge 7, 73
Capital employed 73
Capital gains tax 26
Capital structure 93, 101, 112, 115, 119–122, 148, 231, 232, 237
Capitalisation of costs 10
Cash Flow Return On Investment (CFROI) 8, 78, 79, 97, 122, 237
Cash flow statement 237
Cash tax rate 16, 26
      Capital gains tax 26
       Deferred tax 26

Chaos theory   237
Competitive Advantage Period (CAP)   15, 16, 40, 41, 44, 48–53, 57, 58, 75, 76, 237
Compounding   237
Continuing period   75, 90, 237
Continuing value   237
Core competences   44, 237
Corporate tax rate   103
Corporate value   69, 237
Cost of capital   5, 8, 13–19, 33, 40, 41, 68, 73, 75, 76, 79, 86, 100, 118–122, 132–142, 156–158, 166, 178, 194, 196, 200, 238
Cost of debt   86, 101, 111–123, 137, 138, 196
Cost of equity   77, 101, 102, 108, 110, 111, 115–123, 147, 180, 194–196, 238
Creative accounting   9, 181, 238
      Balance sheet   10
      Capitalise interest costs   10
      Fixed assets   10
      Profit and loss account   10
Critical value appraisal   238
Cross-sectional analysis   195, 238
Cross border valuation   25
Current assets   238
Current liabilities   238

D

Data limitations
Debt:Equity ratio   103, 105, 115, 119, 194
Debenture   112
Debt capital   118
Debtors   238
Deferred tax   26, 238
Depreciation   10, 25, 27, 70, 79, 95, 238
Discount rate   238
Discounted Cash Flow (DCF)   8, 86, 108, 177, 183, 238
Disposal   198
Distinctive capability   43, 239
      Architecture   43
      Innovation   44
      Reputation   43
      Strategic assets   44
Diversifiable risk   105, 239
Dividend   77, 110, 111, 239
Dividend valuation model   101, 108, 110, 239
Dividend yield   106, 108, 121, 239
Divisional beta   121

E

Earnings Before Interest Tax Depreciation and Amortisation (EBITDA)   16, 24–26, 28, 37, 95, 177, 181, 239
Earnings per share   14, 93, 199, 239
Earnings yield   111, 121
Economic depreciation   70, 71
Economic profit   7, 8, 64, 70, 72, 239
Economic value   97
Economic Value Added (EVA)   8, 64, 239
Efficient markets hypothesis   227, 239
Emerging markets   15, 18, 113, 130, 131
Enterprise value   95, 180, 183
Equity   239
Equity beta   103, 121
Equity cash flow   77, 78, 100
Equity risk premium   102, 106, 108, 116, 117, 133, 137, 138, 195, 239
Equity share capital   239
Exercise price   56
Ex ante analysis   108
Ex post analysis   106
Evaluator   16

F

Federal Accounting Standards Board (FASB)   131
Financial drivers   12
Financial engineering   198
Financial leverage   112, 118
Financial reporting   11
Financial risk   240
Financing effects   18
Fisher effect   133, 134, 240
Fixed assets   9, 10, 26, 70, 240
Fixed capital investment   16, 24
Floating charge   240
Flow through accounting   72, 240
Forecast horizon   240
Free cash flow   7, 8, 15, 16, 24, 28–35, 48, 50–52, 55, 66, 74, 76, 86, 87, 88, 89, 90, 142, 145, 148, 165–167, 177, 178, 180, 182, 240
Fundamental beta   105, 195

G

Gearing   77, 118, 148, 194, 240
Goodwill   11, 96, 183, 240
Gordon's growth model   121, 122

H

Harmonisation 11

I

Income statement 240
Incremental Fixed Capital Investment (IFCI) 27, 29, 67, 156, 157, 165, 168, 240
Incremental Working Capital Investment (IWCI) 67, 156, 240
Inflation pressures 133
Inflation, rate of 139
Innovation 43
Intangible assets 183, 241
Intellectual capital 186
Intellectual property 185
Interest payable 241
Internal rate of return 111, 241
International Accounting Standards (IAS) 131
International Accounting Standards Committee (IASC) 12
International Fisher Effect 241
International Monetary Fund 130

J

Joint ventures 15, 19, 164–169, 190

L

Law of one price 109, 241
Leverage 241
Liabilities 241
Life cycle 31, 46
      Product 46
Loan capital 241
London Stock Exchange 14
Long-term liabilities 241

M

Maintenance capex 27
Marginal tax rate 112, 114, 137, 180
Market:Book 92, 96, 242
Market capitalisation 191
Market implied capital advantage period 241
Market implied duration 49, 53
Market relative analysis (MRA) 92, 177, 241
Market risk 105, 132, 241
Market share 13
Market Value Added (MVA) 5–9, 68, 69, 242
Market value of capital 73

Market value of equity 180, 241
Marketable securities 242
Mergers 15, 19, 153, 158, 190
Minority interest 242
Modigliani and Miller 231

N

Net assets 242
Net capital employed 242
Net current assets 242
Net Operating Profit After Taxes (NOPAT) 7, 67, 69, 242
Net present value 53, 54,57, 68, 70, 72, 242
New issues 190
Nominal value 112

O

Operating cash flow 29, 159
Operating effects 18
Operating profit margin 13, 157, 158
Options pricing,
    theory 55, 57, 123, 234
    model 56
        Exercise price 56
        Project volatility 56
        Risk-free rate 56
        Stock price 56
        Time to expiration 56
Options value 233
Ordinary shareholders 100

P

Patents 183
Pecking order theory 232
PE Relative 243
Peer group
    analysis 113, 191, 194, 242
    companies 19, 95, 113, 121, 195, 196
    comparators 92
Peer instruments 113
Performance spread 67, 69, 71, 243
Perpetuity 38, 40, 69, 76, 84, 88–91, 97, 100, 111, 147, 168, 179–181, 243
Perpetuity value 18
Planning period 16, 34, 35, 40, 49, 53, 57, 58, 69, 75, 84, 90, 91, 158, 165, 166, 168, 200, 243
Porter's five forces 41

Portfolio theory   227, 243
Positive spread   5
Predictive beta   105
Preference shares   111
Present value rule   226, 243
Price:Earnings   91–93, 177, 180, 182, 183, 242
Price:EBIDA   92, 95, 182
Price:Sales   92, 96
Product development   28
Profit and loss account   9, 10, 72, 93, 243
Project volatility   56
Published beta   103, 104, 137
Purchasing power parity (PPP)   133, 243

R

Real option   55, 76, 243
Realisable value   243
Reducing balance depreciation   243
Regeared beta   103, 104, 138
Relative valuation models   243
Replacement cost   70
Replacement Fixed Capital Investment (RFCI)   27, 29, 165, 168, 244
Replacement value   244
Reputation   43
Return on equity   121
Research and development   13, 28
Reserves – capital   244
Reserves – revenue   244
Residual value   97, 166, 168, 180, 200, 244
Return on capital   40, 79, 205
Return on equity   14, 111
Rights of access   183, 184
Risk   14, 91, 132, 142, 178, 191, 196
      Market   105, 132
      Specific   132
      Total   132
Risk-free rate   56, 102, 105, 106, 113, 116, 117, 133, 137, 138, 141, 180, 195, 244
Risk premium   107, 180

S

Sales growth   13, 16, 24, 152, 157, 158
Scenario analysis   7
Scenario thinking   50, 132
Scenarios   169, 244
Sensitivity analysis   244

Share capital 244
Share premium 244
Shareholder Value analysis 6, 8, 12, 15, 72, 153, 244
Shareholder's fund 244
Short-termism 9, 244
Sinking fund 159
Specific (unsystematic) risk 105, 132, 245
Spot exchange rate 141
Spread 8
Spread methods 6
Spreadsheet modelling 17
    Operating effects 18
    Financing effects 18
    Tax effects 18
Stability 47
Statement of Shareholder Value Achieved 13
Stock price 56
Straight-line depreciation 245
Strategic assets
Strategic business unit (SBU) 192, 196, 245
Strategic plan 190
Strategic valuation 52
Strategic value 35, 156, 159, 245
    per share 37
Strategic value added 65, 66, 67-79, 245
Strategic Value Analysis (SVA) 5, 15–19, 52, 64, 152, 153, 178, 190, 204
Strategic Value Management 15, 19, 190, 199, 200, 245
Synergies 245
Systematic risk 120

Tangible assets 245
Tax effects 18
Tax shield 147, 148
Terminal value (TV) 15, 18, 34, 35, 48, 49, 53, 57, 58, 69, 75, 78, 79, 84, 89, 90, 97, 147, 148, 179, 246
Time to expiration 56
Time value of money 14, 141, 246
Total assets 246
Total business return (TBR) 246
Total Shareholder Return (TSR) 8, 9, 246
Traded equity options 123
Trademarks 183
Transfer pricing 194
Triangle debts 164

U

Ungeared beta 103, 104, 137, 138
Unsystematic risk 105

V

Valuation methods 5
Valuation metrics 19
Value chains 42, 46
      Dynamic 46
      Evolving 46
      Stable 46
      Unstable 46
Value creation 5, 12, 154, 157
Value drivers 13–16, 24, 179, 187, 198, 247
Value gap 37, 49, 152, 198
Value inflow 47
Value mapping 154, 190, 192, 247
Value migration 46–48
Value outflow 47
Value preservation 5
Value realisation 5
Value reporting 12, 13

W

Weighted Average Cost of Capital (WACC) 7, 16-19, 34, 69, 78, 87, 88, 89, 90, 100, 101, 115–117, 138, 141, 145, 148, 163, 177, 179, 181, 185, 247
What if 51, 163
Working capital 14, 26, 247
Working capital investment (WCI) 16, 24, 27, 29, 33, 157, 165, 168
World bank 130

Y

Yield to redemption 247
Yield to maturity (YTM) 111, 113